Aristophanes: *Frogs*

BLOOMSBURY ANCIENT COMEDY COMPANIONS

Series editors: C. W. Marshall & Niall W. Slater

The Bloomsbury Ancient Comedy Companions present accessible introductions to the surviving comedies from Greece and Rome. Each volume provides an overview of the play's themes and situates it in its historical and literary contexts, recognizing that each play was intended in the first instance for performance. Volumes will be helpful for students and scholars, providing an overview of previous scholarship and offering new interpretations of ancient comedy.

Aristophanes: Peace, Ian C. Storey
Plautus: Casina, David Christenson
Terence: Andria, Sander M. Goldberg

Aristophanes: *Frogs*

C. W. Marshall

BLOOMSBURY ACADEMIC
LONDON • NEW YORK • OXFORD • NEW DELHI • SYDNEY

BLOOMSBURY ACADEMIC
Bloomsbury Publishing Plc
50 Bedford Square, London, WC1B 3DP, UK
1385 Broadway, New York, NY 10018, USA

BLOOMSBURY, BLOOMSBURY ACADEMIC and the Diana logo are trademarks of Bloomsbury Publishing Plc

First published in Great Britain 2020

Cover design: Terry Woodley
Cover image © Nick Rutter - The Cambridge Greek Play, *Frogs*, 2015, ADC Theatre, Cambridge. By permission of the Cambridge Greek Play Committee.

A catalogue record for this book is available from the British Library.

A catalog record for this book is available from the Library of Congress.

ISBN: HB: 978-1-3500-8092-8
PB: 978-1-3500-8091-1
ePDF: 978-1-3500-8093-5
eBook: 978-1-3500-8094-2

Typeset by RefineCatch Limited, Bungay, Suffolk

To find out more about our authors and books visit www.bloomsbury.com and sign up for our Newsletters for Thompson

*Thank you for coming along
and making this a great
occasion.*

Contents

Illustrations

Figures

Table

Preface

In the Warner Brothers cartoon masterpiece *One Froggy Evening* (1957, dir. Chuck Jones), a lonely construction worker finds a frog in a box who can sing and dance, but will do so only for him. The man's ambitions for celebrity and profit are continually frustrated until, old and destitute, he abandons the frog in another building site to be discovered again in the following century. It might be the best seven minutes of film ever made, a sublime tragedy of vicarious ambition and human loneliness, in which the viewer only ever hears the voice of the frog. This was my first singing frog, encountered in childhood on a Saturday morning watching television. The second was Kermit, singing 'Rainbow Connection' at the start of *The Muppet Movie* (1979, dir. James Frawley). It is an unexpectedly beautiful song about the power of hope and dreams, and of wanting to expand one's horizons to find something more for oneself in life. Third came Aristophanes.

Tragedy, beauty, comedy, purpose – these are the associations I have with singing frogs, and consequently I have welcomed the opportunity to write this short book. Unlike Jones's construction worker, I have not been alone in hearing these voices. I have learned about the play from friends, who have discussed ideas on the play over many years. These generous souls include Liz Scharffenberger, Ian Storey, Jonathan Vickers, Amy Cohen, George Kovacs, David Creese, Alan Sommerstein (whose commentary informs much of what I say here), Mary-Kay Gamel, Emmanuela Bakola and Hallie Marshall. Keith Rutter at the University of Edinburgh first taught me the play when I was a doctoral student, and Kerr Borthwick shared his love of Walter Leigh's music and Douglas Young's translation. As a Crake Doctoral Fellow at Mount Allison University, I first raised the idea that now finds its way in chapter 24. A version of chapters 5, 9, 15 and 29 was delivered at the University of Warwick in conjunction with a production of *Frogs*. The cover image comes from the 2013 Cambridge Greek Play, directed by Helen Eastman. I am grateful to her, Stelios Koutsoukos, Platon Mavromoustakos, Magdalena Zira and Eric Csapo for help with images included in this book.

My research has been generously supported by the Social Sciences and Humanities Research Council of Canada for many years. Students at the University of British Columbia and the American School of Classical Studies in Athens have worked through comic fragments with me, which explains one of the emphases in this book. I have benefited from the generous and patient support of Alice Wright, Georgie Leighton, Lily Mac Mahon, Merv

Honeywood, and their team at Bloomsbury, and I am thankful to the anonymous reader who offered feedback on the manuscript. I am continually grateful for the friendship, support and critical insight of the series co-editor, Niall Slater, whose work has taught me so much about ancient comedy.

Joy is granted to me every day by my family, Hallie, Jonah and Thompson.

Hopping: Some Ways to Read This Book

The twenty-nine chapters in this book offer an introduction to Aristophanes' comedy, *Frogs*. One way to read the book is to go straight through, from beginning to end. That's not the way academic books are often read, though, so there are some alternatives. Choose your own adventure. Here are some possible paths one might take to trace a particular theme in *Frogs*, by reading only selected chapters:

Comedies	1–6, 9, 20, 29
Tragedies	1–2, 7, 17–21, 23–5
Religion	1, 3, 8, 11–12
Characters	1, 4, 7, 13, 16, 18, 26
Stagecraft	3, 6, 9–10, 13–14, 16, 21, 25
Reperformance	3, 7, 25–7
Politics	5, 9, 14–15, 18, 22, 29
Major Themes	7, 9, 12, 15, 17, 20, 22, 29
Chorus	10, 12–13, 15, 21
Reception	10, 18, 22, 24–8

In addition, cross references to discussions in other chapters are in bold square brackets. These offer less predictable routes through the text, but they help to demonstrate the deep network of associations Aristophanes builds. The index can uncover deeper connections still. References to line numbers of *Frogs* are in round brackets without further reference; other play titles are given in full. Unless noted, all translations are mine. A short guide to further reading is found at the end of the book.

Achieving consistency in transliteration is a challenge. Several terms are transliterated and not translated, since they do not map cleanly onto a single idea in English. In transliteration, *e* and *o* represent the short vowels epsilon and omicron, *ē* and *ō* the long vowels eta and omega, and either *u* or *y* might represent upsilon. Names of people and places are a particular problem: Latinized forms (e.g. Cleisthenes, Aeschylus, Ceramicus) and direct transliterations (e.g. Kleisthenes, Aischylos, Kerameikos) are both used in scholarship; I have used Latinized forms except for unfamiliar names where the direct transliteration helps with pronunciation, or to avoid confusion with other people (and so I refer to the lord of the underworld as Plouton, to avoid confusion with Plutus [Latin] or Ploutos [Greek] the god of wealth, and Platon to distinguish the comic poet from the philosopher). Also confusing are the names of Aristophanes' plays: *Frogs*, for example, can also be referred to as *Batrachoi* (the Greek title) and *Ranae* (the Latin title), and scholarship might use any of these. In some cases, the Greek word may be used comfortably in English without evoking a misleading cognate. Consequently, I use aulos, stasimon, strophe and antistrophe, but *skēnē*, *orchēstra* and *katabasis.*

1

Dionysus

Dionysus is the largest role in Aristophanes' *Frogs*, and the character appears in almost every scene. Dionysus was a god of exuberance and community building, and these qualities are evident in his responsibility for both wine and theatre. From theatre, however, come impersonation and masks; and from wine comes responsibility for madness and departure from one's self. His rituals could emphasize fertility and vegetation. The worship of Dionysus in Athens recognized all of these aspects and more, and it is a mistake to try to contain the god within too narrow a compass.[1] At the same time, as Albert Henrichs has argued, 'No other Greek god has created more confusion in the modern mind, nor produced a wider spectrum of different and often contradictory interpretation.'[2] Multiple conflicting stories exist about the god's double- or triple-birth, and his death and restoration: Dionysian exuberance embraces life beyond death, and some rituals focus on a happy afterlife for his believers. His name is found on Bronze Age Linear B tablets from *c.* 1250 BCE. In the earliest Greek literature, he is 'a joy for mortals' (Homer, *Iliad* 14.325) who is nevertheless already associated with death (*Odyssey* 11.325 and 24.74); as Heraclitus observed, 'Hades and Dionysus are the same' (fr. 15 DK).

Traditionally, Dionysus was first recognized as a god and worshipped in Attica – the area controlled by the *polis* (city) Athens – in the community (deme) of Ikarion. He taught viticulture to the Athenian Icarius, and he avenged the hero's death when he was killed by drunken shepherds. Ikarion was also supposedly the deme of Thespis, the legendary inventor of tragedy. Dionysus was worshipped annually in a local festival organized by the deme, and the celebration included productions of tragedies. Not every Rural Dionysia included theatrical performances, but many did, and there are indications of theatrical performances in twenty-three demes and the area of Brauron in the classical period, though not all were in existence in the late fifth century.[3] In an early comedy of Aristophanes (*Acharnians* 237–79, dated 425 BCE) a character performs a procession (*pompē*) and song that was recognizable enough to evoke among spectators the procession, accompanied by a phallic song, from a Rural Dionysia.[4] These processions, with an oversized phallus-pole, imagined satyrs as attendants of Dionysus. The Roman writer

Pausanias describes a painted version of the myth in Athens (1.20.3), which provides a model for these processions.[5]

In the Attic festival calendar, the Rural Dionysia begins a season of Dionysus worship that extends through the winter, as '*Rural Dionysia*, *Lenaia*, *Anthesteria*, and *City Dionysia* succeed one another at intervals of roughly a month over the period from about December to March'.[6] In different ways, all of these festivals are relevant to the study of *Frogs*. The Lenaia and the City Dionysia will be discussed later [**2**], as will Dionysus' connection to the Eleusinian Mysteries [**12**], but the Anthesteria, which the historian Thucydides calls the 'older Dionysia' (2.15.4), is also relevant: 'It is a festival at which some social norms are overturned–slaves dine with their masters, young men insult their betters from wagons – and even (so to speak) some cosmic norms: the dead roam the streets, a god visits the city (arriving from the sea?) to take a mortal bride.'[7] The festival lasted three days, each of which is associated with a particular clay vessel: Pithoigia, Choes and Chytroi. It was celebrated at the Limnaion, an old (unidentified) temple of Dionysus 'in the marshes'. Pithoigia celebrated opening large jars (*pithoi*) of wine; Choes poured wine from pitchers (*choes*) and featured a drinking contest, in which silence commemorated Athens receiving the polluted Orestes into its community, and concluded with libations for the dead; Chytroi continued the association with the dead as porridge was made in pots (*chytroi*) offered to Hermes.

This description sidesteps the life of Dionysus, his birth and youthful adventures, his rescue of Ariadne after she is abandoned on Naxos by Theseus, his defeat of pirates by metamorphosing them into dolphins, his arrival from the East and reception in Greece, among many other stories, because from the perspective of *Frogs*, very little of that matters. While Euripides' *Bacchae* can offer a sophistic debate about the nature of his birth (*Bacch*. 286–97), 'the Dionysos of *Frogs* has little or nothing to do with representations of the god in fifth-century sculpture or vase painting, and by his dress alone he would have been recognized as a figure quite distinct from the mythic or cultic manifestations of the god.'[8] Aristophanes' Dionysus drinks no wine, does not carry the *thyrsus* (a fennel staff wrapped with ivy with which Dionysus is associated) and is not attended by dancing maenads or satyrs.[9]

Even his visual appearance in *Frogs* is uncertain. Until the fifth century, Dionysus is always represented with a dark beard. Vase fragments from the 470s begin to show a beardless Dionysus, which may be influenced by a notable theatrical presentation of the god: Aeschylus' lost play *Edonians*, where Dionysus is presented as womanish (fr. 61), is one possible source for this influence.[10] Whatever the case, this was the image the sculptor Pheidias displayed on the east pediment of the Parthenon in the 430s, and subsequent artists could feel free to use either appearance.[11] In Euripides' *Bacchae* (left unproduced at the author's death in 406, and possibly presented a few months after *Frogs*), Dionysus appears disguised as a mortal but is young and unbearded.[12] While the Dionysus of cult presented a mature god with dark hair and beard, the Dionysus of myth, as seen in tragedy and satyr play that often focused on his youthful adventures, presented a young man. Both of these possibilities were available to a comic poet presenting Dionysus onstage in the late fifth century.

Dionysus had appeared on the comic stage before *Frogs*, for example in *Dionysalexandros* ('Dionysus-becomes-Paris'/'Dionys-is-Alexander') by Cratinus, whose theatrical career flourished *c.* 454–423. The play was produced in 430, 429 or perhaps 437.[13] A plot summary preserved on papyrus (the 'hypothesis', *POxy* 663) allows us to say much about this play. Dionysus appears to disguise himself as the shepherd Paris (= Alexander), in order to judge the beauty contest between goddesses that will lead to the Trojan War. The chorus of satyrs tease Dionysus as he appears, perhaps because his beard is shaved and he is dressed as a shepherd:

> After this he sails off to Sparta, takes Helen away, and returns to Ida. But he hears a little while later that the Greeks are ravaging the countryside <and looking for> Alexander. He hides Helen very quickly in a basket and changing himself into a ram awaits developments. Alexander appears and detects each of them, and orders them to be taken to the ship, meaning to give them back to the Greeks. When Helen refuses, he takes pity on her and holds on to her, to keep her as his wife. Dionysus he sends off to be handed over. The satyrs go along with him, encouraging him and insisting that they will not betray him.
>
> *POxy* 663, lines 20–44[14]

Many questions remain unanswered, but the spectacle offered by the play is obvious: Dionysus, perhaps shaved to become Paris (fr. 48, 'I appeared shorn, like a fleece'; cf. *Thesmophoriazusae* 215–48), is somehow also transformed into a ram (fr. 45, 'And the silly fool just walks about going "baa baa"'); Helen, perhaps used to finer living (fr. 42, 'Do you [sing.] want gateposts and fancy porches?'), is indecorously hidden in a basket, allowing a jack-in-the-box appearance when the real Alexander arrives. *Dionysalexandros* also involved political satire: 'In the play Pericles is very persuasively made fun of through innuendo [*di' emphaseōs*] for having brought the war on the Athenians' (*POxy* 663, lines 44–8). Exactly what *emphasis* means is debated, but somehow the appearance of Dionysus or Alexander evoked the general Pericles, without making the connection explicit.[15] Whatever his exact appearance, somewhere in the play Dionysus was described with his usual iconographic attributes (fr.40.2: '<He had> a thyrsus, saffron robe [*krokotos*] with lots of decoration, large drinking cup').[16]

There were, then, many Dionysus comedies.[17] Relevant to *Frogs*, Aristophanes wrote *Babylonians* for production at the City Dionysia of 426 [**3**], in which Dionysus was also a character (fr. 75) and may have been presented as an inept rower, who must learn aspects of seafaring.[18] Dionysus rowing an onstage ship, perhaps assisted by the chorus of Babylonians, again suggests a moment of theatrical spectacle. Indeed, a scene with Dionysus at the oar recurred, in Eupolis' *Taxiarchs* and Aristophanes' *Frogs*, with rowing scenes also attested in plays by Hermippus and Cratinus [**9**].[19] These plays engage with the Dionysus of ritual and of myth, yet they are similarly free to do with him whatever is needed by the plot.

2

Lenaia

The two principal theatrical festivals in Athens were the Lenaia and the City Dionysia. The City Dionysia was celebrated in the sanctuary of Dionysus Eleuthereus on the south slope of the Acropolis, where the theatre can still be seen today. The cult title Eleuthereus evokes 'freedom' from responsibilities, the 'bounty' of the god and the 'liberty' from tyranny that Athens enjoyed after the democracy was established in 508/507, but it was explicitly tied to the town Eleutherai, which bordered Boeotia and came under Athenian control around this time.[1] The cult image of the god was taken to the town, and was returned in a torchlight procession (*pompē*) and celebration that evening. The next day, a *proagōn* ('pre-contest') ceremony announced the competitive events that would follow, and perhaps offered a preview of what was to come. After the mid-440s, this occurred in the Odeion, a large roofed building immediately next to the theatre. Another procession led to the theatre, where pre-play ceremonies might display the richness of Athens and its political control over the smaller cities in the Delian League.[2] Competitive performances followed. Each of the ten tribes of Athenian citizens (tribal divisions were also established after 508/507) would compete with a chorus of fifty men and fifty boys – a thousand amateur male performers singing and dancing in a non-dramatic performance in these competitions alone.

Three tragedians were selected, each to present a tetralogy consisting of three tragedies followed by a satyr play (a shorter play mocking the presumptive seriousness of tragedy and other genres, typically with a satyr chorus), on three successive days. Three or five comedies were also presented; the precise sequence of these events is not known.[3] Ten judges were selected annually, one from each tribe, with the god Dionysus notionally being given a role to play in the adjudication as well.[4]

Central to the effective operation of this festival was civic financing through rich citizens selected as *chorēgoi* ('producers'). Funding was achieved through a wealth tax, whereby rich citizens were selected (or could volunteer) for a liturgy, to provide funds for a tragic, comic or dithyrambic chorus (*chorēgia*) or for a warship (*trierarchia*). These liturgies encouraged civic engagement and fostered competitiveness, especially since the *chorēgos* of a victorious chorus could set up a monument in his own honour.[5] *Chorēgoi* were selected by the eponymous archon (the magistrate who gave his name to the year, an allotted office whose responsibilities included the City Dionysia), and would be responsible for expenses associated with the chorus throughout the rehearsal period (providing recruitment costs, rehearsal space, chorus trainers, food and lodging), costumes, props, masks and (I presume) any extras or backstage personnel. The archon would assign a poet-playwright, and, for tragic and comic productions, a group of actors whose expenses were subsidized by the *polis*, which also apparently paid for the construction of the scene building (*skēnē*).

A similar choragic system was in place for the Lenaia, for which another archon, the *basileus* ('king'), was responsible.[6] This is the festival at which *Frogs* was first performed in 405. Less is known about the performances here, but comedy had been included since the late 440s,[7] where again there were three or five competitors each year, and a tragic competition, in which two playwrights each offered a dilogy (two tragedies), from *c.* 433/432.[8] Both of these competitions also offered prizes for the best actor (an actor's competition had been added to the Dionysia between 451/450 and 448/447).[9] Other features distinguished the Lenaia competitions. Unlike at the Dionysia, metics (resident foreigners who were not citizens) could pay for a *chorēgia* at the Lenaia, giving them the opportunity to achieve social capital while being taxed, and fewer sacrifices were expected.[10] There were also differences in the resources offered by the *polis*: for example, it appears that the *mēchanē* (the crane used for flying heroes and gods) was only available for a Dionysia production.[11]

It is usually assumed that the plays at the Lenaia were also held in the Theatre of Dionysus, but the matter is less certain than is usually admitted.[12] Part of the celebration took place at the Lenaion, the location of which has not been identified archaeologically, and it is possible there was a performance space there. A second-century CE source refers to 'the Dionysian theatre and the Lenaian one' explicitly (Pollux 4.121), but earlier sources also suggest the possibility of a different space (*Acharnians* 504). Three possibilities exist. The Lenaion might have been in the agora (the open marketplace of Athens), but if so it has left no archaeological record in a thoroughly excavated site; it might be 'in the fields', though this seems to conflate the deme settings of Rural Dionysia, or it might be at the *Dionysion en Limnais* (Sanctuary of Dionysus in the Marshes), the location of which is also unknown today but may have been on the banks of the Ilissos river, which ran outside of the city gates.[13] The *Dionysion en Limnais* was also the setting for the third day of the Anthesteria (Chytroi), and while we cannot be certain that there was a performance space there as well, it is possible that this is where plays at the Lenaia were performed.

The comedies of Aristophanes were written for an audience familiar with the ritual calendar. *Acharnians* could conflate elements of Rural Dionysia with the Anthesteria;[14] *Frogs* combines festivals connected to the Limnaion, both the Lenaia and the Anthesteria. These juxtapositions of festivals have led to some confusion about discrete elements: the use of wagons in the form of ships were part of the processions at the City Dionysia, and ritual abuse from the wagons was probably associated only with the Dionysia, though it is attested also for the Anthesteria and Lenaia.[15] While the City Dionysia remained primary in terms of reinforcing Athenian civic identity, it is a mistake to think of the Lenaia as a secondary (or worse, second-rate) festival. Comedies were more prominent at the Lenaia than at the Dionysia, and theatrical victors at both festivals were commemorated. Extant playwrights will have had plays performed at both festivals, as well as at Rural Dionysia, throughout their careers.[16]

Uncertainty about the venue for the Lenaia limits what can be said about the theatre space itself. For our purposes, the layout of the theatre space at both festivals is identical: an *orchēstra* provided a dancing space for a comic chorus of twenty-four individuals. The audience would watch from raked seating (like in a stadium) surrounding the *orchēstra*, with the centrepoint as a focus, at which an altar (*thumelē*) was located (it was likely permanent, but perhaps could be removed if not needed). A one-storey wooden stage building (*skēnē*) with a central double-door would serve as backdrop to the action. The *skēnē* was probably not individuated for each play, but painted with a standard, generic appearance suitable for all plays at the festival, that would be transformed through the suggestion of a play's dialogue.[17] Actors could enter the performance area along *eisodoi* (side-ramps), or through the

Figure 2.1 Theatre of Dionysus in *Assassin's Creed: Odyssey* (UbiSoft, 2018).

central door, which also served as a natural focal point for the audience.[18] I believe a low wooden platform was attached to the front of the *skēnē*, but this is uncertain [**9**].[19] There have been many virtual reconstructions of the Theatre of Dionysus, and (invariably) all of them are inadequate in different ways. One that reflects the latest scholarship on fifth-century production spaces closely comes from the video game, *Assassin's Creed: Odyssey* (Ubisoft, 2018; see figure 2.1).[20] It shows a rectilinear *orchēstra* and *skēnē* together forming the performance area, with actors and chorus using both as the play required. A rectilinear *orchēstra* and a small, wooden *skēnē* with a low platform create a playing space that includes the wider natural environment of the city, with the shape defined by wooden benches (*ikria*). This is imaginative, but it captures many of the features of the most recent scholarship. Admittedly, some of these claims remain unprovable, but they correspond to archaeological evidence and the demands made on theatrical space by extant tragedies and comedies.

3

Aristophanes

Aristophanes, son of Philippus of the deme Kydathenaion (Cydathenaeum), is the best-known surviving Greek comic playwright. He wrote plays that were produced at major festivals from 427 to after 387, which leads scholars to estimate his lifespan from *c.* 446–*c.* 385.[1] Aristophanes was part of a new generation of poets who challenged Cratinus and his contemporaries: when Aristophanes won at the City Dionysia in 426, he was the first new comic playwright to be victorious there in at least nine years; signs of this transition were already apparent at the Lenaia, where new poets had won in 428 (Phrynichus), 427 (Myrtilos), 426 (Eupolis) and 425 (Aristophanes).[2]

Later scholars in antiquity referred to the plays of this whole period (from 487/486 until the death of Aristophanes a century later) as 'Old Comedy', often grouping Cratinus, Eupolis and Aristophanes as a triad to match the tragedians Aeschylus, Sophocles and Euripides (both triads include one senior figure and two successors). There are problems with this periodization of the genre (Old-Middle-New), of which ancient scholarship was so fond,[3] and we should resist any generalizations. Because only Aristophanes has complete comedies surviving, it is easy to assume his practice was representative of his peers. This need not be so. *Frogs*, for all its creativity and imagination, is clearly drawing on a deep knowledge of previous theatre, and is manipulating previous comic successes of Aristophanes and of others.

Eleven of Aristophanes' plays survive, with substantial fragments of many more of the forty that he wrote, and the dates for many plays are certain. Among other things, this list shows that he was active at both the Dionysia and the Lenaia throughout his career (see table 3.1, with extant plays in bold).[4]

Little is known about Aristophanes' life apart from the years of productions.[5] Despite being registered in a deme in the heart of Athens, he may have had a family connection to the island of Aegina (*Acharnians* 653–4). He describes two lawsuits brought against him by the populist demagogue Cleon, that may have arisen from his presentation of Cleon in *Banqueters*, *Babylonians* and *Knights* (*Acharnians* 377–82, 502–3, *Wasps* 1284–91). Aristophanes' plays resist Cleon's hawkish pro-war policies. That Cleon was also from the deme of Kydathenaion made this enmity, whatever its true

Table 3.1 Aristophanes' Plays, with Date, Festival (when known) and Director.

427-L	*Banqueters*	directed by Kallistratos (possibly Philonides)
426-D	*Babylonians*	directed by Kallistratos
425-L	***Acharnians***	directed by Kallistratos
424-L	***Knights***	
423-D	*Clouds I*	
422-L	***Wasps***	
422-L	*Proagon*	directed by Philonides
421-D	***Peace***	
c. 418	***Clouds II***	(partially rewritten, unstaged version of *Clouds I*)
414-L	*Amphiaraus*	directed by Philonides
414-D	***Birds***	directed by Kallistratos
411-L	***Lysistrata***	directed by Kallistratos
411-D	***Thesmophoriazusae***	
c. 408	*Gerytades*	
405-L	***Frogs***	directed by Philonides
404-L (?)	*Frogs*	(revised and reperformed)
c. 391	***Ecclesiazusae***	
388	***Wealth***	
387	*Kolakos*	directed by Araros
c. 386	*Aiolisikon*	directed by Araros

nature, particularly nasty. From the beginning of his theatrical career, Aristophanes will have witnessed significant changes in his city over the course of the Peloponnesian War. He lived through oligarchic coups, the collapse of the democracy and a diminishment of Athenian power **[9, 25]**. Throughout this time, and for at least fifteen years afterwards, he continued to write comedies. Other miscellaneous details are known. Aristophanes may have gone bald at an early age (*Peace* 767–74). An inscription lists Aristophanes once serving as *prytanis* (a civic official) for his tribe.[6] His son Araros directed his play *Kokalos* in 387, which suggests that Aristophanes was married at latest by *c.* 409. Aristophanes had another son who was a playwright, either Philetaerus, who won twice at the Lenaia in the 370s, or Niceratos.[7]

Another feature evident in the table is Aristophanes' regular use of other men as directors of his plays. 'Director,' the person who takes a written script and is ultimately responsible for what appears onstage, is how I translate the Greek term *didaskalos*. For Aristophanes this function must be distinguished from the poet (*poiētēs*) and the producer (*chorēgos*, responsible for funding the chorus and other associated production costs). Most fifth-century playwrights apparently directed their own work: i.e. they were both *didaskalos* and *poiētēs* (and at least in part choreographer and composer, and sometimes actor; for plays without a director listed, we assume it was Aristophanes himself). Whatever his reasons, this choice was not simply a result of Aristophanes' youth or inexperience, despite the poet's rhetorical claims (*Knights* 514–16, 541–6, *Clouds* 528–31): throughout his career, Aristophanes used other men. I stress this to resist generalizations about Aristophanes' so-called apprenticeship, or 'producing' (i.e. directing) plays 'in his own name'.[8]

We know of three directors used by Aristophanes. Kallistratos probably directed Aristophanes' first three plays (*Banqueters*, *Babylonians* and *Acharnians*, 427-L, 426-D, 425-L), *Birds* (414-D) and *Lysistrata* (411-L); he seems also to have directed a play (which he himself wrote) that came second at the Lenaia of 419/418.[9] Philonides directed *Proagon* (422-L), *Amphiaraus* (414-L) and *Frogs* (405-L); he may have been a victor at the Dionysia *c.* 410.[10] Araros, Aristophanes' son, directed *Kokalos* (387) and *Aiolisikon* (*c.* 386); he may have composed plays beginning 376–372. All three therefore had a theatrical career independent of Aristophanes, and we know that other playwrights also used directors in this way.[11] Possibly, using a director frees the playwright to act in his production, though this is speculation.[12]

Philonides, then, as director (*didaskalos*) of *Frogs*, is someone with whom Aristophanes had worked since at least 423/422. Oddly, an inscription lists sixteen members of a *thiasos* (religious dining club) of Heracles, which includes Philonides, Simon of Kydathenaion (Aristophanes' deme) and Amphitheus, which is the name of a character in *Acharnians*.[13] This is an unexpected grouping, that perhaps positions Philonides as a fellow demesman as well (the fact that the chorus of *Banqueters* was also a *thiasos* of Heracles pushes the apparent coincidence further). We do not know how their relationship emerged. Though it is natural to speak of the poet finding a director to propose a play to the appropriate archon in hopes of securing a chorus (and so a producer), the reality might be very different: possibly the *chorēgos* could choose another *didaskalos* when assigned an untried poet (apparently the *chorēgos* also paid salaries for assistants such as the *chorodidaskalos*, or chorus-trainer). Significantly, it appears that a competitive victory would be ascribed to the *didaskalos*. I do not believe the relationship between poet and director was secret, as some ancient sources intimate, but only that the credit for victory went in the first instance to the *didaskalos*, in the same way that in American cinema the Academy Award for Best Director is more prestigious than that for Best Adapted Screenplay. Favouring the *didaskalos* is seen in choragic victory monuments,[14] and would explain the metaphors Aristophanes uses that suggest his supposed subordination in his early career, but also why the poet's name is attached to the plays we have surviving.

Adopting a directorial perspective can be illuminating when considering Aristophanes' career. The first time Philonides was used was for *Proagon*, a play set apparently at the 'pre-contest' ceremony held before the Dionysia (and the Lenaia?) at the Odeion [**2**]. *Proagon* won that contest, with Aristophanes' *Wasps* taking second place and Leucon's *Presbeis* (*Ambassadors*) coming third: it would seem, then, that Aristophanes had written two plays entered in the same contest, directed one himself and let Philonides direct the other.[15] The second time Philonides was used was in 414, a year when Aristophanes had two plays accepted at different festivals: *Amphiaraus* at the Lenaia and *Birds* at the City Dionysia, which was directed by Kallistratos. Set apparently at the recently consecrated healing shrine at Oropos, *Amphiaraus* showed a man being restored to health by the hero of the title (in a plot perhaps similar to *Wealth*). The next play we know Philonides directed was again a Lenaia play, this time in 405, where he was victorious, defeating Phrynichus' *Muses* and Platon's *Cleophon*.[16] That play was *Frogs*.

4

Hero

Is it productive to see Dionysus as the comic hero of *Frogs*? This is not a question of whether he is the protagonist (the lead actor), and it is certainly the largest role in the play (though if Aeschylus and Xanthias are doubled [**16**], the length is comparable to that of Dionysus).[1] Nor is Dionysus a Greek *hērōs*, a dead mortal receiving cult worship. The question is whether Old Comedy typically produces a focal character with whom the audience is invested and to some extent identifies, and whether it happens in *Frogs*. It certainly happens in tragedy (though Aristotle can write *Poetics* without needing a word for hero). For comedy, however, the idea of heroism is different than that, and emerges from Whitman's influential study, which saw the Aristophanic hero as a charming rogue, exhibiting *ponēria* ('wickedness' or 'rascality'): 'A desperate small fellow, inexcusably declaring himself for a social savior.'[2] Whitman's definition draws only on a selection of plays, though, and does not apply to all contenders. More embracing is Sommerstein, who sees a 'fantastic project ("Great Idea") at the heart of each play': 'The initial situation is always one which from the point of view of at least one major character is extremely unsatisfactory; and the Great Idea is this character's plan for putting things right, for achieving *sōtēriā* for himself, his family, his city, or . . . the whole Greek world.'[3]

Dionysus' Great Idea in *Frogs* feels very local: there is a lack of good tragedians in 405, and he has a way to remedy this. There is a struggle to implement the Idea (the journey to the underworld), and its realization has unexpected consequences (the contest between Aeschylus and Euripides).[4] It is not clear to what extent Dionysus exhibits *ponēria* himself – he refers to 'my rascal Euripides' (852) – but it is Aeschylus who eventually offers salvation to the city. By making the *agōn* such a dominant part of *Frogs*, Aristophanes confers elements of comic heroism to each of the three dominant roles: Dionysus, Aeschylus and Euripides. There is also a kind of bait-and-switch, however, because the final decision about the playwright to bring salvation (1448, 1501) is not based on literary merit, but apparently on political advice, though even that, too, is undermined [**21, 22**]. This is unexpected, even as it reinforces the core message that it is poets who help the city [**18**]. Aristophanes uses Dionysus as a stand-in for himself [**7**], as well as at different times,

Aeschylus [**20**] and the chorus [**15**]. Wherever we choose to locate heroism in *Frogs*, Aristophanes is there.

This lack of heroic focus in *Frogs* leads to a problem, though, since 'there remains something deeply appealing and illuminating about the idea of a comic hero, . . . and it is worth asking what accounts for this hold on the critical imagination'.[5] Even though 'the first half of the play focuses on the comic identity of Dionysus',[6] arguments that Dionysus undergoes a mystic initiation and becomes a deserving judge for the contest prove unconvincing [**12**], and his centrality to the play's resolution is suspect. Instead, comic heroism emerges because of Aristophanes' self-identification. Apparent authorial self-positioning (whether genuine or a pose for the purpose of the play) allows the audience to invest likewise. Humour 'arises from the hero's own presumption, indeed, *insistence*, in the work that he really *is* heroic, regardless of whether anyone outside of the fictional world would find anything heroic, in the traditional sense, in his behavior'.[7] The character's commitment to a Great Idea creates heroism which in turn elevates the comic poet and the artistic (literary, civic, political) value of comedy itself.[8]

5

Names

Personal humour is a recurrent feature in Aristophanes' plays, in which individual Athenians – all notionally part of the audience – are identified by name, for the sake of a quick joke. *Kōmōdoumenoi* ('those who are mocked in comedy') are typically living citizens, singled out because of their political prominence, their involvement in poetic performance, or because their egregious behaviour or appearance were in some ways distinctive.[1] Some of them are known from other sources, but many remain unfamiliar to us today. Scholia can record the opinions of Hellenistic or Roman scholarship, but the nature of the joke can remain unclear.

It is easy for a modern reader to be overwhelmed by these names, and so it is worth being alert to the real people that will be particularly important to the play. The tragedians Aeschylus and Euripides appear as characters in *Frogs*, but living literary figures are regularly invoked. These include **Phrynichus** the comic poet, one of the competitors against Aristophanes at the Lenaia in 405. Phrynichus the son of Eunomides (13, whose dramatic career might have extended from 429–*c.* 405) is not to be confused with Phrynichus the son of Stratonides (689), who was a general (*stratēgos*), established the oligarchic coup that brought in the Four Hundred and was assassinated in 411. Nor is he Phrynichus the son of Polyphradmon (910, 1299), the tragic playwright who was a contemporary of Aeschylus (career *c.* 501–*c.* 476), and who wrote *Phoenician Women* about the battle of Salamis.[2] An Athenian would distinguish these men automatically from context, but modern readers might not.[3] Possibly, Aristophanes is even making a joke with all these Phrynichoi, since *phrynē* is a word for frog or toad (even if the title of the play is *Batrachoi*).[4]

Several other names recur in the following discussion.

- **Cinesias** (153, 1437), the dithyrambic poet, is a character in *Birds* (414 BCE), and is mentioned in *Ecclesiazusae* (392 BCE), which establishes the range of his career. He is associated with radical and subversive musical innovations [**8, 20**].[5]
- **Cleophon** (674–85, 1504, 1532) was the chief democratic voice in Athens between the oligarchic coups, from 410 to his execution by the Thirty in 404 [**9, 15, 23**].[6]

- **Theramenes** (541, 967), a politician able to follow changing political winds, was one of the leaders of the oligarchic coup of the Four Hundred (411 BCE), helped ease into the more moderate Five Thousand. He successfully shifted his allegiance to the pro-democracy side and was re-elected as general (*stratēgos*) in 407 and was a trierarch at Arginusae (406). He helped negotiate Athens' surrender to Sparta (404), and then became one of the Thirty, until he was executed by Critias, the pro-Spartan leader of the Thirty [**9, 14**].[7]
- **Archedemus** 'the bleary eyed' (417, 588) began the prosecutions against the generals after Arginusae [**9**].
- **Cleisthenes** (48, 57, 422) is an Athenian politician (perhaps general, perhaps liturgy-paying trierarch), ridiculed from *Acharnians* (425 BCE) to *Frogs* for his sexual preference as a bottom, which as he aged would be increasingly shameful by presumptive Athenian morality [**7, 12**].
- And there is **Alcibiades** (1422–66), the bad boy of Athenian politics, who since 415 had helped Athens, Sparta and the Persians, and caused some sort of significant scandal in each location [**22**].

Many other individuals are known only slightly, such as **Callias** (428–30) and **Cligenes** (706–15). They were recognizable and notorious to the audience, but remain mysterious today. Knowing these names helps as one approaches *Frogs*.

6

Costumes (*Frogs* 1–51)

Two characters walk into the *orchēstra* as the play begins. One is riding a donkey and is carrying comically exaggerated baggage on a stick over his own shoulders. The other, on foot, is the god Dionysus, who presents himself not as the son of Zeus, but as the 'son of *Stamnos* [Winejug]' (22). The baggage-carrier, his slave (1), is Xanthias (his name is first used at 271; the name is also used of comic slaves in *Wasps* and in some vase paintings). The audience can see that these characters are part of a comedy, as if there were any doubt: they are masked, and underneath their costumes is the padded earth-toned bodysuit (*sōmation*) with distended belly, buttocks and chest, and tight sleeves and leggings, as was typically worn by comic actors. Attached to the suit and visible under the costume is a phallus, an oversized, flaccid costume penis perhaps made of red leather. The default male comic body, therefore, was grotesque and ridiculous, far from the citizen ideal.[1] The *sōmation* is not mentioned by the characters (though Dionysus is called 'Belly-boy' at 200), but terracotta figurines and South Italian vase paintings depicting Athenian plays use it as a marker of comic stage identity throughout the classical period.[2]

On top of this costume base are markers of character identity. Xanthias will wear a plain tunic, and Dionysus a flowing saffron garment often worn by women (*krokōtos*). Possibly, this is enough to identify him as Dionysus, who had worn a *krokōtos* as a character previously in tragedy (Aeschylus, *Edonians*, fr. 61, and see *Thesmophoriazusae* 130–45) and comedy (Eupolis' *Taxiarchs*, fr. 270). Dionysus also wears effeminate boots (*kothornoi*).[3] These details are juxtaposed with a third layer of costume the Dionysus actor wears: a lionskin and a club, emblems of the hyper-masculine hero Heracles. This is a disguise, as Dionysus eventually explains (108–11), intended to facilitate a journey to the underworld (Heracles had descended to the underworld and returned to fetch Cerberus), and Dionysus partakes of that heroic precedent, despite his own mythological precedent of descending to the underworld for his mother Semele.[4] The notion of dressing for success, using costume to assume qualities of another person, is found elsewhere (*Thesmophoriazusae* 146–58). In no sense is the audience fooled, however [**13**]: spectators see all three levels of costume covering the actor. The costume of the slave riding the donkey adds a third level as well: the baggage (*skeuē*, a word also used for theatrical props) being carried by the slave is inherently funny, and serves as a launching point for several jokes (1–18).[5]

A vase, formerly in Berlin but lost during the Second World War, appears to depict the scene of these two actors approaching the door to knock (see figure 6.1).[6] The scene is not well painted, and the only photograph poor. One can still see Dionysus on the left, with the leggings of the padded bodysuit clearly drawn, holding a club above his head as he prepares to knock at the door, with his lionskin in his left hand.[7] To the right is Xanthias on the donkey with a huge bag on his shoulder in the top right. Dionysus appears to be floating and it is not clear if the object in the lower centre is meant to be an altar or a low stage on which Dionysus is supposed to stand. Because the characters are drawn stage-naked (i.e. only wearing their bodysuits), there is in fact no indication that this is Dionysus and not in fact Heracles (Xanthias also appears to be naked, and the phallus is hardly visible on both figures). The vase is Apulian, made in South Italy in the second quarter of the fourth century (and so thirty to fifty years after the debut of *Frogs*). The vase therefore points to an early, exported performance of the play, if it is to be at all meaningful for its purchaser. While there is no need to replicate all the

Figure 6.1 Apulian red-figured bell krater, 375–350 BCE, formerly Berlin F3046. Photo: After M. Bieber, *Die Denkmäler zum Theaterwesen im Altertum* (Berlin 1920) pl. 80.

performance details from the earlier Athenian production, other vases do point to a continuity of tradition. The artist can choose to emphasize some features over others: stage nudity points to the comic *sōmation* at the expense of the identity of Dionysus (neither *kothornoi* nor *krokōtos* are painted), which is assumed to be known by the viewer.[8]

If this is a representation of *Frogs*, we can isolate other details about production choices. First, a real donkey was used, which in turn might associate Xanthias with the Return of Hephaestus, depicted in the phallic processions at the Rural Dionysia [**1**].[9] Similarly, the mask of Dionysus appears thoroughly unremarkable: a short-cropped dark beard marks him as a generic middle-aged man, and so neither the heavily bearded Dionysus of myth nor the clean-shaven Dionysus from the Acropolis [**1**].[10] Xanthias' beard, barely visible, is also cut very short. As painted, Dionysus' Heraclean club is quite small (just bigger than his forearm), and so perhaps anti-heroic. The directorial choice in the 1971 production of the National Theatre of Northern Greece (tr. Thrasyvoulos Stavrou, dir. Kostis Mihailidis) plays the humour in a different way, making the club oversized and impossible for Dionysus to wield convincingly. Both possibilities make effective comedy.

As in *Knights*, *Wasps* and *Peace*, the opening dialogue of *Frogs* gives the sense of warming up the audience. The opening lines, 'Shall I tell one of the usual jokes, master, at which the spectators always laugh?' (1–2), immediately challenge the audience with a reflexive awareness: these characters know they are in a play, and they want to ingratiate themselves with the audience through comedy. They are also aware there is a tradition of comedy, of which they are part. This theatrical awareness, one component of a larger process called metatheatre, plays with the conventions of theatre.[11] The actors are supposed to know their lines, and characters do not usually hesitate in this way. Since costuming has been so consciously layered, the theatrical pretence is on particular display. Metatheatre by itself is not inherently comedic (it is also a feature of serious theatrical genres), but here it does add to the sense of playfulness that the comedy seeks to establish, while drawing the spectators into the dramatic world.

In addition to the layering of costume, the byplay associated with props and a donkey onstage and the playfulness of metatheatre, humour is operating on other levels, too. The entire play is in verse, alternating between spoken dialogue (in iambic trimeter, which was thought to match natural speech rhythms), and more elaborate metres that were accompanied by music. Though he is riding a donkey, Xanthias still carries the baggage: by not taking advantage of the benefit a beast of burden offers, he appears foolish, and this is reinforced when he insists that he is still carrying the load, even though he rides (21–32). There is also scatological humour (3–11): Xanthias insists he is not making jokes that equate his burden with a need to defecate, and in so doing receives both the laughs at puerile humour and laughs at being superior to those same jokes. It's a kind of recycling. Further, baggage-carrier jokes are the sort of comedy Phrynichus employs: the first name of a contemporary Athenian being mocked is one of Aristophanes' rivals in the Lenaia contest of 405, the poet Phrynichus (12–14).[12] Aristophanes' dialogue establishes a range of means by which humour might be achieved, and this passage suggests he is indiscriminate about how he will achieve that success.

A sense of the energy of this opening scene can be inferred from this image from a 2012 production by Fantastico Theatro in Cyprus (figure 6.2), from the 16th International Festival of Greek Drama in Cyprus (dir. Magdalena Zira). The donkey has become a bicycle, and so Xanthias will be in constant, precarious motion onstage, in contrast to the corpulent Dionysus in his fancy waistcoat and lionskin festooned with flowers. Only some of the baggage is being carried by Xanthias, but the awkwardness of his large form awkwardly balanced is apparent, and the class difference between the two (god/human slave) is largely eroded through casting and costume.

The premise of *Frogs* at this point seems straightforward. Dionysus and Xanthias are on their way to the underworld, and Dionysus has reasoned that

Figure 6.2 Dionysus and Xanthias, 16th International Festival of Greek Drama in Cyprus (2012). Photo by Socrates Socratous. Set design by Dimitris Alithinos and costume design by Elena Katsouri.

by dressing like Heracles, the trip will be easier. There is a logic to his idea, but it is skewed since the two are both sons of Zeus.[13] Both Dionysus and Xanthias act as if they are ordinary residents of Athens, which increases the tension with their Zeus-born identities.[14] The audience sees the god and his slave make their way to the central door of the *skēnē*, which is the house of Heracles (whether this is to be imagined as a temple for the god or just an ordinary Athenian house is not clear). Heracles appears at the door and, again, mask and costume generate laughs, as the authentic Heracles doubles up at the sight of Dionysus' ineffective costume (Heracles ends three lines with a form of the verb 'to laugh': 42, 43 and 45). The sight of the real Heracles creates a mirror of sorts, as the 'genuine' Heracles' props and costume can be measured against Dionysus' ineffective disguise.[15] All this is preamble, and Dionysus now begins to explain why he has undertaken this quest.

7

Yearning (*Frogs* 52–107)

Dionysus was reading a copy of Euripides' *Andromeda* when he fell in love with Euripides. A seaman serving on a naval ship under Cleisthenes (48, [**5, 27**]), Dionysus was suddenly struck by *pothos* ('a yearning', 53) and *himeros* ('desire', 58). The passion is deep, almost beyond words, and its suddenness will recall, for some spectators, the love-at-first-sight moment experienced by Perseus in that play, when he sees Andromeda chained to a rock to feed a sea monster (fr. 138).[1] Dionysus' *pothos* was not for a woman, nor a man, nor a boy, and so Heracles reasons it must be a sexual desire for the effeminate Cleisthenes who is none of these – a suggestion Dionysus rejects, despite his wearing both hyper-masculine and feminine clothing (56–60).[2] Heracles does not understand, so Dionysus explains, with bathetic ordinariness: has Heracles ever had a longing for pea soup? Heracles understands that kind of yearning perfectly well, and it is that sort of longing Dionysus feels for ... (the name is postponed until the last word of the sentence at the start of the line) ... Euripides (61–7), the tragic playwright who died probably in his seventies within the past year. So, it's necrophilia, suggests Heracles (67).

Aristophanes' Dionysus has decided to undertake a *katabasis* (a descent to the underworld [**8, 11**]) in order to bring back the object of his yearning, Euripides, because Dionysus needs a skilful or clever poet (68–71). The word *dexios* (71) prizes the intellect, and is a quality Euripides himself will praise for poets (1009; and he will use the word in another sense at a climactic moment in 1402 [**21**]).[3] No living poet will do: after listing some suggestions, the rest are dismissed as 'chatterboxes' (92 *stōmulmata*, though this is a quality Euripides admits he uses at 943), 'pissing on Tragedy a single time' (95) before disappearing.[4] Sophocles himself had died even more recently than Euripides, and was undoubtedly successful, but he, too, is excluded. Since he died after *Frogs* would have been proposed, it seems much of this passage (71–88) was a late alteration to the text (Sophocles is also mentioned at 787–94 and 1515–19).[5]

Euripides was a *gonimos* poet, a word suggesting fertility (writing both lots of plays, generating ideas and excitement?) and also innovation, and so 'ballsy' (96, 98).[6] Heracles may be lost amid these literary-critical evaluations, but Dionysus' poetic examples – 'the foot of Time' and 'Heaven, Zeus' bedroom' (100) – are hardly sublime expressions, even if they do sound Euripidean.[7]

Dionysus is undertaking a grand supernatural journey for a clever and fertile poet, but it is not clear at this point he fully understands what that means.

Literature stirs passions: this is a great mystery, that as readers and theatregoers humans care about what happens to fictional characters. Like Dionysus, I get caught up in romantic comedies. Euripides' poetry moves the god in his gut, creating a hunger for the playwright. *Andromeda* with its romantic plot was a popular play and it was reperformed throughout antiquity, but the first person to love the play was Dionysus. *Andromeda*, produced with *Helen* in 412, was not Euripides' most recent play: a scholion on line 52 asks why Aristophanes did not select one of the more recent (i.e. post-412) beautiful plays of Euripides, such as *Hypsipyle*, *Phoenissae* or *Antiope*. The straightforward answer is, apparently, arbitrary personal preference: he loved it (as did Aristophanes, as the extended parody in *Thesmophoriazusae* indicates) and he loved the idea of a sudden, irrepressible yearning which Perseus displays. But it is also a nostalgia, a 'longing for time, years earlier, before the oligarchic revolution'[8] which must have seemed very far away in 405.

What do we make of the fact that Dionysus was reading a play from seven years previous while onboard a ship? Is this a prerogative of the god of theatre, or is it a means of levelling him, suggesting his pastime activity is that of any of a trireme's crew? One answer is given by Xenophon, describing shipwrecks on the coast of the Black Sea: 'Here they found . . . many written books [*bibloi*], and all the many other things ship captains keep in wooden chests' (*Anabasis* 7.5.14). Athenian functional literacy was low, and not everyone could read, and there is little indication people read for pleasure. There were booksellers in Athens (*Birds* 1288–9, Eupolis fr. 327 K-A), and it seems it was possible to get copies of even obscure playwrights (*Frogs* 151 refers to a speech of the tragedian Morsimus, Aeschylus' great-nephew who is also mocked at *Knights* 401 and *Peace* 803). Xenophon does not say the books are plays, but the presence of any written texts means that the scene imagined in *Frogs* is at most an exaggeration of reality, and not a fantastic, unrealizable possibility.

There is another level to Dionysus' *katabasis*, which draws on another lost tragedy, Euripides' *Pirithous* (date unknown).[9] *Andromeda* creates one metatheatrical analogy: Perseus' relationship to Andromeda in Euripides corresponds to Dionysus' relationship to Euripides, as Euripides is associated with the title character of his play. In *Pirithous*, the playwright presented the *katabasis* of Heracles to fetch Cerberus, but while in the underworld he rescues Pirithous, who had come to abduct Persephone but was tricked and stuck to a seat, and Theseus, who stood by his friend in Hades. This creates a second and arguably deeper metatheatrical association: Heracles' descent to the underworld and encountering Theseus and Pirithous corresponds to Dionysus' descent (dressed as Heracles [**6**]) and encountering Aeschylus and Euripides. Pirithous corresponds to Euripides (the possible author of *Pirithous*), and so linking Theseus as the senior Athenian hero and the moral representative of the Athens of the past, with Aeschylus is also straightforward [**18, 24**]).

Though the characterization of Pirithous is not certain, an association with Euripides is natural.[10] Further similarities emerge: the chorus of *Pirithous*, as in *Frogs*, comprised Eleusinian initiates (fr. 2 [**12**]); Pirithous had an encounter between Heracles and the gatekeeper Aiakos (fr. 1 [**13**]); *Pirithous* may have begun on the surface and presented a change of locations to the underworld.[11] As in Euripides' *Heracles*, *Pirithous* presents Heracles as a saviour (*sōtēr*, [**4**]), 'ethically and politically assimilated to traditional Attica'.[12] Casting Dionysus' costume as a metatheatrical evocation of a tragic figure recalls Dikaiopolis-as-Telephus in *Acharnians* or Trygaeus-as-Bellerophon in *Peace*. Though we cannot be certain how the chair or chairs that kept Pirithous and Theseus in the underworld were presented, they both conversed with Heracles onstage (fr. 5a, 7). We should not rule out an association between the lost tragedy and the Chair of Tragedy or Pluto's throne [**16, 17**]. Finally, Pirithous is apparently set out to be devoured by serpents, affixed in a way that Andromeda had been.[13]

Dionysus' desire for Euripides is more than nostalgia for a recently lost playwright. Aristophanes is arguably the most thoughtful and subtle reader the tragic playwright had in his lifetime. Throughout his career, Aristophanes had demonstrated repeatedly an ear for Euripidean poetry and an understanding of the ways the tragic playwright had challenged his genre through performance. Euripides had been a character in earlier Aristophanic plays (e.g. *Acharnians*, *Thesmophoriazusae*) and Euripidean tragedy had shaped earlier Aristophanic plots (e.g. *Peace*, *Thesmophoriazusae*). Euripidean paratragedy, the metatheatrical evocation of tragedy within a comedy, was a specialty (e.g. the citation of Euripides' *Oeneus* fr. 565 in 72, or *Andromeda* fr. 144 in 100). No one in Athens (or, arguably, since) understood Euripides better than Aristophanes. This is why, perhaps more than anything else, Aristophanes was able so successfully to mock and ridicule the tragedian. In some ways, Dionysus' *pothos* is the playwright's *pothos*, as it is that of at least part of the audience. It is alright for us to miss Euripides, because Dionysus does, too. There's a fragment from the Hellenistic comic poet Philemon, the context of which is lost: 'I'd have hanged myself to see Euripides' (fr. 118).[14] This feels like an echo of *Frogs*, directly or indirectly, and the sentiment might reasonably be shared, if we accept the hyperbole, by many theatre fans of their favourite playwright. Dionysus' struggle to identify precisely what it is that he misses about Euripides becomes an open question for the play, as Dionysus takes us with him to Hades.

8

Underworlds (*Frogs* 108–66)

Dionysus asks Heracles for the route he took to Hades during his twelfth labour to fetch Cerberus (108–11). The instructions given will be programmatic for the next 500 lines. The ordinariness of the detail Dionysus seeks, including brothels, bakeries and places with the fewest bedbugs (112–15) belies both his godlike identity and the exceptionality of the journey. Heracles' answer lays out the detail of Aristophanes' underworld, the fullest description in Greek literature since *Odyssey* 11. It is also a showcase for Aristophanes, who 'does not merely make use of a few traditional motifs in his telling, he piles up as many as he can in the narrative, never content with a single allusion if he can make multiple ones'.[1] Though not a traditional underworld geography (and not an afterlife composite anyone necessarily believed in), it should still feel familiar for the Athenian audience.

When asked the ways to get to Hades quickly, Heracles' initial answers misinterpret 'ways' (117 *tōn odōn*) not as 'roads' but 'methods'. He suggests suicide by hanging, by drinking poison hemlock and by jumping from a great height from, probably, the Dipylon Gate, the main access in the city wall, through which the Panathenaea procession passed (120–35). All of these are rejected, since they preclude the return journey Dionysus wishes (again, his mortality is presumed here for comic purposes). If he is to undertake 'the long journey [lit. sailing]' (136 *ho plous polus*), Dionysus will encounter and overcome four obstacles.

The first obstacle is a bottomless lake (*limnē*), Acheron (137–42 [**10**]), which divides the surface and the underworld. Sometimes envisaged as a river, crossing requires paying the old ferryman Charon two obols, twice the expected price. This amount was the price of admission to the theatre, and was the salary for a day of unskilled labour.[2] Heracles envisions risk with the small size of Charon's boat (139–40), and says that the Athenian price hike has made it to Hades brought by the Athenian hero Theseus in *Pirithous*.

Next is 'Withering Heights'[3] (143–53 [**11**]), which includes beasts and snakes, mud and shit, and sinners being punished. Reference to serpents recalls those threatening Pirithous [7], and suggests physical threats on land to mortals descending. Aristophanes' *Gerytades* had a river of diarrhoea in the underworld (fr. 156.12), but the association of mud has specific Eleusinian associations [**12**].[4]

Heracles also lists a number of sinners being punished. A sense that one's choices in life carry over into punishment in death is not clearly attested before this play. Homer refers to the Isles of the Blessed as a reward for heroes like Menelaus, but his underworld offers a bleak afterlife that is largely undifferentiated. Singling out crimes deserving of particular punishment allows Aristophanes to proceed from those who dishonoured the gods, parents and guests (a trio found only in Aeschylus, incidentally),[5] to those copying out a speech from the bad tragedian Morsimus or (Dionysus adds) anyone who has learned the *pyrrichē* by Cinesias (the competitive Pyrrhic dance, performed with a shield, was part of the Panathenaea).[6]

Third is the musical band of Eleusinian initiates (154–61 [**12**]), male and female adherents to the mystery cult of Demeter centred on Eleusis. They will appear in full daylight (*Frogs* is performed in daylight), with pipes (*auloi*) and clapping. This tells the audience (a) that these are likely to be the chorus, (b) that if the audience have made an association with *Pirithous* [**7**] it is reinforced by this choice, and (c) that if spectators know the title of the play is *Frogs* this will create a rival expectation about choral identity. All three are true.

Fourth, and treated almost in passing, is the door guarded by Aeacus (162–3, [**13**]). This is another potential association with *Pirithous*, and will signify Dionysus' arrival in Hades.

This is not the first underworld in Old Comedy, and the Great Idea of returning someone to Athens in order to save the city itself has an important history. Eupolis' *Demes* (*c.* 417?), with its chorus made up apparently of personified Athenian neighbourhoods, presented four dead leaders from the past returning to help Athens at the instigation of the comic hero Pyronides.[7] I accept Storey's argument that their return was accomplished through a necromancy (summoning the underworld spirits to the surface), though an offstage *katabasis* remains possible.[8] The returned leaders – Solon, Miltiades, Aristides and Pericles – all had distinctive political personalities, and perhaps each encountered a contemptible opposite of themselves in contemporary Athens (e.g. Aristides 'the Just' encounters a *sykophantēs*, who makes a living bringing scurrilous lawsuits to court). Solon had previously been summoned in a comedy perhaps from the late 430s by Cratinus, called *Cheirons*:[9] his ghost, referring to Salamis, where his ashes were scattered, says,

I live on an island, as the tale is among men
Scattered across every city of Ajax.

fr. 246

A lost comedy by the poet Nicophon, which might just predate *Frogs*, is called *Back from Hades*.[10]

The dead returning to life seems also to have featured in a comedy by Platon (not the philosopher, but 'Plato Comicus', the funny one) called either *Laconians* or *Poets*:[11]

Speaker 1
Promise me you are not dead.
Speaker 2
In body I am!
But I've brought back my soul, like Aesop.

fr. 70

We do not know the story of Aesop's return (later accounts have him killed by the people of Delphi to avoid a plague), but it seems clear that Speaker 2 has overcome death. We cannot say whether this play predates *Frogs* or not (Platon's career spans the mid-420s to the 380s, very much like Aristophanes'), but he was competing against Aristophanes at the Lenaia of 405 with *Cleophon*.

Two earlier comedies do appear to be set in the underworld, however. Pherecrates, whose theatrical career spanned *c.* 440–410, wrote a play called *Shiners* (*Krapataloi*) in which the silver fish of the title are being used as coins in Hades.[12] Further, Aeschylus is a character, who boasts of the great *technē* (craft) he has built and handed over (fr. 100). Storey suggests that another fragment recalls the instructions for a quick way to get to Hades:

No worries, sir – catch a fever,
eat unripe figs in summer time,
and when you are full, fall asleep until noon.
Then have spasms, burn up, and scream.

fr. 85

Fragments 101 and 102 are explicitly metatheatrical, with references to the audience and the judges.

The other is Aristophanes' *Gerytades*, from 408 or 407.[13] In this play a delegation from Athens is sent to the underworld (perhaps at the instigation of the title character), in a reversal of what happened in *Demes*. Rather than politicians, the delegation comprises three poets: Meletus the tragedian, Sannyrion the comic poet and Cinesias the dithyrambic poet. These are not major figures, though all are alive. Whatever the purpose of their journey, the delegation is selected because they are all 'slight'; this is how I render *leptos*, a term suggesting they are both physically frail and artistically deficient (and so not merely the stereotype of the starving artist; even their hopes are slight, fr. 156.10).[14] This conceit seems to run through the play,[15] as the poets leave the surface where they starve and eat wax from their writing tablets (fr. 159, 163) and head to the underworld (and into the *skēnē*) for a banquet, where they can eat the poems of Sthenelus (fr. 158, another hungry tragic poet, compared by Platon fr. 136 to Morsimus) or fatten themselves with solo songs from tragedies (fr. 162, cf. *Frogs* 939–44; food is mentioned in fr. 164, 165, 167, bread in fr. 156.1172 and 173). While they may be 'praising Aeschylus at banquets' (fr. 161), the humour emerges from the impoverished poets presented.

Meletus the tragedian is almost unknown (he is probably not the accuser of Socrates), but Sannyrion (fr. 2) mocks him as 'the corpse of the Lenaion'.[16] Sannyrion was in turn mocked by another comic poet, Strattis, in his play *Cinesias*. Cinesias, who had been a character in *Birds* 1372–1409, and whose Pyrrhic dance at the Panathenaea in 406 been in some way distinguished (*Frogs* 152–3), was the 'chorus-killer' (Strattis fr. 16).[17] Cinesias was also a member of a notorious dining club called the *Kakodaimonistai* (*Devils*; Lysias fr. 195.2 Carey), and seems to have suffered from severe chronic intestinal distress. More than a decade later, Aristophanes writes a scene in which a man caught in public wearing his wife's robe is asked if his outfit is because Cinesias has defecated on him (*Ecclesiazusae* 330). It is not an accident that the rivers of dung in *Frogs* and Strattis are found near references to Cinesias. A mean joke that is repeated for years (if it is not a scholarly invention[18]), it may be that the bad-boy musician very nearly deserved it. In more sense than one, he was a shitty poet.[19]

This is a deeply layered array of cross references to a wide range of comedies, and it is hard to disentangle. All of these comic underworlds inform the situation in *Frogs*. At the same time, the underworld journey here plotted also corresponds to a walk through Athens along the Ilissos river:[20] beginning at the shrine of Heracles at the Diomeian gate, along the marshy Ilissos, through a meadow (where the 'Lesser Mysteries' of Agrai were celebrated [**12**]), to the sanctuary of Dionysus *en Limnais*. The correspondence is not exact, but the possibility of a kind of double vision is real: the audience is invited to impose a familiar geography on the path, and if Slater is right that there was a separate theatre for the Lenaia [**2**], then the setting for most of the play, Plouton's palace, resonates with the site of the Lenaia festival and the performance of *Frogs*. Dionysus has his route, and is set to proceed. In doing so, he ostensibly leaves Athens behind.

9

Warships (*Frogs* 167–208)

When *Frogs* was performed in 405, the Athenian democracy was not yet at its lowest point. The experiment of radical democracy inaugurated (traditionally) under Cleisthenes in 508/507 had been severely tested throughout the Peloponnesian War (431–404), particularly in the years since it had lost most of its naval fleet in the Sicilian expedition under the reluctant generalship of Nicias (415–413). Syracuse in Sicily, aided by Sparta, was victorious, and more than 10,000 Athenian hoplite soldiers were captured and killed, and over 200 triremes were lost, including a vast number of oarsmen (perhaps up to 30,000): it was perhaps the greatest defeat in classical Greek history (Thucydides 7.87.6, and see 6.31, 6.43, 7.42). In addition, from Spartan incursions into Attica more than 20,000 publicly-owned slaves had deserted (Thucydides 7.27.3). Alcibiades [**21**], who had favoured the expedition, defected to Sparta and then Persia. In 411, in an extraordinary political action, the democracy was persuaded to hand power to 'The Four Hundred', in part because the financial burden on the rich had increased significantly with the losses at Sicily. This oligarchy was short-lived, due to internal division, and the Four Hundred were replaced by the Five Thousand (all those male citizens who could furnish a suit of hoplite armour; Thucydides 8.97), who governed for a few months, before democracy was restored in 410, at the instigation of the lower classes (Thucydides 8.89.2–94.1), celebrated by a public reconciliation held in the Theatre of Dionysus (Thucydides 8.93). The Athenians continued to fight, and were victorious in some naval engagements at Cynossema (411), Cyzicus (410), but not without more losses.[1]

In the months before *Frogs*, the battle at Arginusae (406) should have been another cause for celebration. Ships were manned in part by slaves and resident aliens (metics), because of a lack of capable citizen rowers. Some of these would have been slaves from the mines, incentivized to return. Payment was a problem, and the Athenians lacked coinage. As a result, in 407/406 they melted down all but one of the gold statues of Nike (Victory), in a desperate but irony-laden attempt to persevere (Hellanicus 323a F26). The Athenians were victorious at Arginusae, under the command of eight of the ten *stratēgoi* (generals) elected for that year, but due to a storm immediately after the conflict, it was not possible to rescue all the sailors from the destroyed Athenian warships, and many drowned. The Athenian population found this unforgivable, and sentenced six of the eight *stratēgoi* to death (Xenophon, *Hellenica*, 1.6.1–35; Diodorus 13.101–2). The Athenians soon regretted their decision, and brought charges against the prosecutors. Democratic will was shown to be exceptionally volatile and desperate.[2]

Arginusae is central to understanding the politics of *Frogs*: the enfranchisement of slaves is mentioned three times (33–4, 190–2 and 693–4 [**14**]),[3] even if Xanthias himself did not serve, because, he says, he had an eye infection (192).[4] Concerns about warships are found later in *Frogs*: because of the plays of Euripides (supposedly), no one wants to fund a trireme these days (1065) and the all-citizen crew of the flagship *Paralus* would talk back to their commanders (1071). Theramenes, one of the trireme commanders who had failed to rescue those drowning, is identified at 541 (as an opportunist playing both sides without political repercussions) and 967–70 (as a follower of Euripides); and Archedemus, who began the prosecution of the generals, is singled out (416–21) and called 'the Bleary-Eyed' (588, and see Lysias 14.25). The corrupting influence of Euripides supposedly infects both the rich and the poor, and one is tempted to connect Xanthias' (imagined) eye infection that prevented him serving with the nearsighted ambition of Archedemus, and with the vinegar thrown into enemy eyes during a sea battle (1440–1).

Aristophanes is not shying away from political controversy in addressing Arginusae and its aftermath head-on, and it is inconceivable that he imagined his audience sharing a unified viewpoint on these matters. Indeed, Dionysus was reading *Andromeda* on Cleisthenes' warship (48b, [**6**]), and many in the audience would understand that as a reference to the most recent naval conflict, Arginusae, as well. As soon as five days after the performance of *Frogs*, Theramenes was elected as a *stratēgos*,[5] but he was rejected at the subsequent *dokimasia* (public scrutiny in advance of taking office), possibly as the influence of this play becomes felt. Aristophanes has an obligation to attempt to win audience favour by not alienating everyone, but he does not avoid political engagement, even in the fraught and unpredictable situation of 405. Indeed, he seems to believe such engagement is a central part of being a poet [**18, 29**].

As Dionysus and Xanthias continue their journey to the underworld, a funeral procession (*ekphora*) passes, moving from one *eisodos* to the other. A bier being carried (or perhaps rolled), accompanied by bearers, carries a corpse (170), and there is surely a comic surprise when the corpse sits up and speaks to Dionysus and Xanthias. The short encounter confirms they are on the right path, and the scene is intensified by having the corpse refuse to take up the baggage Xanthias had just put down (160). He demands exorbitant wages (two drachmas, i.e. twelve obols), even though it technically would not be him doing the carrying, we presume, as the corpse for a moment becomes an inversion of the donkey-riding Xanthias. Xanthias feels like 'an ass at the Mysteries' (159, a proverb meaning he feels useless and out of place), but wants Dionysus to hire someone else.[6] The corpse's 'speak of the devil' entry[7] is perfectly timed.

The visual impact of the procession must be inferred. Presumably, the *ekphora* would be recognizable, and this may have included the presence of female mourners, as part of the procession, bewailing the dead. Though not mentioned in the words, there may be considerable spectacle. More pointed, however, is the question of the corpse's appearance. Masks represent broad age categories, and we are by no means obliged to believe the corpse has died of old age. Indeed, given the thousands who had died at Arginusae (twenty-five triremes and most of their crew; Xenophon, *Hellenica* 1.6.34), the greatest loss to Athenian citizenry had been of younger, military-aged men. Though Thrasybulus and Theramenes attempted rescue, they were unsuccessful. Were bodies recovered after they drowned? Whatever the answer, a young corpse (unbearded but with dark hair on the mask, which perhaps was whitened to suggest death) would naturally be read in the light of the sea battle. I suggest, however, that funerals had been frequent enough that any mask would intimate a comparison with the victims of the Athenian naval victory. Any burial would be read in the light of *ekphorai* that had been carried out in recent months, and in the light of many more that had not. The contrast of the corpse with Xanthias, who avoided service, becomes more pointed and possibly quite comedically daring. Even though he is onstage for only a handful of lines, the corpse's personality comes through clearly. He is 'sardonic', willing to haggle over wages, and Dionysus 'finds the Corpse's arrogance intolerable'.[8]

The corpse departs, Xanthias and Dionysus (and their donkey?) follow, and they approach a point where they expect Charon. The ferryman promptly appears, on a boat with oars. Their line of greeting, *chair' ō Charōn chair' ō Charōn chair' ō Charōn* (184, 'Hail Charon' three times) might sound like nonsense syllables in its repetition of *Chai/Cha* and *rō/rōn* (cf. 'she sells seashells'). Is it Dionysus repeating the phrase three times, as if evoking the dead? Is it Dionysus and Xanthias alternating and then both speaking together? Editors disagree,[9] and this points to the challenge facing many lines of interpretation. Additionally, a scholion says the line is paratragic, a quotation from a satyr play by Achaeus called *Aethon* (fr. 11). (Scholia are the commentary that accumulated over centuries in antiquity and are preserved in the margins of several manuscripts **[25]**; an individual comment or scholion is written by an anonymous scholiast.) In terms of stagecraft, the *didaskalos* has a choice in the representation of this boat. Is it 'eensie weensie', as Heracles had suggested (139), and so perhaps represented by an *ekkyklēma* (the low wheeled platform used for revealing interior scenes in the theatre [**17**]) and creating a metatheatrical resonance? Or is it a larger vessel, evocative of a trireme (and so perhaps, like the ship-cart that carried Dionysus at the Anthesteria [**1**])? I prefer the former, though the latter does evoke Arginusae more directly. In Euripides' *Alcestis* 252 and 444 (439 BCE), Charon is said to have a two-oared boat, and this may have been a wider belief reflected in the design choices. Whatever was decided, the scene plays on an incongruity, as the vessel either defies Heracles' description, or is too small for the language of the trireme which is applied, as Dionysus prepares to climb aboard.[10]

Xanthias is not permitted to travel this way, since he is not a citizen, not having fought at Arginusae (191–2). This Athenocentric perspective is funny in itself, but it is overshadowed by the drowning corpses in the sea battle. Xanthias will have to run around the lake instead (193, an option which should make Charon superfluous for anyone).

As he boards, Dionysus straddles the oar, as (I imagine) its shaft and grip rise up between the actor's legs, a momentary and surprising replacement for the costume phallus. He must be taught to row, told even how to sit in a boat, as he is put to work. This inversion anticipates a later scene [**12**] but more importantly, it evokes another scene from the comic past. Dionysus had been taught to row a trireme in Eupolis' *Taxiarchs* (428 [415?]; fr. 268.53–4, 'You, at the front; won't you stop splashing us?'),[11] and possibly in Aristophanes' *Babylonians* (426; [**1**]). He is shown how to pull an oar, which he is able to manage even though he is 'unexperienced, unseamanlike, unSalaminian' (204).[12] As Xanthias departs with the donkey, Dionysus and Charon row into the centre of the *orchēstra*, and music begins to play, and they begin to hear what Charon has promised, 'amazing things from frog-swans' (207a).

10

Croaking (*Frogs* 209–68)

According to Gilbert and Sullivan's *Pirates of Penzance* (1879), one of the desirable qualities for a Modern Major-General is the ability to 'quote the croaking chorus from *The Frogs* of Aristophanes'. Eleven lines of the song that follows are the *Brekekekex koax koax* (209–10, 220, 223, 225, 235, 239, 250, 256, 261, 267): eight syllables (short-short-short-long, short-long, short long; what metricians call a *lekythion* [**19**]) that define the sound and initial appearance of the chorus.[1] It is an uneven rhythm, and we might want to provide a short pause at the end to help regularize it. Even then, the rhythm will not easily fit with Charon's anapestic *ō opop, ō opop* (208 'Heave-ho-ho! Heave-ho-ho!'; long-short-short, long-short short), which has just set the rhythm for rowing.[2] This conflict, between the regular rowing rhythm and the less regular syncopations of the chorus, establishes a conflict, an *agōn*, between the chorus and Dionysus that the song will have to resolve. Dover notes that this rhythm sounds nothing like the actual lake frogs found in Greece, *rana ridibunda*.[3] He suggests that the *br-* and *-x* serve as written markers for the beginning and end of sounds, but may not have been voiced, and so the croaking may have been closer to an 'ek-ek-ek'.

Any discussion of ancient theatrical music is hamstrung by the lack of score, tempo, rhythm, modes, tempering – anything, in fact, apart from the words and metre (leaving aside corruptions in the manuscripts that arise from recopying, and other obstacles to interpretation). Throughout *Frogs*, all musical passages are accompanied by a single instrument, the aulos, a double-pipe played by an *aulētēs* (aulos-player).[4] Vase paintings show the *aulētēs* in elaborate robes, and it is probable that he enters the performance area as the music begins.[5] Choral entries are often spectacular and more elaborate than subsequent songs. In this case, the chorus of twenty-four singers (the standard size for comedy in the fifth century) adopt the persona of frogs in Lake Acheron.

A lot occurs simultaneously in this short scene, and the following snapshots are necessarily selective and incomplete. In terms of the narrative, it brings Dionysus closer to Hades, overcoming one of the anticipated obstacles [**8**]. The journey may represent travel across the *orchēstra* (from stage right to stage left, perhaps), but it may equally be from a point that designates 'the shore' (where Charon pulled up) back to exactly the same point after a wandering journey within the *orchēstra*. If there is a low wooden platform attached to the *skēnē* [**2**], the division between shore and lake would be visually clear: at this point in the play, departing from shore into the *orchēstra* leaves one place, and returning, even to the same point, redesignates that point as somewhere else. Whatever the decision, I believe it is certain that the same door that had represented Heracles' house in Athens will come to represent the gate of Hades. This flexibility of comic space in the early part of a play, as locations morph as needed by the plot, is central to understanding the stagecraft of Old Comedy.[6] Meanwhile, Xanthias, having led the donkey [**6**] along an *eisodos* (side entrance) either walks the perimeter of the *orchēstra* in full view of the audience, or the actor circles behind the *skēnē* (leaving Dionysus in the performance area) and returns along the other *eisodos* at 269.[7]

Dionysus is in a contest with the frogs, though the basis of the competition is not explicit in the surviving script. As Wills spelled out, it cannot simply be based on volume (Dionysus is not out-shouting the frogs, though in the *orchēstra* centre his voice could benefit most from the theatre acoustics) or on violence (he is not swatting frogs with his oar).[8] Part of the answer may lie in rhythm, as Dionysus seeks to assert his regular rowing rhythm onto the frogs' more musical alternative, which proves to be contagious as Dionysus subconsciously adopts their rhythms and accelerated pace.[9] That, however, does not grant Dionysus a victory, since the chorus never accept his metrical structure. It is he who adopts *koax* into his speech (222, 226–7, 250, 261, 266–8). Wills's suggestion, adopted from P. J. Cosijn in 1685, that Dionysus conquers the frogs with the sound of a tremendous fart is plausible,[10] but again only as a partial solution.

By calling them 'frog-swans' at 208, Charon had signalled the musical elegance (an expectation that of course does not need to be fulfilled in performance), while at the same time pointing to the transition between life and death (Plato, *Phaedo* 84e–85a, notes the belief that swans sing most beautifully before they die – their swansong):[11] 'The comic quality of the scene is due in part to the incongruity of elevated lyric on the lips of frogs.'[12] Being amphibians, frogs also exist in a liminal state between the surface and below, and the choice of a *limnē* (137, 181, 193; a lake, rather than a river) as the transition point marks this liminality clearly. Even the festival of the Lenaia was associated with the cult worship of Dionysus *en Limnais*, 'in the Marshes', which further ties the character Dionysus to the particular geography of Athens and the worship of Dionysus at the Anthesteria,[13] regardless of where precisely theatrical performances at the Lenaia were held [**2**].[14] It also establishes a contrast between marshy shallows and the bottomless abyss Heracles had described (137–8). As MacDowell notes, the frogs themselves are not dead, but represent a midpoint between Athens and the underworld.[15] The contest within the play is one of aesthetics, and elements of artistic beauty are central. The contest operates in both high (elite, literary) and low (common, corporeal) registers simultaneously.

That distinction, between high and low, inevitably evokes associations of hierarchy and class, and to some degree every spectator wants to feel sophisticated, when they get the jokes. Class was explicit in the master/slave relationship with Dionysus and Xanthias, but at the same time it was undermined by the grotesque comic bodysuits **[6]** and comfortable banter with each other (and see **[13, 14]**). In contrast to Dionysus' buffoonery, it might be natural to accept that the frogs evoke the opposite, i.e. high cultural values against which Dionysus' gastrointestinal response may be contrasted.[16] Choral beauty can be accomplished through music and choreography, and the sight of a large group moving in sequence can be enthralling. As the tradition of musical theatre in the twentieth century has shown repeatedly, song and dance in a comedy can achieve the sublime.

Costumes also require decisions. It is possible that previous comedies by Callias and Magnes also employed a frog chorus,[17] which perhaps are evoked here. Were there flippers? Did they leap? Were they corpulent or agile? We do not know, but the possibilities for physical comedy are many.[18] The amphibian choreography could include elaborate and elegant acrobatics, as perhaps is indicated in the pun at 245, *polukolumboisi melesin* (evoking both 'many-diving melodies' and 'many-diving limbs').[19] Possibly, the chorus operated as two semi-choruses, with twelve singing *brekekekex*, answered by a dozen *koax*.[20] Verbal gymnastics are also required, as with the invented word *pompholugopaphlagasmasin* (249 'with bubble-splutter-plops', the sound of frogs diving).

Above all, the scene must be spectacular. The arrival of twenty-four singing and dancing choristers (the *parodos* or entry-song) is always a significant moment in the structure of an Old Comedy, and spectacle is important. The 2013 Greek-language production of *Frogs* for the Cambridge Greek Play (dir. Helen Eastman, a photo from which appears on the cover) demonstrated the energy and exuberance possible in a *parodos*: choreographed dancing frogs with umbrellas leap behind Dionysus in his dinghy, while green balloons float over the stage and an acrobat swings from a ring upstage.

An additional dimension is given to the scene by a performance conceit, that Dionysus, despite being surrounded by frogs, hears them, but never sees them (except, arguably, at the end in his eventual triumph). The emphasis on hearing led an ancient scholiast on line 211 to suggest that the chorus of frogs do not appear physically in the performance area, an idea I find unpersuasive.[21]

This is not a question about the uncertainty of the frogs' location: within the dramatic world, there are frogs in the lake Dionysus and Charon cross. Rather, the issue is one of stagecraft: do the chorus-members remain behind the *skēnē* as they sing, or do they have frog costumes and appear visibly to the audience?[22] Both are conceivable. My conviction for onstage frogs recognizes the importance of the *parodos* to comedy, and recognizes the humorous possibilities to be gained through costume, choreography and staging in this particular scene.[23] It is funnier for the audience if they can see the singing and dancing frogs but the god of theatre cannot. Dionysus struggles, turns around, and yet somehow misses the twenty-four other bodies in the *orchēstra* with him. It may even be that the chorus performers are physically manipulating Charon's boat to make its physical journey easier (and the staging more efficient), as they sing. Aristophanes both recognizes the comic tradition of Dionysus-learning-to-row found in Eupolis [**9**], while at the same time elevating the level of spectacle and inverting the expected authority of a god in the theatre being upstaged.

The *aulētēs* stops playing after 267 – Dionysus' triumphant and final adoption of the frogs' croaking – and the final line, as the boat pulls ashore, is 'I was going to stop your *koax* eventually!' (268). The chorus, perhaps surprisingly, exit the *orchēstra* (they would be expected to stay), taking Charon with them, and neither is seen again after line 270, as all the performers assume other roles.

11

Monsters (*Frogs* 269–322)

Dionysus disembarks from Charon's boat and immediately calls Xanthias. A feeling of loneliness is instantly created when the chorus exits the *orchēstra*. Dionysus pays Charon at 270, and Xanthias appears (presumably along the other *eisodos*) at 272. How much time does line 271 occupy? 'Xanthias! Where's Xanthias? Hey, Xanthias!' For that moment, Dionysus is alone, on a foreign shore, in the underworld. His victory over the frogs is taken away by circumstance, and he has no time to celebrate. In the scene that follows Dionysus' cowardice is foregrounded (according to a scholion on *Peace* 741, Eupolis had also presented a cowardly Dionysus, presumably in *Taxiarchs*), and the audience is invited to see the god as a superstitious man, uncertain in his dealings with uncertainty. If Dionysus has been making a journey from East to West (stage right to stage left), any further advance is denied by what they would find there: mud and darkness (273). Here be monsters.

Cowardice is an acceptable quality in a comic hero,[1] and its expression in this scene helps to further the play's metatheatrical resonances, Dionysus' relationship with Xanthias, and the play's representation of Athenian popular religion. A fearful Dionysus raises the stakes for the journey, helping to mark the momentous weight of what travelling to the underworld should represent. Dionysus and Xanthias look for father-beaters and oath-breakers, recapitulating the details Heracles had described (143–53, [**8**]). Both of these are significant offenses in Athens, and Aristophanes' joke that he still sees them now (274–6) neatly sidesteps any direct accusations of individuals by having the characters scan the audience. The spectators for a moment become the inhabitants of Hades. This in turn allows Dionysus to try to use Xanthias as a personal shield, positioning him on different sides, but always remaining in some way vulnerable (285–7). The sense of being surrounded would be more effectively achieved if Dionysus and Xanthias are in the *orchēstra* and no longer near the door. Since they are alone onstage, this poses no conceptual difficulty: comic space is fluid, and once the lake is no longer required for Charon's boat and the frogs, it can be redesignated as a new area. While not necessary, one way this could be done would be if Dionysus and Xanthias' steps were slow and gloopy, as they traverse the mud. That is when they see the Empousa (288–96).

Our understanding of the Empousa is incomplete, because she was a monstrous creature of popular superstition – what weary or lazy parents might use to frighten children into good behaviour. Specifics are appropriately amorphous, and most of our knowledge comes from scholia on this passage. The Empousa is associated with the worship of Hecate, had a fiery face[2] and was capable of shape-shifting. Her devouring of her victims was voracious, and so Demosthenes claims his opponent Aeschines' mother was nicknamed Empousa, from her sexual appetites (Demosthenes 18.130).[3] Again, the sea of faces in the audience likely becomes what the characters see, reinforcing the spectators' inclusion in the underworld. Dionysus' cowardice is shown with each new form, except when she becomes a very attractive woman, at which point all is forgotten and Dionysus steps forward (290–1), until she changes into a dog (an animal associated with Hecate). Humour is achieved when the character Dionysus has no short-term memory and is purely reactive to the most immediate situation.[4]

Reaction to the Empousa occurs in three stages. First, the characters look for protection, and Dionysus runs to the downstage edge of the *orchēstra* and supplicates the actual Priest of Dionysus sitting in the front row (297–300). It is a wonderful joke that a modern production can only replicate imperfectly, as a character seeks protection from an audience member whose authority derives from the extra-theatrical version of the character. Meanwhile, Xanthias calls upon Heracles, another protecting divinity, but also the disguised identity of his terrified master.

Next, after they are sure the Empousa has departed, Dionysus quotes a line from Euripides' *Orestes* (408): 'After the waves, I see calm sea [*galēn*] again' (303, cf. *Orestes* 279). Infamously, this line when delivered by the actor Hegelochus three years earlier was pronounced so that some in the audience heard the key word as if a vowel at the end had been elided, and so, 'After the waves, I see the weasel [*galēn'*] again.' This seems a remarkably subtle difference, which if nothing else points to the precise diction actors were expected and normally able to produce,[5] despite the open-air theatre and the use of masks. The weasel [*galē*] was a symbol of bad luck, and so maps onto modern understandings of a black cat, and like a skunk it was known to have a foul odour (*Acharnians* 255–6, *Plutus* 693). Weasels were another symbol of Hecate, and so Aristophanes' reuse of the line here is contextually appropriate for warding the Empousa away, especially after the evocation of theriomorphic shape-shifting, as well as being a theatrical evocation of the quality of a particular recent tragic actor.[6] Borthwick suggests that the characters might throw three stones in front of their path at this point, an apotropaic gesture to avert evil, and what Theophrastus, *Characters* 16.3, has his Superstitious Man do at the sight of a weasel.[7]

The third consequence of seeing the Empousa is that Dionysus has soiled himself. Correcting Dionysius' claim that he went pale, Xanthias invents a word for the truth of the matter, saying 'you yellowed yourself completely' (308 *huperepurriase sou*).[8] In this light, the paratragic dignity that Dionysus attempts to achieve with his *katabasis* is doomed to failure, a failure repeated when he suggests the responsibility for his woes should lie with 'Heaven, Zeus' bedroom' and 'the foot of Time' [7].[9]

Music from the *aulētēs* is again heard, which the characters hear, accompanied by the 'most mystic' (314 *mustikōtatē*) breeze smelling of torches. The word *mustikōtatē*, accompanying torch-lit singing, signals an Eleusinian context [**12**]. Brown's recognition that the preliminaries to Eleusinian worship included the warding away of evil spirits such as the Empousa means that the identity of the chorus as Eleusinian Mystics will be unmistakable.[10]

12

Mysteries (*Frogs* 323–459)

Religion in Athens was a *polis*-religion: the city had its gods, and worship involved participating in city sacrifices and rituals in different ways.[1] This included attending the theatrical events at the Lenaia [**3**]. Neighbourhoods (demes) had religious practices, too, as did households. Polytheistic worship was communal and did not for the most part require specific doctrinal beliefs from its practitioners. In addition to this, however, there were mystery cults, which one did voluntarily join (one became initiated), and which consequently did expect specific beliefs and behaviours. The Greater Mysteries of Demeter and Kore (the maiden Persephone) at Eleusis – the Eleusinian Mysteries – constituted the most widely-practised mystery cult in classical Athens, and had adherents from across Greece. Every audience member watching *Frogs* would either be an Initiate or would know many friends and family members who were. Initiation offered a promise for a better afterlife that the *polis*-religion never did.

Several features of Eleusinian worship can be identified, even if precise details remain elusive.[2] 'Lesser' Mysteries were celebrated in the month of Anthesterion day 20, a week later than the Anthesteria festival of Dionysus, on Anthesterion 11–13.[3] The Lesser Mysteries were celebrated at Sanctuary of the Mother at Agrai, and served as a pre-initiation for the Greater Mysteries at Eleusis.[4] These preliminary rites were tied specifically with Heracles, who was initiated before his *katabasis*, and this is surely why the chorus of Euripides' *Pirithous* comprised mystic Initiates [**8**]. After preliminary rites, a procession (*pompē*) for Mystai led 22 km along a particular route to the sanctuary in the deme of Eleusis, escorting a representation of Iacchus – Greek *Iakchos*, used as a name of an Eleusinian deity and a ritual cry, and pronounced with three syllables (*ee-ak-khos*). Individuals would walk beside a heavily laden donkey, which explains the proverb of being, like Xanthias, 'an ass at the Mysteries' (159, [**9**]).[5] In 405 the identification between Iacchus and Dionysus was partial and incomplete, but they were, in some sense, the same.[6] At Eleusis, worshippers would be led into the sanctuary where 'mysteries' would be revealed. This was a secret, and one that was mostly kept, though it may have been something like a symbolic ear of grain, for example, as a representation of Persephone's annual descent to the underworld and return in the spring. Words, sounds, smells, darkness, all combined to provide some transcendent, uncanny experience that would lead initiates into a new understanding of life. It was a ritual that one could repeat annually if one wanted to renew the experience, evoking the annual journey of Kore herself. Significantly, anyone could become an initiate: though there would be costs involved that would preclude some participating, in principle one could be slave or free, male or female, Athenian or not. Here, in a society governed by rigid class distinctions (and living in the wake of an oligarchic coup), worship at Eleusis was a great social leveller.[7]

Aristophanes chooses to give his chorus a second identity in *Frogs*, and when they return to the stage for a second *parodos* (316), they assume the role of Eleusinian worshippers. They enter in a procession, and the nature of their song would inevitably invite comparisons with the Iacchus procession that audience members had witnessed. At least some of the chorus hold torches, and they are dressed simply. A 2014 production by the National Theatre of Greece directed by Yannis Kakleas conveys the exotic other-worldly feel of an obscure ritual with the solemnity associated with genuine prayer: the initiates, both men and women, are dressed in long white skirts and matching open blazers, and lit candles sit on their shoulders, as wax drips down. The contrast with the performers' previous appearance as leaping frogs is apparent. The poet and director contrive to present a second stunning entrance-song.[8]

This *parodos* consists of seven distinct parts, and it is helpful to think of each as a discrete musical composition, with occasional interruptions by Dionysus and Xanthias, who remain in the performance area throughout the song, even if they initially do not participate:[9]

1. Hymn 1: Invocation to Iacchus 316–53
2. Anapaests 354–71
3. Hymn 2: Soteria 372–82
4. Hymn 3: Demeter 385–93
5. Hymn 4: Iacchus 394–413
6. Ribaldry 414–39
7. Hymn 5: Conclusion 440–59

As eavesdroppers, Dionysus and Xanthias have a privileged position, secretly watching what might be thought to be private or secret rites (an idea also explored in *Thesmophoriazusae*). The audience is invited to share in this perspective because they can hear both parts of the split-focus scene. Though the performers were all male, the chorus is costumed as both male and female: in *Lysistrata* this creates the feel of two tragic choruses of twelve.[10] The gender division offers an opportunity for sexist and heteronormative humour (337–9): Xanthias smells pork (*choiros*; a word also meaning vulva, as at *Acharnians* 771–96), and Dionysus warns him to beware of sausage (i.e. an anally penetrating penis).[11]

Each of the five songs I have labelled 'hymns' (in that they are in the form of cultic religious songs) are strophic: that is, they include a strophe ('turn') consisting of a particular melody with a specific, unique metrical pattern, and an antistrophe ('counter-turn') that repeats that melody and metrical pattern precisely. Strophic choral songs allow choreography to be repeated as well, with a strophe's actions being repeated (or reversed) in the antistrophe. This is a regular feature of Greek theatrical music. Two features distinguish the songs here. First, the strophic pairs are quite short, and sometimes they are repeated more than once. While this is a long *parodos*, the strophic length is closer to the length of a sympotic (drinking) song than to typical theatrical melodies. Secondly, the verb 'to play' (*paizein*) is used repeatedly, which is nowhere else associated with Eleusinian worship.[12] This suggests Aristophanes is giving the feel of Eleusinian worship,[13] but in a distorted (more popular, quicker, possibly more dynamic) form than actual Eleusinian singing. This prevents him from revealing the Mysteries to the uninitiated, which was a prosecutable offense [**17, 22**].

The first hymn, addressed to Iacchus, stresses the night-time, torch-lit dance in the meadow, that is somehow also in daylight. Several elements of this idyllic setting have been identified in the afterlife promised by the Orphic mystery religion.[14] The strophe (324–36) is answered in the antistrophe (340–52), and the repeated *I-ak-ch', ō I-ak-che* (316, 317, 325, 341) appears to contain within it reminsences of the frog's *ko-ax* ('one a natural sound heard at the Anthesteria, the other a meaningless human cry at the Eleusinia').[15] The blurring of Iacchus with Dionysus is metatheatrical: the chorus members, singing in a performance in honour of Dionysus (at the Lenaia), play a role in which they sing a song in honour of Iacchus, as an actor playing the role of Dionysus looks on.

Iacchus returns as the subject in the fourth hymn, where the strophe is (unusually) sung a total of three times (397–403, 404–8, 410–13), with a refrain at the end of each verse; Sommerstein suggests the men sing, then the women, and then both semichoruses together.[16] This song teasingly stresses the cheapness of the costumes, and how they are torn and consequently risqué. This is another joke, at the play's *chorēgos*, as if this was all that could be afforded. In the light of the frog costume just seen, it is understood as a ridiculous claim, and is obviously not true. The scholiast on line 404 notes that in 406/405 at the Dionysia, special provision was made for two individuals to share a *chorēgia* (Aristotle, fr. 447), but there is no evidence that it applied to the Lenaia as well.[17] Even if it did, this should not be understood as a diminishment of expense for a comic chorus: if anything, it affirms that (as with vase-painting) even in its most desperate political and economic straits, Athens maintained its funding for the arts.[18]

The second hymn to a personified Salvation (Soteria) is appropriate for Demeter-Kore, and brings a sudden shift to the music, as the strophe offers thirty-nine consecutive long syllables (372–6; the antistrophe at 377–82 is the same except for a substitution of two shorts in 382 for the name Thorykion). Dionysus as a comic hero is seeking a means to save the city [**4**], and so this short song resonates beyond the *parodos*, but its slow, languid pace represents a deliberate effect by Aristophanes.

This is followed by the third hymn, apparently to Demeter. The subject is announced clearly by the *koryphaios* (the 'head-speaker' of the chorus, who is responsible for all of the spoken lines in the play) at 383–4; yet spectators may reasonably doubt this, since the content would be equally appropriate for a Dionysiac chorus praying for victory in the comic contest. After the strophe (385–8), the antistrophe reads:

> And may I speak many funny things [*geloia*]
> and many serious things [*spoudaia*], and,
> worthy of your festival
> having played and mocked
> and won, may I be crowned.
>
> 389–93

Note the ambiguity of 'your festival' in 391, appropriate for both Demeter and Dionysus. The contrast of *geloia* and *spoudaia* is central to Old Comedy.[19]

By the end of the fourth hymn, Dionysus and Xanthias leave their hiding spot and join the dancing of the chorus.[20] Being caught up in the enthusiasm of the revellers incorporates the two, and prepares them for the next part of their journey.[21] Their three-line stanza is almost identical to that the chorus now adopts for the jesting, which replicates another part of the Eleusinian procession, the Jesting from the Bridge (*gephurismos*).[22] There remains a feel of something strophic even in these short stanzas, as the first two refer to Archedemus (416–21), who had begun Arginusae prosecutions [**5, 9**], and the next two to Cleisthenes (422–7), who had been one of the Arginusae generals [**5, 7**]. It would seem a third pair is begun on the subject of Callias (428–30), a priest of the Mysteries, who possibly had been caught having illicit sex while costumed as Heracles.[23] Additionally, it is possible to see reference to similar jesting evident in the extant fragments of Eupolis' *Demes* [**8**].[24] Maintaining the rhythm, Dionysus and Xanthias ask for directions, and Dionysus again instructs Xanthias to pick up the baggage (431–9).

The final hymn serves as an send-off, concluding this musical medley. The *koryphaios* appears to separate the chorus into two groups in different sections of the *orchēstra*, as Dionysus and Xanthias make their way for the door upstage. The underworld for initiates is not dark and gloomy, but bright and pastoral, for 'all we who are initiated and lead a life that is righteous [*eusebē*] to strangers and individuals' (456–9). These final words, perhaps surprisingly, seem to introduce a new theological dynamic to Eleusinian worship: this is the earliest Greek source where a believer's actions, and not simply initiation, have a positive outcome on one's afterlife. Was this understanding widespread, and simply not attested otherwise? Or is this Aristophanes the theologian? We simply do not know.

Scholars have hinged interpretations of the play on this *parodos*. In an influential article, Segal asked 'how the rather timorous and almost despicable figure of the first part of the play [Dionysus], can serve as arbiter in a contest of the gravest import at the end'.[25] Dionysus changes 'into a god of communal solidarity',[26] who embodies the Spirit of Comedy. This approach, seeing the development in the Eleusinian initiation of Dionysus, is developed further by Bowie and Lada-Richards.[27] This interpretation adheres to a familiar ritual pattern, whereby *katabasis* is a symbolic death and rebirth. This understanding has been aggressively challenged by Edmonds.[28] While this ritualist approach is attractive, it does not lead to a new Dionysus: Dionysus does not possess the dignity claimed for him in the second half, and he is not an abstracted Spirit of Comedy.[29] For Edmonds, a *katabasis* can exist as a literary device without necessarily implying ritual initiation. He challenges Bowie, claiming that the elements depicted do not map onto Eleusinian ritual clearly enough to constitute a recognizable initiation.[30]

This is an important critique, and it may be that Aristophanes is seeking to have it both ways. Dionysus-as-Heracles performs elements of an initiation, because Heracles had done so, and the Eleusinian context is the initiation most recognizable to Athenians. The preliminary rituals blur into other mysteries and rites, some of which are geographically contiguous with the Lenaia festival. Dionysus is both a comic buffoon and the god Iacchus, and the recipient of cult worship in the present festival and elsewhere. Aristophanes gains nothing by imposing limits on this interpretation.

I therefore question the interpretation of Bremer who characterized the *parodos* as 'a rather shallow and repetitive piece of poetry'.[31] There is great tonal variation in the short stanzas that draw the audience away from any expectations of theatrical performance to less elite musical form. The many hymns introduce a broad melodic variety without ever becoming turgid or repetitive. The emphasis on play and enjoyment (*paizein*) is a clue that sombre worship is not characteristic of the afterlives of those who had been initiated.

Two matters remain. First is the practical question of what happens to the Initiates' torches between the end of this song and the next mention of them (459–1525)? If they are removed by stagehands, there is virtually nothing in the intervening thousand lines that identify the chorus in their character as Mystai.[32] Alternately, if they are kept (positioned around the *orchēstra* perimeter, or at the *thymelē* in its centre), the underworld setting is continually reinforced visually, but also without any textual support. It is not clear which of these is more desirable as a directorial choice, but flames at the *orchēstra* centre would limit the staging choices for subsequent scenes.

Finally, the *parodos* also contains an extended passage, spoken by the *koryphaios*, in anapaests, a metre associated particularly with the regular marching of a choral entrance (354–71).[33] It is an appropriate metre for a *parodos*, used regularly in tragedy, but that is not the chief association here. In Old Comedy, anapaests are associated particularly with a central portion of the *parabasis* [**15**]. Their form here is contextually appropriate to the entry song: the *koryphaios* offers *prorrhēsis* ('the forbidding'), part of the Eleusinian rites in which there was a public announcement excluding the uninitiated from participating. The list rapidly shifts from the expected exclusion of the uninitiated to a literary level, as an expected reference to the bull-devouring god Dionysus has the Old Comic poet (and former rival of Aristophanes) Cratinus substituted (357). Cratinus is particularly appropriate since in his play *Wine-Jug* [*Pytine*] (Dionysia 423 BCE), he had presented himself married to a personified Comedy and enraptured by Drunkenness. Those not seeking to mend the civic strife in Athens or who are war profiteers or take bribes or are traitors (359–62), or who is a corrupt official like Thorycion (363), or (climactically?) anyone who prevents comic poets being paid a living wage (367–8), is forbidden from participating. As Bowie notes, 'Political crimes are thus set in an Eleusinian context.'[34] The attacks on individuals and groups of people in Athens are presented in the metre associated with the comic poet's direct advice to the citizens of Athens in the *parabasis*. *Spoudaia* and *geloia* are not opposites: they coexist, in a constant and uneasy tension whereby Aristophanes makes jokes which possess a serious resonance. In 405, he can do nothing else.

13

Disguise (*Frogs* 460–533)

Dionysus approaches Plouton's door and knocks, recapitulating the earlier scene at Heracles' door [**6**]. The individual who answers is never named, but is clearly a slave. The surprising association with Aeacus, one of the three traditional judges of the underworld, can be made with confidence. In Euripides' *Pirithous* [**8**], Heracles had a scene with Aeacus, and so for many spectators, there will be a programmatic expectation that such an encounter would be repeated here. Though the scholia provide contrasting identifications, Lucian regularly presents Aeacus as the gatekeeper in the underworld, and that is likely informed at least in part by this play [**26**]. Artistic depictions suggest the identification could be reinforced by giving Aeacus a knobbly staff.[1] As soon as the doorkeeper sees Dionysus, he is fooled by the Heracles costume and believes that this is Heracles returned. Aeacus the judge has been made a slave, and the Dionysus playing the part of a slave will be made a judge.[2] This topsy-turviness exists in the Athenian world of 405 where slaves become citizens and citizens are enslaved. We do not need to draw more significance than this, except to see that Aristophanes is creating resonances between his laughter-inducing scenes and his political message.

Thus begins one of the funniest comic scenes in Aristophanes. Despite the audience's ability to see all three layers of costume, characters in the underworld will only see what is on top. The Heracles disguise is, in that sense, perfect, and the scene will be more successful the less persuasive the illusion is for the audience. Aeacus' instant response is one of vehement anger, as he recalls how Heracles had taken his dog (Cerberus) the last time he was there. His bombastic paratragic verbal assault (470–8) is overwhelming as Aeacus storms off, leaving a frightened Dionysus behind.[3] Comically inverting a familiar religious formula (an example of bedpan humour), Dionysus proclaims 'I've shat myself [*enkechoda*]; call the god' (479). He borrows a sponge, supposedly for his weak heart, but uses it to wipe himself. The disgusting corporeality of human bodies, as a physiological extension of moral cowardice, is again reinforced through the body of a (supposed) god. Dionysus then gives the lionskin and club to Xanthias, who assumes the mantle of Heracles, and Dionysus, now playing the slave, picks up the baggage, just as the door opens again (492–502). Xanthias claims to be

'Herakleioxanthias' (499), which prompts Dionysus to label him the 'whipped slave [*mastigas*] of [the deme] Melite'. The scholia indicate that Heracles had a temple there (so *mastigas* is a comic substitution for 'god'), but since Callias also lived in Melite [**5**], and may have at one time appeared in a lionskin on the battlefield, there may also be an embedded reference to him as well.[4]

The next character at the door is not Aeacus, but an enslaved woman (503–20). She has come from Persephone, who is presented as working in the kitchen (as if expected Athenian gender roles were practised in the underworld as well).[5] She calls him 'dearest', offers him pea soup and, when Xanthias demurs, she suggests other appetitive delights, including food, female companionship, entertainment and almost certainly sex (soup had been used to explain *pothos* to Heracles previously, and the sexual implications of such desire were not avoided). The promised women include two or three dancers and 'a most attractive female aulos-player' (513–15 *aulētris … ōraiotatē*).[6] Xanthias, adopting the role he plays, gives instructions for Dionysus to carry the bags after him, and the woman leaves. Dionysus, equally aroused by the enslaved woman's offer, forcibly takes back the lionskin and club (521–33).

This exchange exploits the comedic dynamics of a master–slave relationship. Having established that one's innate social position (Dionysus as god, Xanthias as slave) is independent of one's moral fibre (Dionysus is a coward, Xanthias relaxed and unflappable), the scene shows that relationships with others are similarly contingent. Whoever has the disguise of Heracles is treated as if he has more status than anyone else in the scene. The humour develops because the elite but undeserving Dionysus is treated as a hostile high-status character, who demands an immediate and powerful contrary response, whereas the arguably deserving slave Xanthias is treated as a beneficent high-status character, who deserves fawning and appreciation. Dionysus fights to assert higher status than his slave, and when he is given it, the response is negative. Xanthias dutifully obeys his master, and when given high status, the response is positive. 'Status' in this sense is borrowed from Keith Johnstone. Status shows relationships, typically between characters, and clearly marks a hierarchy that expresses itself in terms of gesture, posture, voice and movement.[7]

Status relationships are always present between two characters, and this always gives actors clues for performance, even if they are unaware of Johnstone's vocabulary. Heracles laughing at Dionysus (42–6) established Heracles as higher status (he had the power, and possessed information that Dionysus needed). The corpse (170–7) established himself as higher status when he refused to accept the wages Dionysus offered. The frogs (209–67) were higher status than Dionysus, since he was struggling to see them even though they were in plain sight to the audience. Arguably, Dionysus' victory, appropriating their rhythm, raised his status with respect to them, and his claiming of high status drives them away, whereupon he is left scared and alone and low status. And so forth. Status is a powerful analytic tool that can be used to describe any theatrical scene, scripted or unscripted. Further, narrative interest is generated when two characters reverse the status they had over the course of a scene: here, multiple reversals, with different results, drives the action further, as Dionysus exerts his natural social position in hopes of achieving the specific high-status response that Xanthias is receiving. If the actors know the point when their status positions reverse, and they let it inform their performance, their instantiation of their characters will communicate to an audience.

14

Torture (*Frogs* 534–673)

Two more short scenes follow, and though the subject matter of the first (549–89) repeats and escalates what has just happened, the structure of the play ties it more closely to what follows. These structural elements create a pattern of expectation in the audience. The *ABAB*-pattern is known as an 'epirrhematic syzygy': choral lyric (in this case a strophic pair), *epirrhēma* (lit. 'that which is said afterward'), strophic pair, *epirrhēma* [**15, 18**]. For now, what is important is that the expectation created focuses audience attention on the second half, favouring it:

A1	strophe	chorus	534–40
A2	antistrophe	Dionysus	541–8
B	spoken scene	D, X, female crowd	549–89
A3	strophe	chorus	590–7
A4	antistrophe	Xanthias	598–604
B	spoken scene	D, X, male crowd	605–73

These technical elements are often obscured in translations, but they provide important non-verbal information to the audience about how the play is unfolding. It is, admittedly, complex, but in the same way that the return of a musical leitmotif can shape audience expectations about an individual character, so these structural features are worth recognizing because of the information they convey extra-dramatically to the audience.

The musical components are straightforward, and in fact represent the same strophic structure each time. The chorus members 'have altogether lost the character of the initiates they had in the parodos'.[1] The aulos-player accompanies the chorus and then a soloist each time, and (assuming that a few words have dropped in the manuscripts from 592), the metrical pattern of the stanza is sung a total of four times (each of the four A elements above). This pairs Dionysus' song with that of Xanthias, and gives an implicit weight to the latter.

The first strophe (534–40) has the chorus identify the cleverness (540 *dexiou*) of a man who adapts his position to ensure the greatest personal comfort, rather than enduring his lot. The example given is Theramenes, who had been part of the oligarchic coup in 411, had then helped in its overthrow, and who had failed to rescue survivors at Arginusae. This reality casts a dim light on the nautical metaphor used, where sensible self-care is abruptly reframed as political opportunism. Theramenes is crucial for understanding *Frogs* [**5, 9**], and his ambivalent presentation here does not make clear Aristophanes' personal views of him. As the passage is being sung, the character maintaining his comfort could be either Xanthias or Dionysus. Dionysus removes this ambiguity in his antistrophe (541–8): from his perspective, he thinks it ridiculous that an upstart slave would enjoy sex and a bowel movement (543–4) as Dionysus voyeuristically watched while masturbating (544–5), which is the presumptive response of domestic slaves as imagined by their masters (see *Knights* 24–9). Dionysus' fixation on hierarchy as he sees it is both pathetic and puerile, given his divinity.

Dionysus resumes the Heracles disguise, and three women enter – an Innkeeper, Plathane (a common Athenian woman's name derived from *plathanon*, 'bread-pan', appropriate for a baker) and her slave – all rushing the one they suppose is Heracles. They probably enter along an *eisodos* rather than from Plouton's door (it could be either, as neither has been used since the location has refocused in the underworld), suggesting that news of Heracles' arrival has spread.[2] Of course, they are not the female company Dionysus had wanted when he reclaimed the lionskin and club, as comic reversals continue. They harangue Dionysus, while Xanthias offers various unhelpful comments for his own, and the audience's, amusement (552, 554, 563, 568). The women remember Heracles in the past had shown himself a glutton, but also that he had drawn his sword in (mock?) madness (564). No other mention of a sword is made, and it is not clear if Heracles earlier would have carried one. Regardless, the unexpected reference evokes the filicidal and uxoricidal madness of Heracles dramatized in Euripides' play *Heracles* (*c.* 418 BCE), which was one of the few times he had appeared as a tragic figure. Determined to do something, the women each go (in separate directions?) in search of an advocate (579 *prostatēs*, a male citizen with the right to represent them in court). The Innkeeper seeks Cleon, and Plathane seeks Hyperbolus. These men were both pro-war Athenian demagogues in the 420s and 410s, now deceased (and so conveniently available in the underworld), and were regular targets of Old Comedy and Aristophanes.[3]

There is no way to stage this exchange with fewer than four speaking actors [**15**], which I believe was not allowed by the normal rules of the contest. There are ways that both characters could be voiced by a single actor, with the intent to deceive the audience, but more likely, if I am correct, the scene as it stands will have been adapted when the play was reperformed [**25**]. There is indication that other sections have been adapted [**19, 21**], but there is no direct evidence for adaptation here other than Plathane speaking.

Dionysus' immediate reaction to the harangue, of course, is to want to return the club and lionskin to Xanthias. Using a 'wheedling diminutive'[4] *Xanthidion* (582 'Xanthy-baby'), Dionysus implores his slave to resume the role that he had earlier forbidden him to play. Xanthias' prophecy at 532–3 ('perhaps sometime you might have need of me again, if the gods wish it') is fulfilled. The strophe and antistrophe (590–604, repeating the melody from 534–48) confirm the transfer of disguise: the chorus notes that Xanthias acts the part, 'glaring terrifyingly' (592), and that Dionysus is likely to change his mind again. Xanthias acknowledges that is likely, and draws attention back to the central door, which opens.

Dionysus' treatment of the disguise has been consistently reactive: giving it away when threatened (Aeacus, the Innkeeper and Plathane) and taking it back when Xanthias was offered food and sex by the domestic slave. As the syzygy moves into its final element, there is a moment of satisfaction for Dionysus when he sees that Aeacus is returning: he has finally got it right, and Xanthias is finally going to suffer instead of him (605–15). Dionysus' delighted quips (606, 610–11, 612) recapitulate those of Xanthias in the previous spoken section. The audience is rewarded by seeing the pathetic coward finally on top, until Xanthias takes it away with a single sentence, using the Heracles disguise to reassert his high-status position: 'Take my slave boy here and torture him [*basanize*]' (616).

In Athenian law, slaves were unable to testify without being tortured. This process was called *basanos*, and was supposedly needed to avoid testimony that was biased (whether in favour of their masters or against them depends on circumstances). Surviving legal speeches have owners rejecting the torture of their slaves by others (presumably because it risks reducing their value, in addition to revealing what the torturer wants to hear). Though it has been disputed whether *basanos* was a real procedure or a legal fiction, never actually used in practice (or only rarely),[5] the present scene argues for its familiarity to Athenian audiences. Xanthias-as-Heracles' offer of his slave for torture to determine the truth immediately reverses the status dynamic, and returns Dionysus to his comically low-status position. Again, the underworld assumes features of real-life Athens, as Xanthias places no limits on the torture allowed (618–22).

Now desperate, Dionysus attempts to assert high status by claiming he is a god (629–34). Aeacus is shocked at this insolence, and Xanthias suggests that he should be flogged all the more, since a god would not feel it. Dionysus responds, 'Well then, since you say you are also a god, why don't you also get blows equal to mine?' (635–6). 'Good point,' is all Xanthias can respond (637).

The status-games [**12**] continue, but now that the two have been levelled with each other, rather than reversal of status positions, they enter into a contest for high status:[6] both will be whipped, and the one who does not cry in pain is (obviously) the god. 'From this point the rationale of the torture-scene changes,' Sommerstein observes. 'Its original object was to establish whether Xanthias-Heracles was guilty of stealing a dog; henceforth the issue is whether Xanthias-Heracles or Dionysus is really a god.'[7] This shift in focus anticipates the similar shift in the motivation for Dionysus' *katabasis*.

Aeacus accepts this proposal and begins whipping Xanthias and Dionysus alternately. Both men remove their clothes (and are stage-naked, wearing only the *sōmation*, as they had appeared on the Berlin vase [**6**]), and the whippings begin.

- The first blow, against Xanthias (645 mid-line), does not register. Dionysus insultingly calling him *mastigas* (501 [**13**]) has proved true.
- The second blow, against Dionysus (646 mid-line), also causes no audible response.
- The third blow, against Xanthias (649 mid-line), produces the exclamation, *iattatai*,[8] which Xanthias covers by pretending he is remembering a deme festival of Heracles at Diomeia.[9] The club and lionskin may even be lying on the ground before his face as he hunches over to receive the whipping.
- The fourth blow, against Dionysus (652 line-end), causes him to shout *iou iou*, which he claims is a shout of delight at seeing approaching cavalry, and that his tears are because he smells onions. The same phrase is found for pain at Sophocles, *Trachiniae* 1143 and *Oedipus* 1071, but for joy at Aeschylus, *Agamemnon* 25. It is possible that the placement of the blow at a line-end allows for a bigger physical wind-up, as the poetic line is completed.
- The fifth blow, against Xanthias (656 line-end), evokes an *oimoi* (another standard tragic exclamation). He claims to have a thorn in his foot.[10]
- The sixth blow, against Dionysus (658 line-end), makes him shout 'Apollo', which he completes as a line of the poet Hipponax (though the scholia attribute it to the poet Ananius; fr. 1).
- The seventh blow, also against Dionysus (663 line-end), is in the belly, at Xanthias' request. Dionysus shouts 'Poseidon,' and completes it with a lyric from Sophocles' lost *Laocoon* (fr. 371). The sudden introduction of a snatch of familiar music (performed unaccompanied, I presume) is the largest reaction, and least plausible attempt at masking pain yet.

Both Xanthias and Dionysus struggle to maintain composure, and increasingly fail to do so as each blow reduces the status of the victim. Finally, an exasperated Aeacus defers to Hades and Persephone (here called by the Athenian form of her name, Pherephatta). The syzygy ends with everyone departing, and Dionysus closing with a joke, saying he wished that Aeacus had thought of this resolution earlier (672–3).

This exchange constitutes a second contest (*agōn*) in the play: the first was Dionysus in competition with the Frogs [**10**], the third will be Dionysus judging a competition between tragic playwrights [**17–23**]. The narrative of *katabasis* can represent the journey as a symbolic conquering of death. Konstan argues that the play exhibits three modes of transcending death through initiation for him, this confusion between Xanthias and Dionysus reflects the uncertain personal identity in this liminal stage.[11] My sense is that the initiation of Dionysus is not prominent here. The scene's humour is generated on a number of levels, and the contrast with the first element of the syzygy, when the women were attacking Dionysus, is what is foregrounded structurally. Earlier, the women's verbal assault (accompanied by them hitting him?) showed Dionysus failing to assert himself as a god. In the second spoken scene, the whippings from Aeacus similarly failed to distinguish Dionysus, who received more blows and seemed less able to govern his pain response.[12]

The parallelism is perhaps reinforced by Aeacus' attendants. He has at least two slaves obeying his orders (605), and he calls for reinforcements from Ditulas, Skebluas and Pardokas, who are three Scythian archers (such as were used in Athens as constabulary). At least five extra bodies increase the threat posed by Aeacus. Perhaps Aeacus delivers the blows, but it may be the Scythians: Athenian archers carried whips (*Thesmophoriazusae* 933, 1125, 1135), and while Aeacus assumes legal and moral responsibility for the interrogation regardless (using first-person verbs, e.g. at 646 'I will go to this guy and strike him'), the actual whipping could be done by the experts.

15

Parabasis (*Frogs* 674–737)

The chorus is central to the appreciation of any Greek play, even when its role is minimized, as it is arguably in *Frogs*. In Old Comedy, there are two choral sections that help define the audience experience. These are the *parodos* (when music begins and the chorus first enters) and the *parabasis*, when the chorus 'steps aside' from its dramatic persona and addresses the audience directly. These two points articulate the structure of the comedy. Because our evidence comes from one poet, however, it is not clear that this is generally applicable. Cratinus' *Dionysalexandros* [**1**], for example, appears to contain parabatic material in the *parodos*.[1] Aristophanes' early plays seem to presume an expected structure for a *parabasis*, even if it is not always followed.[2] That structure is built around the anapaests, spoken by the *koryphaios*, and the epirrhemmatic syzygy (an *ABAB*-structure [syzygy], where a strophic pair alternates with speeches [*epirrhēmata*]). In *Frogs*, the anapaests appear as part of the *parodos* [**11**], and here, at the expected moment for the *parabasis*, we have only the syzygy: a strophe sung by the chorus as a whole, twenty lines in trochaic tetrameter spoken (or chanted) by the *koryphaios*, an antistrophe (repeating the same melody as before), and another twenty trochaic lines by the *koryphaios*.[3]

The strophe (674–85) focuses on Cleophon, the most influential democrat since the restoration of the democracy in 410 [**5, 9 15, 25**].[4] Cleophon had been the chief architect in rejecting a Spartan peace proposal, after the battles of Cyzicius in 410 and Arginusae in 406 [**9**], as he would again in 405 after Aigospotamoi, [**25**]. Determined to continue the war regardless of the cost, his democratic, pro-war position was opposed to the elite perspective with which Aristophanes aligns himself.[5] Cleophon would be executed during the second oligarchic coup of 404. The sacred chorus is called to witness 'the mob of people, where ten thousand [*muriai*] brains are sitting who are more ambitious [*philotimoterai*, literally 'honour-loving'] than Cleophon' (676–8). This might also provide a ball-park estimate for the size of the audience at the Lenaia. Estimates for theatre audiences are now assumed to be between six and eight thousand for a single performance at the Theatre of Dionysus, though new archaeological investigations may revise that.

Pericles' citizenship law of 451/450 decreed that children needed two citizen parents to be a citizen.[6] It would be easy to cast aspersions on the true citizenship (and so the true allegiance) of anyone born just before that time, since near contemporaries, only a few years younger, would have been subject to the new law (as might have been the case for Aristophanes himself [**2**]). This is a guess, but such a situation would fit for an ambitious politician and general in his late 40s at the time of *Frogs*. Cleophon's lips are 'babbling on both sides' (679 *amphilalois*), suggesting he does not speak proper Greek (or proper barbarian, for that matter), which is appropriate for a Thracian swallow (681). The imagery shifts again and Cleophon is now a nightingale, whose song of lament indicates he will die 'even if they [i.e. the votes] are equal' (685).[7] Cleophon is not going to escape legal redress through a hung jury (Orestes in Aeschylus' *Eumenides* avoided execution through a split vote). At the same time, another play at this competition of the Lenaia is Platon's *Cleophon*. Aristophanes suggests metatheatrically that Platon's dramatic entry will die even if votes are tied, and (reflecting back on the use of the name earlier in the strophe), those watching the performance rightly expect more than they are going to get from the comedy *Cleophon*.

Paired with this, and marking the syzygy structure, is the antistrophe (706–17). This stanza is focused on Cligenes, who is probably Cligenes of Halae, who served the Athenian Boule (deliberative council) in 410/409 [**5**]. If his name is rightly restored to Lysias 25.25, he was responsible for organizing several executions that year, which would not have made him popular with the elite. The fact that he may have owned a public bath and a fullery (the latter of which would smell of urine, an association that could easily be transferred to him in popular thought) explains the emphasis at 710–13 on the watered-down detergents (712 *pseudolitrou*, 'sham-shampoos'). He is a monkey (708), he was short (709), prone to fight, prone to drink, and liable to be attacked at night for what he did (714–17). He does seem to be a target ripe for mockery.

Similarly paired are the two speeches by the *koryphaios*, each of which is twenty lines long and accompanied by the *aulētēs*. These speeches, positioned in the *parabasis*, would be recognized as the poet's advice to his city. Because it is still delivered in a context where persuasive advice is likely to appeal to the judges of the theatrical contest, the views here cannot be accepted as Aristophanes' personal opinions without question, but there is an alignment between this advice and the poet: it purports to be from him, through the *koryphaios* his mouthpiece, and the passage begins by asserting this as a right: 'It is right for a sacred chorus [*hieron choron*, cf. 674] to advise and teach the best things to the city' (686–7). The advice concerns Athenian citizenship. Given that slaves who fought at Arginusae had been given Plataean rights [**9**], which the speaker is emphatic is a great decision (693–6), other citizens, who also have fought in sea battles should be pardoned and forgiven (697–9). These men are presumably the same as those described earlier who need their fears alleviated. They had been deceived by Phrynichus the oligarch, son of Stratonides, who had established the Four Hundred in 411, and who was later assassinated [**5**]. Aristophanes praises the enfranchisement of slaves who fought for Athens and at the same time entreats for mercy for the oligarchs: Can't we all just get along? 'Let go of your anger' (700), he pleads, as he again compliments the spectator's intelligence, calling them 'most wise' (701).

The companion speech to this reinforces the same message, establishing a parallel with the debased coinage Athens had been using. Sparta, having taken advice from the traitorous Alcibiades [**21**], had occupied the countryside town of Decelea in 415, before the Sicilian expedition [**9**]. This affected trade but also limited the Athenian ability to access their silver mines in Laurion, leading to the defection of up to 20,000 slaves (Thucydides 7.27). Without silver, the Athenians were minting cheaper copper coins for internal use, since silver would be needed for external trade. In this allegory, the Athenians are keeping the debased coins for themselves (730 'copper', i.e. slaves granted citizenship), and not caring for 'the old coins' (720, i.e. the landed elite associated with the Four Hundred). The old families are from the 'best and brightest' (728 *kai kalous te kagathous*), trained in choruses; the new citizens are base, red-headed foreigners (730; like the Thracian Cleophon). These final lines are aggressive, defying the audience and calling them 'fools' (734 *anoētoi*). The wisdom they earlier possessed (676, 700) has gone. 'Change your ways and use the useful again' (734–5). Implicit in this, Moorton has argued, is a cautious argument for the recall of Alcibiades [**22**].[8]

This is not the advice I want Aristophanes to be giving. It is a message that offers forgiveness to those who overturned the democracy for their own benefit, at a time when Athens was desperate in war and had suffered great losses. Now, six years later, the desperation was worse and the losses even greater. The elitist perspective in the coin allegory still accepts the newly minted citizens, notionally ascribing the same value to them as the old stock, but it does qualify the earlier claim that their enfranchisement had been a great idea. It had been a practical solution to an otherwise intractable problem.[9] As *Frogs* refuses to let us forget, Arginusae and its aftermath had been a disaster for democracy. Perhaps Aristophanes was exhausted, or merely reflecting his own preferences as a landowner himself. Perhaps forgiveness of all citizens, treating the old ones equally with the new, was the only way ahead he saw as viable. But this sentiment will not have sat well with all spectators. The fact that there were individuals on the pro-war democratic side such as Cleophon – corrupt, contemptible political opportunists – meant that neither side possessed a moral high ground. Aristophanes is willing to use the *parabasis* to challenge the assumptions of the audience that they could do without those who had been associated with the Four Hundred.

We live in a world where politics are becoming more divisive, and right-wing parties drive voters increasingly towards the extremes of the political spectrum as the left struggles to present a coherent and unifying vision of itself.[10] This is the case in several countries, not just my own. If there is no common ground to be found, there can be no political advance, and no progress. I cannot say that Aristophanes is arguing for a centrist position, but he is using the public choral space in Athens to urge his listeners to find some common perspective from which to speak: *Let go of your anger*. We do not need to agree on everything to be able to talk meaningfully. But you cannot expect only one side to compromise: *Change your ways*. These are lessons for both factions, but anger and resistance to change seem ever to increase. Citizenship conveys democratic responsibilities, whether you are a new citizen or from an established family. Respect your fellow citizens, participate in the city, and do not exclude those with whom you disagree.

Within a year, it would be clear that this was terrible advice [**25**].

16

Xanthias (*Frogs* 738–829)

The comedy duo of Dionysus and Xanthias, a god and his slave who happily change roles in their impersonations, is 'the first of western comedy's great master-servant double acts'.[1] If I were acting in the play, I would want to be Xanthias. Heiden suggests that it is a role Aristophanes himself played,[2] which is an appealing thought, even if there is no evidence to support it.

All Greek and Roman theatre employed doubling, in that actors would play multiple parts in any production. In fifth-century tragedy, three speaking actors were used in each production, in addition to the chorus and its leader. In Old Comedy, the number is not known: I have argued that three were also used (and that has implications for the text of *Frogs*, discussed below); MacDowell argues that there were four allowed; others effectively set no limit for the number of actors in competition, allowing for 'extras' to take small speaking roles as needed.[3] If we for the moment assume that the minimum will be used (and that the same actor plays a given role wherever possible; i.e. we do not have three Dionysus actors), then until the end of the second *parodos*, the role-division in *Frogs* is straightforward (when a character is not onstage for the full range, I have indicated when they are present):

	A	B	C
1–459	Dionysus	Xanthias	Heracles (38–164)
			Corpse (170–7)
			Charon (180–270)

The actor I have labelled C (it is not clear that the terms protagonist, deuteragonist and tritagonist were in use at this time) is responsible for some quick changes, particularly from the Corpse to Charon. (Note that this concerns speaking actors only; the bier-bearers would be unspeaking extras paid for by the *chorēgos*.)

	A	B	C	D (?)
460–673	Dionysus	Xanthias	Aeacus (464–78)	
			Maid (503–20)	
			[Innkeeper (549–78)	Plathane (549–78)]
			Aeacus (605–73)	

For thirty lines (549–78), four actors are needed to perform the surviving script [**12**]. We cannot say whether the third actor takes the Innkeeper or Plathane (it could be either). Following the *parabasis*, the division remains straightforward, but options are introduced.

738–813	A	B	C
		Xanthias	Slave

I assign the role of the slave to actor C rather than A, so that the Dionysus actor has a longer break and because C has played several roles already; but the part could be performed by A.

830–1527	A	B	C	D (?)
	Dionysus	Aeschylus	Euripides	Plouton

Again, I have indicated a choice in giving Aeschylus to B, the Xanthias actor. Euripides to C. This could be reversed, but future chapters argue [**17–23**] Aeschylus offers some showcase opportunities, and I am happy to follow the judgement of Pickard-Cambridge, Russo and Dover.[4] Plouton is sitting in the performance area throughout this long section of the play. That again seems to point to the use of a fourth speaking actor. Significantly, however, Plouton only speaks from 1414–1527 [**22, 23**], and this, I believe, can be traced to the revision of the text for reperformance [**25**].

There are three obstacles to seeing *Frogs* as a three-actor play. The first is the quick change required of the Corpse to Charon (177–80), at the end of one *eisodos*, while Xanthias picks up the baggage again. The second is the scene at Aeacus's door from 549–78. The humour emerges from the confusion as multiple characters contend for Dionysus-as-Heracles' attention [**12**], and I believe the lines could be performed by a single actor, if the scene was not expanded when it was reperformed, which is also possible. The third is Plouton. While my understanding of the second and third of these points depends on an understanding of the reperformance conditions, the first is not, I feel, an obstacle in practice. It is, rather, another opportunity for actor C to demonstrate his versatility amid the many characters he plays.

If *Frogs* is not a three-actor play, the efficiency that is otherwise shown in the assignment of roles becomes much less focused. For example, there is no need to map the Xanthias actor onto either Euripides or Aeschylus; that becomes merely one possibility among many. I find this less aesthetically satisfying, and believe that there is a virtue in seeing the Xanthias actor excel in another major role within the same play, which is an aesthetic required in the assignment of parts in other ancient plays. Strict actor limits (of either three or four speakers) create constraints that allow for meaningful doublings.

Whatever the case, this scene constitutes a farewell to Xanthias. If he does return later [**22**], it is without mention in the script. Lines 738–813 allow the Dionysus actor time to pause, while it affords an opportunity for spectators to see two slaves speaking with one another. Xanthias' interlocutor is likely a character not previously seen onstage, and so it is not Aeacus [**13**].[5] Spectators will not know that Xanthias will not return, though it may be possible to guess that from the conversation.

The dialogue begins with a description of Xanthias' divine master as *gennadas anēr* (738 'a well-bred man'). 'How could he not be well-bred [*gennadas*], when he only knows how to drink and fuck [*pinein kai binein*]?' (739–40): Xanthias' response immediately undermines a sense that Aristophanes is unquestioning in his apparent support of the political views of the elite. In what follows, the two enumerate the many pleasures available to an enslaved person, which particularly feature dunning their master one way or another (741–55): badmouthing one's owners, meddling, eavesdropping and gossiping are all deserving of punishment, but a joy nonetheless. The joy is a sexual one: when gossiping about his master, the unnamed slave says, 'I come in my pants' (753 *ekmiaisomai*, lit. 'I stain myself out').[6] The two end this discussion by giving each other a hug and kiss to affirm their friendship. Of course, the dialogue is written by someone who is not enslaved, and the dialogue is idealized (and artificial) in many ways. Nevertheless, Aristophanes gives Xanthias a warm send-off, valuing him as a human being.

A great commotion is heard inside the *skēnē*, and the exposition explaining it will shape the remainder of the play. It is all new information: the noise is coming from the tragedians Aeschylus and Euripides (758), and their dispute has led to a civil war (760 *stasis*) among the dead.[7] It is a deft touch if the two characters talking about the tragedians, and hearing the noise within, are played by the actors who will shortly adopt those roles. As the slave explains, there is a law (761 *nomos*) in the underworld that for each craft (762 *technē*) the best practitioner gets free meals at the Prytaneion (764, a public dining hall in the Athenian agora, here transferred to the underworld) and the right to sit in a chair (765 *thronos*) next to Plouton. Aeschylus had held the Chair of Tragedy (769; I capitalize it to suggest what is at stake is more than a physical object, but social position in the underworld), but now that Euripides has died, there is popular demand for a trial (779, 785) because Euripides had given a demonstration of his sophistic, wily speeches for the wide assortment of criminals already dead (771–6). Did this correspond to anything one could see in Athens? Were there demonstrations by playwrights of their forthcoming dramatic works? Possibly this evokes the process of pitching plays to the relevant archon for production, seeking a right to compete [**2**], but we do not know if spectators were allowed to witness such proposals.[8] Plouton's decision is to have a contest (785 *agōn*), a word that became attached to a regular structural element of Old Comedy, comprising a formal contest between two opposing ideas.

Aristophanes establishes expectations for the playwrights. Euripides wants to measure and build: the language used makes imagery literal, with reference to physical objects and measuring devices for assessing poetic skill (796–802). This plays on the word *technē*, which can be used of the professional knowledge of any master craftsman. Aeschylus, in contrast, bellows like a bull at this prospect (803–4). He is associated with strength and nature. Finally, as judge for the contest, it is Dionysus, Xanthias' master, who has been selected (810–11).

Similar images are taken up by the chorus in the short hymn of four brief stanzas that will follow the departure of the slaves from the performance area (814–29), during which the actors will change costume and mask. Euripides has the sharpened tooth, whittling his craft with deft words that will drown the roar of the thunderer Aeschylus, who is a blasting force of nature with whirling eyes and a shaggy mane. Sophocles, the third likely contender, has excused himself from the contest, agreeably deferring to Aeschylus (785–94; these lines may have been late additions to the script in the light of Sophocles' death).[9] Scharffenberger's examination of this hymn notes that in many ways it creates a 'sound portrait' of Aeschylus, which presages the response he will regularly receive in the *agōn* that follows.[10] The presentation of Aeschylus is not entirely negative: the thundering imagery evokes Paphlagon in *Knights* (236), and the storm imagery evokes both the positive image of Zeus and the negative image of Cleophon, mentioned at 681–2 (238).

All this exposition is new, and with it Dionysus' Great Idea specifically to fetch Euripides has been refocused [**4**]. There is no sense that the idea of an underworld technical Chair pre-exists this play, and yet its introduction feels natural and is accepted without question. The purpose for which Dionysus embarked on his *katabasis* has been abandoned in favour of holding an *agōn* between two great tragedians: one who had died long before, and one who had only recently passed away. The slaves depart, heading into the *skēnē*, where the actors will (I believe) adopt the roles of the rival playwrights.

As Dover describes,[11] Xanthias appears to represent a new character type on the comic stage: a slave that emerges as a distinct individual, not merely following orders and serving as a stagehand (as in *Acharnians*), nor appearing a coded representation of an historical figure (as in *Knights* or Eupolis' *Marikas*). A similar character is found in Karion in *Wealth*. Xanthias gains the upper hand over his master, and remains jovially unflappable in the light of ever-increasing danger on this fantastic journey. His level-headedness reinforces Dionysus' cowardice, and his self-assured demeanour is charming. 'Xanthias never openly defies his master,'[12] conscious that the status quo will return, but willing to enjoy transient moments of authority. While the genesis of Xanthias can be attributed to the enfranchisement of slaves at Arginusae,[13] I am not sure this is necessary. The comic potential of an assured slave serving a weak, hesitant or indecisive buffoon of a master – even when that master is the god Dionysus himself – offers comic potential waiting to be discovered.

17

Contest (*Frogs* 830–94)

The contest in the middle of the play begins *in medias res*. It is the third *agōn* in *Frogs*, and by far the most substantial. It anticipates the tone and sets the foundation for the nature of the tragedy-based humour that dominates the rest of the play. As the chorus finish their song, Plouton's door opens, and out rolls the *ekkyklēma*, a wheeled platform used in tragedy for revealing interior scenes.[1] It presents a marvellous tableau: on a throne, centrally, sits Plouton himself, silent and stately. Though there is no textual mention of him, the character speaks at 1414 and this is the natural place for his entry. Like so much else in the play, Plouton also had Eleusinian connections.[2] Next to him is Dionysus, in his adopted role as judge of this contest. He is no longer disguised as Heracles (there is no reference to the lionskin and club, and the attempted disguise is no longer needed), but is still recognizable by his *krōkotos* and *kothornoi* [**6**]. He may also be sitting, but I would not insist on that.[3] There is at least one other chair, Aeschylus' Chair of Tragedy [**16**], on which presumably Aeschylus sits as Euripides attempts to wrestle the chair away (830; possibly Euripides has picked up the chair and holds it away like a spoilt child). The precise dimensions of the *ekkyklēma* and the width of the double door are not known, but the visual impact of the four figures emerging at once, mid-struggle, is dynamic.[4]

The energy and intensity of the scene are very high from the start. Euripides is already desperate and the characterization of both playwrights in broad strokes happens quickly. Euripides will be arrogant (831, 835). In his plays he makes heroes into lame beggars in rags (842, 845–6), a jibe aiming particularly at *Telephus*, the play that will drain from Euripides' skull if Aeschylus attacks him (855).[5] *Telephus* (438 BCE) had been a regular source of humour for Aristophanes throughout his career (*Acharnians* 410–79, *Peace* 146–8, *Thesmophoriazusae* 689–764).[6] His songs are 'Cretan monodies' (849), a reference to the solo songs by scandalous female heroines such as Phaedra, Aerope and Pasiphae.[7] Though his mother sells vegetables (840, parodying a Euripidean line),[8] Euripides is proud of 'the words, the songs, the sinews of [his] tragedies' (862). In contrast, Aeschylus will be solemn and dignified, like his tragedies (833–4), but also overflowing with anger (844, 856). He is a force of nature, a typhoon (848), a hailstorm (852) or a burning oak tree (859). His speech is bombastic, using long invented words (837–9, where seven of ten words begin with the letter alpha, and the last line consists of only two words making a single verse, *aperilalēton kompophakelorrēmona*, an 'uncircumlocutory megabombastolocutor'.[9] Where Aeschylus' words are 'torn chunks', Euripides offers 'whittled sawdust' (881): neither of these is a compliment, but it reveals the contrast between unbridled nature and urbane precision.

This introduction to the playwrights ends with a good joke from Aeschylus, who claims the contest is not equal (867),

> since my poetry did not die with me
> but his did with him, so he will have it to read.
>
> 868–9

Aeschylus boasts of posthumous reperformances of his plays [**18, 24, 25**], which are still alive on the Athenian stage. The fact that Euripides had left unperformed plays at his death (*Iphigenia in Aulis*, *Bacchae* and the now fragmentary *Alcmaeon in Corinth* were all performed a few months after *Frogs* at the Dionysia in 405) is conveniently omitted.[10]

Dionysus calls for fire and incense (871), and the *orchēstra* is ritually purified, by the choristers and perhaps other stagehands as the chorus sings a short song to the Muses (875–84). Smells trigger memory powerfully, and the introduction of a ritual scent into the dramatic world incorporates the spectators into that experience.[11] The 'great contest of wisdom' (882/3) is about to begin, and each playwright invokes divine assistance. Aeschylus prays to Demeter, that he may be worthy of her Mysteries (887): this is appropriate not only because of the Eleusinian identity of the chorus, and the fact that Aeschylus' home deme was Eleusis, but it is also as a joke. Demeter might be the least appropriate god for Aeschylus to invoke, since it was thought that he had revealed the secrets of the Mysteries in his plays. Aristotle suggests that Aeschylus accidentally revealed secrets (*Nicomachean Ethics* 3.2, 1111a10).[12] Sutton's guess, that Aeschylus included the sacrifice of a piglet in these plays, which was a feature of Eleusinian worship (337–8 [**12**]), is plausible.[13]

When Euripides prays, he does not invoke any of the usual gods, but personal divinities: 'The Sky [*aithēr*] my Nourisher, Axle-pin of my Tongue, Comprehension, and Smell-challenging Nostrils' (892–3). In *Clouds*, Socrates prays to his own divinities (*Clouds* 265, 423–4), and the charges at his trial included inventing new gods (Plato, *Apology* 23d). This is a mark of a modern Athenian intellectual, challenging the received *polis*-religion [**12**] and thereby associates Euripides with the sophists. It is natural for us today to think of

Euripides as middle-aged and Aeschylus as old (with a white beard,). To the Athenians, for whom Euripides was a familiar face, it would be natural to present Euripides as they most recently remembered him, which is (if the biographical tradition that he began competing in 455 BCE, the year after Aeschylus died, can be trusted) as a man in his 70s. Both playwrights would likely have appeared in 'old man' masks.[14] The stakes for the conflict are now clear and precisely delineated: old vs. new, nature (*phusis*) vs. culture (*nomos*), monstrous rage vs. sophistic weaselling.

18

Teachers (*Frogs* 895–1098)

The *agōn* between the poets begins with a very precise structure. While the detail can seem intimidating, and the terminology obscure, what is important is to recognize that there is a parallelism at work that carefully structures the audience experience of the poetry. At heart, it is another epirrhematic syzygy [**14, 15**], an *ABAB*-structure where the B component (the *epirrhēma*) comprises not a single speech, but a wider range of elements:

A	Choral Ode (strophe)	chorus	895–904
B_1	*keleusmos*	*koryphaios*	905–6
B_2	spoken dialogue	E, D, A	907–70
B_3	*pnigos*	E, D	971–91
A	Choral Ode (antistrophe)	chorus	902–1003
B_1	*keleusmos*	*koryphaios*	1004–5
B_2	spoken dialogue	E, D, A	1006–76
B_3	*pnigos*	A, D	1078–98

The architecture of this section is deliberate, and each half uses the full range of performers onstage. A strophic choral ode is followed by the *koryphaios* (chorus leader) announcing the transition with the *keleusmos* ('command' or 'bidding'). There follows a stretch of dialogue, which is concluded with two characters each delivering a *pnigos* ('choker', a feature also found in a full *parabasis*, but omitted earlier), which is a patterned speech that was meant to be delivered in one breath (Euripides and Dionysus in the first half, Aeschylus and Dionysus in the second, again creating balance). The effect of this structure is to foreground the content of second half.

The choral strophe (A, 895–904) continues the balanced perspective of the two playwrights established in their previous exchange [**17**]. One, Euripides, will be elegant while the other, Aeschylus, will be excavating root-and-branch.[1] Following this, the *koryphaios* bids both of them to begin speaking (905–6). When the antistrophe comes (992–1003), while it is metrically and musically identical to the earlier song, its content is addressed entirely to Aeschylus. Using an elaborate sailing metaphor (warships are never far away from what happens in this play), Aeschylus is encouraged not to reply in anger, but to hold the course of his argument. The song even begins with a quotation from the opening lines of Aeschylus' tragedy *Myrmidons* (fr. 131), which equates Aeschylus with the wrathful hero of the *Iliad*. For now, at least, the chorus seems won over. Similarly, the *keleusmos* (1004–5) is directed solely at Aeschylus. By addressing the antistrophe to Aeschylus, the chorus indicates its preference between the playwrights.

The same is true of the *pnigos* in each part. Intended as a kind of showpiece, the *epirrhēmata* end with a 'choker,' with each speech at least notionally meant to be delivered in one breath (and so at speed). This is a feature found in the patter-songs of Gilbert and Sullivan (where the tempo can accentuate the singer's precise diction and the use of a single breath, as in the 'Major-General's Song' [**10**]), but also in non-theatrical songs such as the Merry Macs's 'Breathless' (1942) and Shankar Mahadevan's 'Breathless' (1998).[2] Significantly, both *pnigoi* are about the content of Euripides' tragedies. In the first, Euripides claims that as a result of his plays, Athenians understand more and manage their households better, protecting their property (971–9): this is 'the achievement he most vividly takes pride in'.[3] Dionysus concurs, and imagines a series of banal concerns masters might now bother their slaves with (980–91). In the '*antipnigos*' Aeschylus enumerates the faults Euripidean drama has brought to Athens, continuing from line 1069. The political context makes it clear that art is presumed to influence life:

> Of what woes is he not the cause?
> Did this guy not show whorehouse madames, [like the Nurse in *Hippolytus*]
> women giving birth in temples, [like Auge in the lost *Auge*]
> women having sex with brothers [like Canace in the lost *Aeolus*]
> and women saying life is not life? [like Pasiphae in the lost *Polyidus*]
> And then from this our city
> was filled with junior administrators
> and mass-monkey beggar-buffoons
> always deceiving the masses?
> No one can carry a torch
> any more from lack of exercise.
>
> 1077–88

The quickly-stacked allusive references to four tragedies shows the density of Aeschylus' literary reference, and the effect is overwhelming. This final reference is to the torch race at the Panathenaea [**8**], and Dionysus' response is directed only to that point. He describes a particular racer who was pale and overweight, being slapped by onlookers as he ran, farting, and blowing on his torch to keep it lit (1089–98). Possibly, this refers to an actual participant in the Greater Panathenaea in 406, but it might equally be an invented anecdote. Human bodies are gross and funny, and are an appropriate subject for laughter. Again, Dionysus seems to miss the point, even as he gets the final word. The epirrhematic structure foregrounds Aeschylus' contribution, and the negative assessment of Euripides' verse replaces that which Euripides himself had provided. All of this frames two spoken scenes.

The first exchange explores general features characteristic of each playwright's style.[4] Euripides sets the tone for the discussion, and in doing so probably comes off better. At 907–36, Euripides castigates Aeschylus for introducing figures at the start of a play who sit motionless without saying a word – what are now known as 'Aeschylean silences'.[5] While the examples of Niobe in the lost *Niobe* and Achilles in the lost *Myrmidons* are provided, the silent and immobile presence of Plouton on the *ekkyklēma* would serve as an immediate trigger for spectators, cuing them that he is performing another Aeschylean silence. When these Aeschylean characters do speak, their invented compound words represent big ideas but are incompletely understood. In contrast to this, Euripides put tragedies on a diet (937–70), and introduced a set of features designed to increase accessibility to tragedy: his plays had expository prologues, ordinary characters discussing ordinary things, and this was fundamentally 'democratic' (952 *dēmokratikon*). This is obviously a loaded word (perhaps it should be translated 'populist'), and with it comes not only an association with support for the lower classes, but also associations with pro-war demagogues. The claim that Euripides introduced 'everyday household objects' (959 *oikeia pragmata*) into tragedy along with ordinary, non-elite characters will become important later in the play [**18, 20**]. Euripides lists individuals who have followed his example, Clitophon and Theramenes, who were both oligarchs who abandoned their party to help restore democracy.[6] This positions Aeschylus against free speech, recalling the days when not everyone had this right (and so implicitly with the oligarchs).[7] Dionysus gets caught up in the debate, playing a yes-man to whoever is speaking, admitting he was deceived by these theatrical tricks. He has goofball answers, and displays almost no authority to serve as the judge beyond what the audience attribute to him in his role as patron of theatre.

The second exchange attempts to isolate the specific qualities that make a poet admirable (1009).[8] Euripides' answer is immediate: 'Cleverness [*dexiotētos*] and being thought-provoking, and because we improve people in the cities' (1009–10). The first two of these qualities are clearly Euripidean, and again associate him with the intellect [7]. The third is the rhetorical climax: poets improve (literally 'make better') people in the cities. It is an awkward periphrasis for citizens. The choice of *anthropous* ('people') would seem to include women, too, and the plural *poleis* ('cities') suggests not only Athenians benefit from publicly performed poetry. Is this too broad a claim in 405? Apparently not: the answer is accepted by Aeschylus and Dionysus, who then ask what fate should await a poet who has done the opposite, making people worse. Dionysus suggests nothing less than death (1012, the same penalty that Aeschylus had suggested Euripides deserved for allowing a wider range of characters to speak). Yes, it is hyperbole, but it is also uncomfortable for anyone to be this keen on public execution. This might be funny, but I think in the light of the generals at Arginusae [**9**], the extreme penalty is potentially upsetting in its rashness.

Should the stakes of poetry really be so high? As the dialogue continues, Aristophanes' characters would seem to say yes. When asked what Aeschylus has done to improve citizens, he answers that he 'made a play full of Ares' (1021), *Seven Against Thebes*. He then directed (1026 *didaxas*) *Persians*, in which 'I taught [*exedidaxa*] them to desire to defeat their opponents always' (1026–7). The didactic element of tragedy as presented here is simplistic: spectators will emulate behaviour they witness onstage. The possibility for any influence of this sort, however, is important to Aristophanes. He makes a point of blurring the role of the theatre director with that of the teacher (*didaskalos* is the word for both functions), and he cites plays by name, which he expects his audience to recognize. This is significant, especially since it suggests plays could be known by their individual titles, separately from their tetralogies. Both *Seven* (from 467) and *Persians* (472) survive, and so we can evaluate the comic responses to these examples from Dionysus: he jokingly suggests that Thebans (rather than Athenian spectators) were made more aggressive by *Seven against Thebes*, and that the memorable part of *Persians* was bringing a soul back from the dead, which is exactly why Dionysus has come to Hades in the first place.[9] Aeschylus continues by presenting himself in a long line of poets (Orpheus, Musaeus, Hesiod and Homer, 1032–6, with 1035 *edidaxen*) and claiming to have used the hero Lamachus as a model for his characters (1039), not whores (1043 *pornas*) like Phaedra and Sthenoboea, who had appeared in Euripides' *Hippolytus* and the lost *Sthenoboea*.

Aeschylus articulates his role of the poet-as-teacher:

> The poet must hide what is base [*ponēron*],
> and not bring it onstage and not teach it. For young children
> have a teacher [*didaskalos*] advise them, but on becoming men they
> have poets.
> It is absolutely necessary for us to say useful things [*chrēsta*].
>
> 1053–6

These much-quoted lines are framed from Aeschylus' perspective, but Euripides does not disagree. Any qualifications raised concern what constitutes being 'useful', arguing that his natural dialogue is more human (1058). Again, the two senses of *didaskalos* overlap, especially since tragic poets typically directed their own works. People need teachers, and this is the civic function of the poet. Aeschylus then provides two examples of the way in which (he feels) Euripides has not fulfilled this purpose. By bringing on beggars in robes, he has provided an example to the elite on how to avoid paying liturgies, and particularly outfitting triremes [**2**]: the fact that Aeschylus brought Xerxes on in rags, in *Persians* no less, does not diminish the cumulative effect of again signposting *Telephus*. By teaching (1069 *edidaxas*) Athenians to gossip, the crew of the flagship of the Athenian fleet, the *Paralus*, talk back to their officers. The *Paralus* had a crew of all citizens, and so both of these concerns are tied directly to the responsibility of citizens to the Athenian navy. The stipulation shows that Arginusae was not the only time slaves had served on other ships, and that the innovation in 406 was by granting (Plataean) citizenship to them.

A final detail invites some speculation. Aeschylus is playing loose with chronology, and when it has been noticed, it has not aroused concern: Sommerstein suggests Aristophanes 'did not know (and probably did not care) which of these two plays was actually produced first'.[10] The use of *eita* (1026 'then') creates a chronological relationship between *Seven* and *Persians* that is not accurate.[11] Though not all the poets listed (1032–6) were historical individuals, they are in what seems to be reverse chronological order. There is no way that Lamachus (a general from the 430s and 420s, who had appeared as a character in *Acharnians*) could be the historical model for any Aeschylean character. There is a way that these inconsistencies can be understood, however. Lamachus had been a general from the 430s to the Sicilian expedition (Plutarch, *Pericles* 20.1 and *Alcibiades* 18.1), when he was killed in battle in 414 (Thucydides 6.101.6). *Acharnians* is also the earliest we know of Aeschylean plays being reperformed [**25**], and for the *Frogs* audience, it is the time around which they will have begun to see Aeschylean plays in performance. Knowledge of *Persians* and *Seven* (and the *Oresteia*, also mentioned by name [**19**]) may therefore be thought to derive from the period of Lamachus, and it may be that the history of reperformance did restage *Persians* and then *Seven Against Thebes*. Aristophanes and his audience may not know about the dates of the original production (though that information will have been available, and may be hinted at in the reversed list of non-theatrical poets), but many might remember the sequence in which they has been reperformed, in the lifetimes of the audience members.

19

Prologues (*Frogs* 1099–1247)

Frogs is often considered 'the earliest work of genuine literary criticism',[1] and this is true in several senses. The play explicitly thinks about the place of literature, and of publicly performed poetry, in society. It is self-aware as a comedy, questioning from its opening line what makes a comedy effective. More than this, however, it offers critical comment on specific elements of the genre of tragedy, and it is these passages to which the belief in the play's literary-critical strengths reside. The observations are funny, and they are not as substantial as is sometimes thought. They do, however, point to what a close reading of tragedy could offer to a contemporary. As the *agōn* continues beyond the confines of the epirrhematic syzygy [**18**], the tragedians turn to prologues, how tragedies begin. Following a short choral song (stasimon) to set this next portion apart structurally (1099–118), Euripides attacks Aeschylus' openings (1119–76) and then Aeschylus attacks those of Euripides (1177–250).

The stasimon consists of a strophic pair, and for the most part its content is unexceptional. In the strophe, the chorus address the tragedians and encourage them to continue their discussions. The contest is explicitly framed as an inter-generational conflict (1106 'both the old [*ta palaia*] and the new [*ta kaina*]', though this might equally be a judgement call, 'both the old-fashioned and the newfangled'), and their critiques are to be both subtle (1107 *lepton*; not 'slight' as in *Gerytades* [**8**]) and clever (*sophon*, cf. 1104 *sophismatōn*). The joke comes in the antistrophe, as the chorus continues its encouragement, saying that it is not the case that spectators lack learning (1109 *amathia*) and will not understand subtleties (1110 *ta lepta*),

> For they are war veterans
> and each has a book [*biblion*]
> and understands clever things [*ta dexia*].
>
> 1113–14

Spectators are veterans both literally and figuratively, old hands at tragedy. Evaluative terms for literature are frequent, and audience members are flattered as the chorus talk about them. Exactly what is meant by *biblion*, however, is anybody's guess. Even allowing for comic exaggeration, what is it that each spectator supposedly possesses: a programme? a strip of papyrus for taking notes or recording bon mots? a personal scroll of a play, like Dionysus' copy of *Andromeda*? None of these seems right, but whatever is intended points to a degree of functional literacy being important to play-going – understanding the written word is important for appreciating performance.

Euripides' critique of Aeschylus' prologues begins, at Euripides' request, with the opening to the *Oresteia* (1124),[2] Aeschylus' set of plays from the Dionysia of 458, the three tragedies of which survive (*Agamemnon*, *Libation Bearers*, *Eumenides*). This is the earliest attestation of the term '*Oresteia*' for Aeschylus' plays, which, as with the play titles mentioned earlier [**18**], demonstrate the ways plays could be discussed in everyday Athens. Problematically, however, the lines cited come from the second tragedy (*Libation Bearers*) and consist of lines that aren't in the manuscripts. The latter issue can be explained by the textual transmission of Aeschylus' plays in the manuscripts, but the former issue appears to be an inconsistency. I have suggested that perhaps *Libation Bearers* and *Eumenides* were remounted for performance at the Lenaia at some point soon before *Frogs*, and that it would be natural for Aristophanes' audience to think of that stage performance as 'the *Oresteia*';[3] that is speculation, however. Aeschylus recites the first three lines of *Libation Bearers*, to which Euripides claims he can find 'more than a dozen' (1129) errors, quickly rounded up to twenty errors per line (1131).

In the end, Euripides lists five mistakes. He suggests that word choice is inappropriately positive for a god witnessing Agamemnon's murder; that the cult title used of Hermes is inaccurate; that Aeschylus uses pleonasm and says the same thing twice, using more words than are needed; and that he does so again; and that one of the words repeated is not technically accurate (1137–76). Aristophanes has Euripides undercut the elevated style of Aeschylean tragedy. Aeschylus' response is, predictably, haughty and indignant anger, which is appropriate. The effectiveness of this sort of close reading, however, depends in part on the audience knowing the lines already, whether they read them in school or heard them onstage. And, given that the plays are from more than fifty years earlier, any aural familiarity is most likely from reperformance. The choice of the *Oresteia*, then, is not random: these are Aeschylean plays to which Athenian theatrical culture had already given a prominence, and which were to some extent familiar to the *Frogs* audience. Dionysus' contribution to the debate is consistently to lower the tone, introducing bathos. He makes joke interruptions that do not advance the criticism (about tomb robbers, borrowing from neighbours and yelling at the dead). More importantly, however, he encourages exposition by asking for clarification and additional details. In this way, he retains his low-status position (in relation to the playwrights), and provides smooth transitions for Aristophanes from one critique to the next:

> **Dionysus**
> And you, how do you make prologues?
> **Euripides** I'll tell you . . .
> 1177

Aeschylus' critique of Euripides' prologues begins in the same tenor as Euripides' critique. When challenged to recite a prologue, Euripides chooses *Oedipus* (a play from the past ten years, well after Sophocles' *Oedipus Tyrannus*),[4] and Aeschylus diagnoses logical faults, such as whether Oedipus could ever have been truly happy (1178–97). Like the *Oresteia*, the example is cherry-picked by Aristophanes to be both familiar and vulnerable to this sort of critique. Aeschylus then raises the stakes, and claims 'I will ruin your prologues with an oil flask' (1200).

This passage, and the nature of the joke, is one of the most discussed in Aristophanic scholarship, and no agreement on its meaning has emerged. Euripides begins reciting his prologues, and Aeschylus interrupts, interjecting the phrase *lēkuthion apōlesen* ('[he] lost his little oil flask') – what Goldhill calls 'semantic hooliganism'.[5] With increasing frustration, Euripides tries prologue after prologue, and the phrase can be inserted in the first three lines to complete a verse and still maintain syntax (twice in the case of *Meleager*, though two opening passages were known to Alexandrian scholars, 1237–42).[6] The apparent repetitive sentence structure of Euripidean prologues is being criticized, though again these are cherry-picked examples, and the critique (that a noun or noun phrase ends at the caesura of an iambic line, so that the verb and object can be placed after the caesura) is hardly identifying a major stylistic flaw. Humour emerges from the repetition, and Euripides' inability to perceive which of his own verses will be able to be completed with this clause: Dover speculates that over the course of the six prologues given, the audience might even begin participating, completing the line along with Aeschylus.[7] Further, the *lēkuthion* is an everyday object (cf. 959 *oikeia pragmata*), and so Aeschylus is adding a Euripidean quality to the Euripidean verses, in order to ruin them. Sansone argues that the verb *apōlesen* should be understood to mean not 'broke' or 'misplaced' but rather 'had stolen' (an interpretation confirmed in 1242), and that this undercuts the claim Euripides had earlier made about teaching Athenians how to protect their own property (979 [**17**]).[8] Dionysus' interjections reinforce the banality of the resulting sentence, and add to the humour when he blames Euripides for having written his verses in this way.

The greatest controversy is whether there is an additional layer of meaning in the phrase: whether the *lēkuthion* is equated with the penis (or, since the vase shape is not the long thin container archaeologists today call the lekythion but rather the small bulbous aryballos, the scrotum). This idea was proposed by Whitman, and has found many adherents, including Borthwick who draws out the connections with the fourth-century Athenian youth gang called the *Autolēkuthioi* (Demosthenes 54.14, 'Hard-ons').[9] Certainly when Aeschylus says that he could use a tuft of wool, a little sack, or an oil-flask (1203), the grouping invites genital associations. Aeschylus' interjections would then be emasculating Euripidean tragedy.[10] Further, this is an appropriate fate for mythological figures like Aegyptus (1206–8), who fathered fifty sons. Importantly, however, Aeschylus symbolically castrating Euripidean verse is present regardless of whether *lēkuthion* itself suggests a penis. Though finding possible sexual double entendres in literature is not a difficult sport, and some spectators might hear such a nuance in this passage, I am persuaded that we should be sceptical that this is how the joke operates for most listeners in antiquity.[11]

20

Songs (*Frogs* 1248–1364)

As Dionysus wearies of the oil-flask's power to disrupt Euripidean prologues, he signals that Aeschylus has been victorious in that round of the contest. As the previous episode closes, he suggests that sung lyric (1248 *ta melē*) should be the next battleground, a prospect Euripides is eager to seize (1249–50). Again, the segment is blocked off by a short choral song (1251–60), which is insubstantial, but, in a view that evolved over several generations of scholars, is now rightly seen to contain two versions, one of which (likely 1251, 1257–60) originates with the performance in 405, and the other (1251–6) with reperformance [**25**].[1]

Euripides' interest in sung lyric derives from the association of his plays with New Music, a set of compositional and performative innovations which, though they found their roots as early as the mid-fifth century, became particularly prominent in the tragedies of the 410s, influenced in part by the dithyrambs of non-Athenian composers such as Timotheus.[2] These innovations included the possibility of a greater separation of vocal and instrumental melodies, the use of melisma (holding a single syllable over several notes), elaborate metaphors and imagery, and indirect periphrases. This was seen as a generational difference, and the aulos came under suspicion for its ability to imitate other sounds (compare the 1950s and 1960s suspicion of the electric guitar at the birth of rock and roll).[3] While traditional tragic songs were strophic, with strophe and antistrophe repeating melodies in responsion, one feature of New Music song was the increased use of astrophic lyric (without responsion), particularly in solo song (monody). As such, lyric melodies become an important differentiator of old-fashioned and newfangled styles, from traditional choral music to the increased professionalism of the late fifth century.

Aristophanes' comedic brilliance in this scene is achieved not by having the tragedians boasting of their own musical accomplishments, but by having them imitate the other's lyric styles. By putting songs in the wrong mouth, as it were, Aristophanes allows the mockery to emerge more clearly, and allows Aristophanes the creative freedom to invent songs in the style of each playwright. It invites spectators to laugh at the features a rival identifies, rather than cringe at a playwright's misplaced pride in something shown to be deficient. Four songs are sung: two by Euripides in an Aeschylean style, and then two by Aeschylus in the Euripidean style. It would be natural to see these as escalating, a crescendo leading to Aeschylus mocking the New Musical style of Euripidean monody. In all four songs, the character singing works with the aulos-player, the supposed spontaneity of the songs being undercut by the musical support the singer receives from the aulos.

The first song (1264–77) consists of apparently random lines of Aeschylean tragedy alternating with a refrain, 'Oh no! A blow! Will you not come to their rescue?' (1265, 1267, 1271, 1273, 1275). The selection of individual lines are dactylic, recalling the (even more old-fashioned) poetry of Homer, and the first two, if the audience could place them, were relevant for *Frogs*: 1264 is from *Myrmidons* (Aeschylus fr. 132, which had Achilles' Aeschylean silence [**18**]), 1266 is from *Psychagogoi* [*Soul-Raisers*] (Aeschylus fr. 273, which staged Odysseus' *katabasis* in *Odyssey* 11).[4] The song's opening words, 'Phthian Achilles' (1264), are a subtle evocation of the 'slight' poet Cinesias.[5] Disjointed, dactylic, hard to follow and with a regular refrain that evokes early Greek ritual, Euripides' first version of the Aeschylean style is slow, measured, stately and perhaps turgid or pompous.[6]

The second song (1285–95) removes the refrain, but instead inserts *phlatto-thratto-phlatto-thrat* ('strum-a strum-a strum-a strum'), a vocal imitation of a lyre being played.[7] The old-fashioned feel is suggested in an anecdote about Sophocles, who was said to have played the lyre when he acted the title role in *Thamyras*, accompanying himself to epic hexameters (*Life* 5, Athenaeus 1, 20e–f). Since Sophocles retired from acting because of *microphonia* ('a little voice,' *Life* 4), *Thamyras* is often placed early in his career, in the 460s or 450s (and so roughly contemporary with Aeschylus). There is something potentially ridiculous in having a human voice sing the words *phlatto-thrat* while miming accompaniment to the lyre, rather than actually strumming a stringed instrument (and further, that there is aulos accompaniment for the stringed music). The lines again are adapted from Aeschylean tragedy and satyr play, drawing primarily on *Agamemnon* 108–11 (and so continuing the *Oresteia* associations in 1124–76 and 1276). All of this is above Dionysus' head, who wonders if the *phlattothrat* comes from duplicitous con men (or, possibly, from those singing work songs) from Marathon.[8] Aeschylus is said to have fought at Marathon, and this associates the elder playwright with this tradition of Athenian heroes ('Marathon-fighters' is used in a way similar to 'The Greatest Generation' in reference to Americans who fought in the Second World War). Though Aeschylus' association as a *Marathonomachos* is not certainly attested before this (an epitaph of Aeschylus records the fact, but many think it is later), the detail, however, predates this play, as this line jokingly suggests his role there was not military but either as a con man or a menial.

Aeschylus is silent throughout Euripides' imitations of him, and when he does speak, he stresses the uprightness of his compositions (1298 'for the good, from the good'), tying himself to the tragedian Phrynichus (1299, cf. 910 [**5**]).[9] In contrast, according to Aeschylus, Euripides draws on brothel songs, drinking songs, and Eastern pipe-music and dances. He calls for a lyre, but abandons it, both because it would confirm that Euripides had a point with his *phlatttothrat* joke, but more importantly to allow him to call on the Muse of Euripides, an unspeaking character who comes onstage.

That Euripides should have a personal Muse inspiring his poetry, in this context, means that her appearance should be immediately identifiable and funny. For Sommerstein, 'she is an old and ugly woman, heavily made up, and dressed like a prostitute'.[10] For Dover, she might be 'an old hag, an extremely ugly younger woman in dowdy and patched clothing, or a garishly made-up prostitute . . . the only thing we can be sure of is that she is neither dignified nor attractive'.[11] This is one way the joke can work, but not the only way. The introduction of a non-speaking female character is frequent in Aristophanes, and this one has potsherd (or seashell?) castanets, to provide non-traditional musical accompaniment. The scholiast suggests castanets are an evocation of the music made by Hypsipyle to soothe the infant Opheltes in Euripides' *Hypsipyle* (*c.* 409 BCE). Further, the Muse will remain onstage dancing to at least the first of Aeschylus' Euripidean parodies. While grotesque dancing of a man wearing a padded bodysuit and an old woman mask is possible, that limits the joke to one only of laughing at the woman, who is simply unMusical.

An attractive Muse, possibly even a real female dancer appearing naked (but wearing a bodysuit), would allow for her dancing to complement the song and not distract from it. Such women are found throughout Aristophanes, and Euripides' Muse could easily be among their number.[12] An attractive female figure dancing well would enhance the Euripidean song, which increases the effectiveness of Aeschylus' parody.[13] Dionysus' instinct is to assume that a Muse should not *lesbiazein* (1308): a verb that puns both on a 'Lesbian' or Aeolic style of music, but more immediately suggests giving oral sex to men.[14] There is then another level at which the humour is operating. On the one hand, Euripidean music is being presented as both erotic and exotic, drawing on Eastern melodies, Aeolic metres and musical innovations.[15] In contrast, Aeschylus is being compared to the older, traditional Doric musical tradition. The contrast between Doric and Aeolic is fundamental to Greek music, but can be confusing: the names associated with Doric music (which supposedly flourished in Sparta, Delphi and Crete), include the Spartan Alcman but also Terpander, a seventh-century (pre-Sappho) musician from Lesbos.[16] Spectators hear the verb *lesbiazein*, and following the initial meaning, think also of Aeolic music but not necessarily music from Lesbos.[17]

The third song (1309–22) is an astrophic choral number showcasing features of New Music. The imagery of seabirds and ships sailing and dolphins leaping evoke several extant Euripidean songs, particularly from *Electra* and *Hypsipyle*.[18] Unlike Euripides' parodies of Aeschylus, this is (mostly) an original song and not a patchwork of excerpts. The distinctive melismas of New Music are here spelled out in the comic text, as spiders are suddenly introduced, so that *heilissite* ('you wind [your webs]') becomes *hei-ei-ei-ei-ei-eilissite* (1314, where each repeated syllable would be sung with a different note). The imagery barely coheres, with 'oracles and racetracks' (1319 *manteia kai studious*) thrown in as representative tragic fare not needing a context (both are present in Sophocles' tragedy, *Electra*, from *c.* 412).[19] The final line, 'Throw your arms around me, baby' (1322 *periball' ō teknon, ōlenas*), apparently evokes the end of a monody in *Hypsipyle*, and may have involved Euripides' Muse giving an embrace to one of the characters onstage. Sommerstein suggests Dionysus (who was a character in *Hypsipyle*),[20] but it could equally be one of the playwrights, either Euripides (since she is his Muse) or, better still, Aeschylus as he appropriates the persona of his rival, 'winning' her with his song. Though Aeschylus is dignified and pompous, while he is imitating Euripides he sheds that pretence and adopts the style (and apparent morals) of the man he mocks.

At the end of his turn as Euripides, Aeschylus regains his composure and calls attention to a metrical feature, which Dionysus misunderstands as an anatomical one: when the playwright asks if Dionysus noticed that foot, the god (again) misses the point and examines the foot of the Muse. At this point, she can leave the stage, or go to Dionysus, or get ready to dance to the next song. Borthwick additionally detects an allusion to Euripides' mockery of the recognition tokens from Aeschylus' *Libation Bearers* in *Electra*.[21] Aeschylus compares Euripidean 'melody' (1326 and 1329 *melē*, which given the preceding also puns on 'limbs,' as at Cratinus, *Seasons* fr. 276) to the 'twelve tricks of Cyrene' (1327–8), an image that connotes the sexual versatility of a famous sex worker (*Thesmophoriazusae* 98, Platon fr. 134) and the New Musical innovations offered by a twelve-string lyre (Pherecrates fr. 155). In Pherecrates' *Cheiron*, Mousikē, personified as a woman, describes being physically violated by composers of New Music (fr. 155).[22] With the Muse's embrace, then, Aristophanes creates a complex layering of images. When the audience sees the Muse embrace one of the stage figures, it additionally perceives a paratragic evocation of Euripides' Hypsipyle embracing her son, another of Euripides' Electra embracing her brother Orestes, and finally a sex worker (like Cyrene or Euripides' mother or Pherectrates' Mousikē) embracing 'Euripides' (the role Aeschylus is playing, or possibly Euripides himself).[23]

The fourth song (1331–63), Aeschylus' second Euripidean parody, is an elaborate astrophic monody.[24] Unlike the other numbers which were notionally choral songs, this one highlights the professionalism of New Music and makes the most musical demands on any of the speaking actors; these songs are the standout moment for the Aeschylus actor. Earlier, Euripides had boasted that his plays introduced *oikeia pragmata* (959 'everyday things') but had also questioned the appropriateness of Aeschylus' use of compounds like 'horse-cock' (932 *hippalektruona*, cf. 937) for a heraldic device, as he apparently did in *Myrmidons*: 'Was it also necessary to write about a cock in tragedies?' (935 [**18**]). This song picks up on both of those questions, and presents the trauma of a young woman lamenting the loss of her pet cockerel.

The singer begins by addressing the Night (as does Euripides' Electra in her opening song, *Electra* 54) which has sent a dream from Hades (the characters are in Hades), a vision 'cloaked in corpse black' (1336 *melanonekueimona*, a compound expanding on one in Euripides' *Hecuba* 705). She calls for assistance from her slaves (1338), Poseidon (1341), those in her household (1342), the nymphs (1344) and Madness herself (1345), because Glyke ('Sweetie') has stolen her cockerel (1343–4). She was 'wi-i-inding' (1348 *eieieilissousa*, repeating the joke from line 1314) a skein of flax to sell at the market when the bird (metaphorically?) flew away (1352). She calls on Cretans (citing a line from Euripides' *Cretan Men*, cf. 849) along with Dictynna, god of the hunting net, her hunting puppies and finally the goddess Hecate, leading with a torch in each hand, while she searches Glyke's home (1356–63). Stanford stresses that the song represents the ever-changing mood of Euripidean monodies,

> especially their exaggerated emotionalism, sensationalism, triviality of association, lapses into prosaic style, and quick changes of feeling (reflected in the rhythms). ... Many stylistic features are parodied, notably E.'s emotive repetitions (1336, 1352–5), *Oxymoron* (see on 1331), references to dimness and gloom (in the manner of 19th-century 'gothic' romanticism ...). The touches of *Bathos* in 1342, 1345, 1360, 1364, are ... not typical of E.'s lyrics elsewhere and may simply be Ar.'s method of throwing the hysterical character of the rest into relief.[25]

Her foreboding dream is 'a soul that has no soul' (1333 *psuchan apsuchan echonta*), a poetic effect reinforced by excessive anadiplosis, the repetition of words for intensifying effect. When the bird has 'flown away, flown away' (1352 *aneptat' aneptat'*),

it left pains, pains [*ache' achea*] for me
and tears, tears [*dakrua dakrua*] from my eyes
did I shed, did I shed [*elabon elabon*], wretched me.

1353–5

There is no final judgement given; Dionysus rapidly moves on to the next part of the contest, but the effect of these musical parodies will have been clear. Aeschylus-as-Euripides is effective and funny, and even if one was not a fan of New Music, one would recognize and measure the success of the parody by its ability to reproduce the experience of hearing it in a Euripidean tragedy. Aeschylus has gone second in the opening syzygy, in the contest of prologues, and the contest of lyrics [**18–20**], and each time Euripides is unable to cap or close the scene. Aeschylus even sets the terms for the next stage of the contest, which is to weigh words in scales (1365–9).

21

Scales (*Frogs* 1365–1410)

A short choral lyric again sets off the next scene, while a balance is brought into the performance area (1370–7). If Plouton continues to sit on his throne at the door (having been rolled out on the *ekkyklēma*, in a silent tableau at 830), then it would be awkward to use the door to bring the balance into view.[1] Bringing it to the centre of the *orchēstra* gives it a prominence appropriate for the approaching end of the play, keeping it in the focal point of the audience, as Plouton watches from the doorway.[2] In form the scales will have been an upright post, supporting a horizontal balance, from which were suspended two pans. The technology is shown on a black-figure vase from the 530s BCE by the Taleides Painter (Metropolitan Museum 47.11.5),[3] but the pans would be empty. As Dionysus says, it is like weighing cheese in the market (1368–9).

At Dionysus' instruction, both playwrights hold a pan and deliver a line onto it (1378–81). In the same way that Euripides has used material imagery to describe his poetic *technē* (939–44), now the poets will weigh their verses literally, and the weightier poetry will win. Spectators who remember that earlier passage will recall that Euripides had put tragedy on a diet, and so the outcome of this part of the *agōn* might be predetermined, but the fun of the metaphor being literalized maintains theatrical interest.[4] The Slave had promised that music would be measured (797; *mousikē* can also include art, poetry and literature), but the literal understanding of what that phrase promised has been delayed until now. The scene almost certainly resonates paratragically with a lost play of Aeschylus, *Psychostasia* (*The Soul-Weighing*), in which Zeus weighs the souls of Achilles and Memnon as they fight, while their mothers plead for them with Zeus.[5]

There are three rounds, each of which Aeschylus wins by having his pan go down with the weightier line. In the first (1382–8), the Spercheius river (from Aeschylus' *Philoctetes*, fr. 249) is deemed heavier than the (metaphorically) flying hull of the *Argo* (from Euripides' *Medea*, line 1). In the second (1389–98), Aeschylus' Death (*Niobe*, fr. 161.1) outweighs Euripides' Persuasion (*Antigone*, fr. 170). Aeschylus has caught on quicker than Euripides, realizing that this has nothing to do with poetic accomplishment, but only to do with the weight (literal or figurative) of the objects being designated by the words. For his third attempt, Euripides starts with the promising word 'iron-loaded' (*sidehrobrithes*), in a periphrasis for 'spear':

> He took the iron-loaded wood in his right hand.
>
> 1402, from *Meleager* fr. 531

Aeschylus responds,

> Chariot upon chariot, corpse upon corpse.
>
> 1403, from *Glaucus of Potniae*, fr. 38

Again, a clear winner in the terms by which the contest is operating, even if Dionysus misunderstands the line, mistakenly thinking that it is limited to two chariots and two corpses (1405–6). When this scene was staged by the National Theatre of Northern Greece in 1971 (dir. Kostas Mihailidis), a woman standing on wooden blocks held a pan in each hand to represent

Figure 21.1 The Weighing Scene in *Frogs*, Theatro Technis of Karolos Koun (1966). Photo by Tassos Koutsoukos, from the Elite archive.

the scales. This avoids the mechanical problem of empty scales which must always tip in the same direction, but several practical solutions are possible to achieve the needed effect.[6] Karolos Koun's 1966 production with his company Theatro Technis[7] shows something much closer to the probable ancient aesthetic (see figure 21.1). With Dionysus in the middle and the chorus in half-masks standing in the background, the intensity of the tragedians glaring at each other while holding their pans conveys the stakes of the scene.

Defiant, triumphant, Aeschylus proclaims that two lines of his poetry could outweigh Euripides, his wife, his children, Cephisophon, and his books (1409 *biblia*). Euripides' library had been mentioned earlier (943, 1313), as had Cephisophon (944, and see 1452–3). Mention of Cephisophon is by itself humorous, and his name appears to have been a staple in Aristophanic parody of Euripides (fr. 596). Though he has been thought of as a slave or an actor of Euripides, humour seems to reside on his friendship with Euripides (which was close enough to allow the suggestion he had slept with Euripides' wife) and that he had helped write Euripides' lyrics (indirectly pointing again to the professionalization of the New Music [**20**]).[8] Here, Cephisophon is associated both with Euripides' professional and personal life, and the presumption that he would contribute to the weight of Euripidean poetry undercuts the playwright further.

Dionysus stops the contest, without explanation. If my interpretation is correct, Aeschylus has gone second at each stage of the *agōn*, and has consistently shown himself superior, even if Euripides was the original object of the quest. Yet Dionysus does not want to offer a verdict:

> The men are my friends, and I will not judge them,
> Because I don't wish to endure hatred from either of them.
> For I think one to be clever [*sophon*], and I delight in the other.
>
> 1411–13

The language does not make clear which playwright is which in 1413, and though it may have been made clear with a gesture, even that is uncertain. The word *sophon* (also at 1107), which can mean 'clever' (like the Sophistic Euripides) or 'wise' (arguably appropriate for either poet), is ambiguous, and Dionysus' delight in Euripides has been clear since he described the sudden *pothos* he felt while reading *Andromeda*. When ancient and modern scholars have made a decision, it has been that Euripides is the clever one, but English commentators have preferred to keep the line ambiguous.[9] The term is a moving signifier, serving as a marker of poetic ability, but with its referent shifting. The contest was introduced as an *agōn sophias* (884 'contest of wisdom'), and it is the chief virtue for which their poetry aspires. A similar confusion is found at 1434: one speaks *sophōs* ('cleverly'), the other speaks *saphōs* ('clearly'). Given that nothing Aeschylus has said (in *Frogs* or in his plays) can be said to be particularly 'clear', I think if Aristophanes wants Dionysus to indicate one or the other, it is Aeschylus who is *sophos*, even if Euripides continues to bring Dionysus delight.

22

Alcibiades (*Frogs* 1411–66)

What is your opinion on Alcibiades? Seemingly out of nowhere, the literary contest between tragedians shifts gears with a political question concerning an individual who has not explicitly been named in the play so far. Alcibiades (451/450–404/403) was the most notorious and ambitious politician in late-fifth-century Athens. Following the death of his father in 447, Alcibiades became the ward of Pericles, which had ensured his prominence among the Athenian elite. Alcibiades had fought for Athens alongside the philosopher Socrates at Potidaea (432) against the Corinthians, and at Delium (424) against Boeotian allies of Sparta.[1] He had been appointed as one of the commanders of the Sicilian expedition (415), but was recalled for a trial concerning religious offences associated with the mutilation of the herms in Athens immediately before the expedition sailed (Thucydides 6.27). The defacing (or rather castrating) of these statues was a huge scandal, and rather than face trial Alcibiades defected to Sparta. He advised the Spartan occupation of Decelea [**15**], but by 412 he fled to the Persian satrap Tissaphernes, who controlled western Anatolia. He did not acquire Persian support for the oligarchic coup in 411 but in 410, after the Four Hundred were overthrown, he was given joint command of an Athenian fleet, which won a decisive victory at the battle of Cyzicus (Diodorus Siculus 13.50–1). He returned to Athens in 407, and was appointed *stratēgos autokratōr* ('supreme commander'; Plutarch, *Alcibiades* 33). For the first time in several years, he ensured that the procession of the Greater Mysteries could be celebrated (Xenophon, *Hellenica* 1.4.18 [**12**]), but he was ultimately responsible for the naval defeat at Notium (406) and so was sent into exile in Thrace during Arginusae [**9**] and when *Frogs* was staged.

For some, Alcibiades was responsible for Athenian failures in Sicily and Notium, an extravagant aristocrat who was nothing more than an opportunist. At the Olympics of 416 BCE, he had entered seven chariots, and had taken first, second and fourth place in an ostentatious display of personal wealth and ego (Thucydides 6.16.2–5, Isocrates 16.34).[2] When he returned to Athens in 407, his trireme had expensive purple sails, and an *aulētēs* and the tragic actor Callipides running the ship (Athenaeus 12.535d). For Alcibiades, life was art, and poetry had a place in military affairs. All this suggested elite, oligarchic sympathies and personal advancement before anything else. And yet, Alcibiades was also a tactician and orator who could rouse the Athenians and achieve victories, a potential help to a desperate city if his many vices were indulged. How do you solve a problem like Alcibiades? Aristophanes raises this question, but because of textual difficulties the answers given are not especially clear.

Dionysus, an inept judge, has failed to make a decision. Suddenly a new voice is heard. Plouton, who has been seated silently since he appeared at 830, suddenly speaks. It is a surprise use of another speaking actor, and a particularly Aeschylean moment, as the 'Aeschylean silence' is broken by a character who has been onstage motionless (911–13). As discussed, here again a fourth speaking actor is apparently needed [**16**]. Yet the interruption is surprisingly banal:

Dionysus
... For I think one to be clever, and I delight in the other.
Plouton
Then you will not do what you came for.
Dionysus
And if I choose?
Plouton
You will leave, taking whichever
one you choose, so that your trip won't be a waste.
Dionysus
Bless you. Come then, learn this from me:
I came down here for a poet. Why? ...

1413–18

Plouton then says nothing until 1467 ('Make a choice'), and then at 1479 and 1480, when he invites Dionysus and Aeschylus inside. The surprise intervention of Plouton causes Dionysus suddenly to shift the standards by which the contest was being judged. It had been, in the words of the Slave, 'which of the two was cleverer [*sophōteros*] in the craft [*technē*]' (780), and both playwrights have a claim to be *sophos*.

Dionysus' reason to retrieve a tragedian is not what it was at the start of *Frogs*. Then, it was his yearning (*pothos*) for Euripides. Now, he claims to be acting for the city,

So the city might be saved and continue to produce choruses.
And so, whichever of you is going to advise
the city best, him I am resolved to bring with me.
So, first: what opinion does each of you hold
about Alcibiades? The city is in labour over him.

1419–23

The startling image of birth pangs is jarring, and the sudden shift in gear as the literary contest turns political unexpected.[3] On one level, the concern remains about salvation (*sōtēria* [**4, 12**], and see 1419, 1433, 1436, 1448, 1458, 1501),[4] and the benefit of saving Athens is framed immediately in terms of choruses (and so religion or entertainment or self-concern for the god of theatre). Dionysus summarizes for Aeschylus that Athens 'yearns for him [*pothei*], it hates him, it wants to have him' (1425). Euripides answers in three lines that are carefully structured:

> I hate a citizen who to help his homeland
> seems slow, but is quick to cause great pain
> and is resourceful for himself, but for his city useless.
>
> 1427–9

Line 1428 begins and ends with 'slow' and 'quick'; the chiastic structure (*ABBA*) of 1429 is a flourish. Aeschylus' answer is not so clear:

> (A) You must not nurture a lion cub in the city
> (B) It'd be best not to nurture a lion in the city
> But if someone rears it, they must get ready to row [*hupēretein*] with its turns.
>
> 1431a, b, 1432

The first two lines are alternates, and it seems probable that the speech was changed when the play was reperformed; only one version will have been spoken in any given performance. Aeschylus recommends recall, cautiously, seeing value in a lion rather than a swallow like Cleophon (679) or a monkey like Cligenes (709).[5] The verb *hupēretein* means 'do service as a rower'. Its extended meaning, 'to serve, follow orders', or (here) 'to endure its ways', is more idiomatic, but loses yet another reference to the naval situation in 405.[6]

'One speaks cleverly [*sophōs*], the other clearly [*saphōs*]' (1435), Dionysus says, still not deciding, nor indicating which is which. I believe that Euripides' anti-Alcibiadean advice is clear, while the lion image from Aeschylus urging tolerance and perhaps acceptance of Alcibiades is to be seen as clever [**21**]. At the same time, in *Agamemnon* 717–36, Aeschylus had used the image of a lion cub being raised in the home as a pet turning savage when it grew (727–8, taking on the character [*ēthos*] of its parents), bringing slaughter and grief to the house as the lion becomes 'a Priest of Destruction' (735–6 *iereus tis Atas*).[7] Alcibiades as the lion cub is a natural identification not only because of the question asked: Pericles' mother had dreamed she would give birth to a lion (Herodotus 6.131.2), and so the cub is the foster-son Alcibiades. Just as

Paris brought ruin to Troy in *Dionysalexandros*, so Alcibiades might be thought to anticipate a future Athenian destruction.

It is hard not to connect Aeschylus' advice and the passage in the *Oresteia*, and, once made, the suggestion that this advice is clever might not be a compliment. Has Euripides scored his first point in the *agōn*? Possibly. At any rate, Dionysus asks a more general question, how the city is to achieve salvation (1436 *sōtērian*).[8] And again, the manuscripts preserve a doublet from the encore performance: lines 1437–41 and 1451–3 contain a cockamamie idea involving the 'slight' poet Cinesias [**5, 8**], and blinding the enemy during a sea battle with vinegar, an idea Euripides has poached from Cephisophon. Lines 1442–50 instead suggest trusting the untrusted and not trusting the (currently) trusted:

> If we do badly now with these guys, how
> could we not be saved by doing the opposite?
>
> 1449–50

This advice, despite its linguistic contortions (as Dionysus observes, it could be clearer, 1445 *saphesteran*), is similar to that in the parabasis. Lines 1454–62 contain Dionysus in conversation with one of the playwrights who is attempting to postpone giving advice until he is back on the surface. Lines 1463–6 contain more cryptic advice:

> When they consider their enemies' land
> to be their own, and their own to be their enemies',
> ships are a resource, and resources are resourceless.
>
> **Dionysus**
>
> That's good, except that the juryman drinks it all down himself.

The first two lines presumably refer to the Spartan occupation of Decelea and the losses of tribute-paying islands to Sparta. The speaker urges investment in the navy, to which Dionysus counters that jury pay (a constant drain on Athenian finances that war does not interrupt) interferes with that.

Three pieces of advice, from two playwrights, in a text that is recording performance variants. Can this be sorted through? There have been many assignments of these lines, but for present purposes, it makes sense to consider only two, both of which accept both that there is a blending of two performance texts and that there has been some transposition of lines. For Sommerstein (who believes 1442–50 are Euripidean), in the first production, the scene ran 1437–41, 1451–66; in the second production, 1442–50, 1454–66; this has been followed by Henderson and Wilson.[9] For Dover (who believes 1442–50 are Aeschylean), in the first production, the scene ran 1437–

41, 1451–66; in the second production 1437–41, 1451–60, 1442–50.[10] In both these sequences, the advice both playwrights give in the original performance is the same: Euripides says use vinegar; Aeschylus to trust in the navy. In both of these sequences, the advice to change politicians because they cannot be any worse than the present ones is found in the reperformance, though the speaker is different. While the assignment of individual lines is still open to discussion, these two shared conclusions are enough to proceed.[11]

In 405, both playwrights are giving advice that concerns warships [**9**]. Euripides had urged rejection of Alcibiades and adopted a hawkish stance that continues to align him with the demagogues. Though this is the 'democratic' side, which like Euripides' plays gives voice to the people, it is also the pro-war position in a city that (in its silliness) is increasingly desperate. The suggestion of throwing vinegar in the eyes of the enemy suggests this is rash and unthought through. Aeschylus had urged a conciliatory attitude to Alcibiades, accepting him as an Athenian responsibility, but also as an opportunity. The navy had been the traditional strength of Athenian military power, and the wording resonates with a political position held by Pericles (as the scholiast notes; cf. Thucydides 1.140–4) and Themistocles (who had fought at Marathon) before him, which is appropriate for the conservative Aeschylus: 'they should spend money on ships, because money which is never spent serves no useful purpose.'[12] This is not necessarily an oligarchic position, but rebuilding and adopting a defensive stance (and not spending extravagantly on jury pay, a populist position) could be seen that way. Aeschylus' advice is to treat Alcibiades as he had been treated in 407, which, with the advice at 1431–2, might 'represent a coherent naval policy that was not impracticable, and which, if implemented, seemed to have a chance of producing an honourable peace in an Athens released from the grip of radical populist hawks'.[13] Like Alcibiades, however, the Athenian elite need to be appeased and cannot be ignored. As the parabasis advised, so here Aeschylus seems to advocate finding a place for the former oligarchs in Athens.

The association of Aeschylus with Pericles is perhaps surprising, but it is not unnatural.[14] Pericles' first public act as a citizen had been to volunteer as *chorēgos* for Aeschylus in 472, for the tetralogy that had included *Persians*. Valerius Maximus, a writer under the emperor Tiberius, also makes the connection through an interesting slip (7.2.ext.7):

> Deeply shrewd is Aristophanes' advice. He put the Athenian leader Pericles into a comedy, brought back from the underworld and giving a prophetic warning: 'Don't rear a lion in the city, but if one is raised, best do what it wants.' He is telling them that young men of exalted birth and lively turn should be reined in, but if fed on overmuch popularity and lavish

> indulgence they should not be hindered from holding power; for it is foolish and useless to carp at forces which you yourself have encouraged.[15]

Valerius is apparently reading a version of the play with line 1431b–32 (but not 1431a), which he interprets as applying not to Alcibiades specifically, but the class of elite young Athenian men of which Alcibiades was a prominent member. He cites the lines in Latin, and it is not clear whether he has done the translation himself, or is looking at a translated script (or, more likely, excerpt). Whatever the case, the passage is in some way 'memorable' and would be known to others in first-century CE Rome. This makes the attribution of the lines to Aeschylus so interesting. Was Aeschylus understood to be a coded Pericles at Rome? Or perhaps the mistake is with the name Aristophanes: Eupolis' play *Demes* had featured politicians from the underworld offering advice, including Pericles. In that case, Aeschylus' advice at 1431–2 would be quoting, apparently verbatim, the advice Pericles had offered for the city in *Demes*. Either way, Aeschylus is in some way Periclean.[16]

23

Aeschylus (*Frogs* 1467–1533)

Plouton presses for a decision: Dionysus chooses Aeschylus, and Euripides is outraged (1467–78). Nevertheless, the resurrection of Aeschylus 'is far less cheery than it seems'.[1] The god had come to the underworld because of his passion for Euripides, but, as the Great Idea of the play shifts (as it inevitably does [**4**]), the god becomes arbiter in a contest he seems ill-equipped to understand.[2] The audience gets it, though. This is not a play about whether Euripides or Aeschylus is the better playwright. The audience knows that Aristophanes has a deep understanding of Euripidean poetry, is its most subtle reader, and consequently can use it to great comedic effect, as he has done throughout his career [**2, 7**]. This play is about something more [**29**].

The choice of Aeschylus as the winner of the *agōn* is not unexpected. It has been anticipated throughout:

- At the beginning of the contest, Aeschylus held the Chair of Tragedy [**16**].
- In the epirrhematic syzygy, Aeschylus is foregrounded structurally by being given the final *pnigos* [**18**]. It is here that Aeschylus' understanding of poets as improvers of citizens is made explicit.
- When discussing prologues, Aeschylus exposes the supposed weaknesses of Euripides with an emasculating *lēkuthion*, again in the stronger concluding position [**19**].
- When discussing lyrics, Aeschylus's songs in the style of Euripides are given prominence by position and length, and are accompanied by a dancer [**20**].
  When weighing lines on scales in an evocation of an Aeschylean play, Aeschylus won three for three [**21**].
- When giving political advice for how to save Athens, Aeschylus offers a serious suggestion for internal conciliation [**22**], which echoes the parabasis [**15**], and, in 405, might have seemed sensible.
- As Tarkow observes, the characterization of Aeschylus as an Achilles figure, and the association with Aeschylus in Pherekrates' *Shiners*, implicitly anticipates his victory over a (hectoring) Euripides.[3]

Even still, the decision could go either way: if Dionysus should choose Euripides, then Aeschylus (rightly) retains his Chair; if Aeschylus is chosen, then he gets to be resurrected (which is also a good prize, presumably). Aristophanes has drawn out the decision in order to create a level of suspense. In spite of all of this, when the choice comes, it is presented as arbitrary: even though he swore to bring back Euripides, he says 'My tongue swore . . .; I'll choose Aeschylus' (1471).

Dionysus' answer begins with an allusion to an infamous line of Euripides, *Hippolytus* 612: 'My tongue swore, but my heart [*phrēn*] is unsworn.' Aristophanes had drawn attention to the line in *Thesmophoriazusae* 275–6, and it was alluded to at *Frogs* 101–2. For *Hippolytus* (428 BCE), it is crucial to the play that though he says this, indicating that not words but one's mental disposition at the time is what seals an oath, Hippolytus in fact does honour his vow. Nevertheless, the line seems to have been used in antiquity to indicate that Euripides would be prepared to forswear himself, because a character of his did. Aristotle preserves an anecdote about a man called Hygiainon accusing Euripides of impiety in an *antidosis* trial (associated with someone trying to avoid paying a liturgy [**2**]), and mentioning this line in support (*Rhetoric* 1416a28–34).[4] The historical details of the trial (or even if it happened) are less important than the fact that Aristotle was talking about it a century later. It was a plausible story, and it showed that *Hippolytus* 612 was seen to be shocking. Given the brief, incomplete allusion here, that notoriety was already established. It also presumes that Euripides was understood to be part of the liturgical class (and therefore rich).

Dionysus chooses Aeschylus because of personal preference and because it is funny to do so, quoting a Euripidean line at Euripides to justify changing his mind.[5] Neither poetry nor politics is the sole basis for this determination, and Dionysus does not explicate which factors have governed his choice. Aristophanes has introduced multiple vectors for preferring Aeschylus, but for Dionysus it is almost a whim, the same arbitrary personal preference that had struck him when reading *Andromeda* [**7**]. He then quotes two further lines (1175 from *Aeolus*, fr. 19 with a small change, and 1177 from *Polyidus*, fr. 638), to show he sees it as a game. Plouton invites Dionysus and Aeschylus inside 'before you sail away [*apoplein*]' (1480). He invites only the two of them inside (1480 *sphō* is a dual form), which excludes Euripides from the (official) hospitality.[6] Perhaps he has stormed off in defeat, along an *eisodos* (1478).[7]

Alone in the performance area for the first time since the parabasis, the chorus of Initiates sings a short strophic song (1482–99). Sommerstein suggests the balance is removed during the song, but if it is in the *orchēstra* it need not be a distraction.[8] The strophe praises Aeschylus, indicating him with a gesture pointing inside the *skēnē* (1485), and praising his wisdom. While the term *sophos* is not used here, many of the terms are ones that might more naturally be thought to be appropriate for Euripides. They fit Aeschylus, however. He has proven himself (within the terms the play has provided) and he is going to bring goodness to the citizens of Athens. The antistrophe disparages Euripides, again without naming him. He is the one sitting beside Socrates (here a stand-in for all the sophists and Athenian intellectuals), 'casting aside art [*mousikēn*] and leaving behind most of the craft [*technēs*] of tragedy' (1493–5). This does not fit how Euripides has been presented, but it is part of the play's conclusion which is framing Dionysus' choice as a reason to celebrate.

The music does not stop, and Plouton, Dionysus and Aeschylus return to the performance area (possibly the *ekkyklēma* is used again to reveal the interior scene, but they could as easily just walk out). Chanting anapaests (as a means of marking the oncoming end of the play), Plouton bids Aeschylus farewell, and gives him props representing various means of committing suicide, to pass to deserving Athenians when he returns (Sommerstein suggests a dagger, a mortar and pestle, and a hanging rope). The request recapitulates the advice Heracles had given (120–5), a comic call-back. Some of the names of those Plouton hopes to see soon are unknown, but among them are Cleophon [**15**], who will be mentioned again at 1532, in the play's final sentence,[9] and Nicomachus, known to us primarily from a prosecution in 399 (Lysias 30). Aeschylus agrees, and asks that the Chair of Tragedy be given to Sophocles, but never to 'the rogue, the liar, the buffoon' (1520–1) Euripides. Plouton then invites the chorus to escort Aeschylus back to the surface, praising him as they lead with torches. The mention of torches recalls the second *parodos*, when the Initiates first arrived [**12**]. New torches are provided (or picked up wherever the original ones had been left), and lit again. Their final refrain prays that Aeschylus will be able to help the city. 'Save our city' (1501) Plouton had said. It is a hopeful ending.

It is not a celebration, though. Many of Aristophanes' plays end with a *kōmos*, a revel, but the audience does not see the actual celebration. There is still no drink for Dionysus. Athens has not yet been saved – that salvation, outside of the theatre, is still to come.[10]

Though Dionysus does not speak, he, too, is present. Sommerstein suggests that others are as well.[11] There are additional performers available backstage: the individuals who had carried the Corpse's bier, for example. First, Sommerstein suggests Persephone appears standing beside Plouton. The underworld gods together would help integrate the chorus, who are Initiates of her Mysteries. Additionally, there is a servant to carry the suicide implements Plouton provides Aeschylus, and Sommerstein suggests that it is

Xanthias. This is possible, and would again provide recapitulation, though I doubt the audience would be concerned if they did not see Xanthias return to the surface. If the actor who played Xanthias is already onstage as Aeschylus [**16**], such a move provides some narrative closure, with the return of a character (a costume and mask), but it is not needed as a curtain call for the actor who had delighted the audience during the *katabasis*.

24

Euripides: A Heresy

The selection of Aeschylus to save Athens was not a certainty. The logic of *Frogs* would have allowed either outcome, and the premise of Dionysus' *katabasis* for Euripides shifting into an *agōn* between two tragedians was Aristophanes' design. Aristophanes, working with his director Philonides, chose Aeschylus and Euripides as the rivals for several reasons. They each had a distinctive poetic and theatrical style, and Aristophanes had demonstrated his understanding of (and, I would say, love for) Euripides' poetry throughout his theatrical career (especially in *Acharnians*, *Peace* and *Thesmophoriazusae*) [**7**]. The two playwrights represented different theatrical eras, and so map conveniently on the generational conflict that also had been an important patterning device for Aristophanes (especially in *Knights*, *Clouds* and *Wasps*, and, still to come, *Ecclesiazusae*). Throughout the contest, Aeschylus had appeared stronger than Euripides (consistently 'winning rounds' if a perspective from modern boxing is appropriate), in part because of his understanding and appropriation of Euripidean elements [**23**]: '*Frogs* is, of course, preoccupied with Euripidean theater and Euripides himself.'[1] Though the shift in perspective towards the political security of Athens during wartime was not completely unexpected (see especially *Acharnians*, *Knights*, *Peace*, *Birds* and *Lysistrata*), it is sudden, and even that focus was not determinative. In the end, Dionysus decides things (apparently) because it allows him to poke Euripides – for a laugh, using a Euripidean line against Euripides.

I believe there is another level to the contest, one that suggests in some ways the outcome of the conflict was inevitable. I call this interpretation a heresy because I can offer no proof; for some readers it will be persuasive, and will add to their appreciation of *Frogs*, and of Euripides, but I do not insist on it.

Aeschylus' plays had been reperformed posthumously since at least the mid-420s, when Dicaeopolis could say that he was at the theatre hoping for an Aeschylus production to be announced (*Acharnians* 9–11, 425 BCE). *Frogs* 866–70 had Aeschylus claim that his plays had lived on after his death [**17**]. These passages had been connected to a claim that 'The Athenians so loved Aeschylus, that they voted, after his death, that if someone wanted to direct plays of Aeschylus, they could receive a chorus' (*Life of Aeschylus* 12); The next section concludes, 'After his death, he carried off not a few victories' (*Life* 13). This biographical information at least partly informs other discussions in the scholia and later sources, but it is notoriously unreliable.[2] Nevertheless, the Suda, though late, claims that Aeschylus' son Euphorion won four competitive victories with his father's plays.[3]

The case for reperformance is strong. The two Aristophanic passages are hard to interpret if there was no reperformance of Aeschylus, and the claims in the *Life* can be extracted from this information alone. Further evidence is provided by allusions to Aeschylus within Euripides' own plays.[4] Many of these focus specifically on the *Oresteia* [**19**]. *Hecuba* (424–420 BCE) concludes with Agamemnon being told the plot of *Agamemnon*. *Electra* (*c.* 418) and *Orestes* (408) revisit *Libation Bearers*. *Iphigenia among the Taurians* (*c.* 416) offers a skewed sequel to *Eumenides*; *Helen* (412) reframes the satyr play from the *Oresteia*, *Proteus* (now lost).[5] *Iphigenia in Aulis* (405) reframes the relationship between Agamemnon and Clytemnestra in decidedly anti-*Oresteia* terms; when Polymestor is blinded in *Hecuba*, and Polyphemus is blinded in *Cyclops* (408), both cry out quoting *Agamemnon*. This represents an intense, sustained engagement with the *Oresteia* over two decades, which is able to be traced selectively due to surviving plays. As Zuckerberg has observed, the fact that this engagement is not mentioned in *Frogs* is itself telling.[6] *Clouds* (423, or perhaps only *Clouds II c.* 418) also shows a deep dependence on the *Oresteia*. In addition, Euripides' *Phoenissae* (*c.* 409) and the fragmentary *Hypsipyle* (*c.* 409) seem to resonate with *Seven Against Thebes* [**18**].[7] All these plays presume close audience familiarity with Aeschylean tragedy, and I believe it is a familiarity gained from reperformance.

We do not know the circumstances for such a reperformance, and there is no need for the original tetralogies to be preserved: as *Frogs* demonstrates, plays could be thought of as individual works as well as sets by the end of the fifth century. As I look at the dates for these works, I suggest that they indicate the possibility of a reperformed *Oresteia*, all four plays, in the 420s. When *Frogs* talks about the *Oresteia* as beginning with *Libation Bearers* [**19**], this may indicate another performance as a dilogy (just *Libation Bearers* and *Eumenides*) in the decade preceding 405 at the Lenaia [**2**]. The possibility of a reperformed *Seven* (with what other plays? possibly *Persians*?) before 409 should also be considered. West has argued that other Aeschylean or partially Aeschylean productions were directed by Euphorion, and these include *Myrmidons* [**18, 20**] and *The Soul-Weighing* [**21**].[8] *Peace*, *Birds*, *Frogs* and *Ecclesiazusae* all refer to *Myrmidons*, which might suggest a performance for that before 421.[9] A fragment of Aristophanes (fr. 696, Athenaeus 1.21E) suggests that a lost play (possibly *Gerytades*) had a character claim to

Aeschylus that they had seen *Phrygians*, which may have been produced alongside *Myrmidons*.

Biles provides the most sceptical reading of all this evidence. While he allows reperformance of plays at rural Dionysia,[10] he denies 'that Aeschylean drama was regularly reperformed in competition in Athens and was victorious' or that his plays 'were a regular feature of the City Dionysia'.[11] The question of regularity, however, is subjective, and it enters his argument subtly. I do not think anyone believes Aeschylean reperformance was 'regular'. There is indication, however, that in the twenty-five years preceding *Frogs*, a handful of such remountings may have occurred:

1. *Oresteia* tetralogy, 420s (Dionysia);
2. *Persians* (pre-421, since it is alluded to in Eupolis' *Marikas*)
3. *Seven Against Thebes* (pre-*c.* 409)
4. *Oresteia* pre-405 (Lenaia).

Any of these might be attributed to Euphorion (that is irrelevant to my argument), and it is possible this number could be expanded by adding Myrmidons and *Phrygians* (pre-421) and *The Soul-Weighing* (*Psychostasia*, at the Dionysia, given that the play requires the use of the *mēchanē*).[12] The total number of productions that Aristophanes seems to indicate might be only two Dionysia performances (half the number of victories Euphorion supposedly won with his father's plays), and only five productions total, including Lenaia performances and possibly even deme performances (which might still attract substantial crowds, especially if a classic were being restaged; this provides another way a single play might achieve an independent identity).

This number could be increased: surviving evidence is sporadic in any case. Biles describes a supposed posthumous remounting of *Persians* in Sicily, which he also discounts.[13] I am not as sceptical, but for now it is significant only that this, too, is a play mentioned by name in *Frogs*. Further, when Aeschylean plays were remounted, the *didaskalos* was under no obligation to present it without any changes (even assuming original production decisions, music, choreography, etc. could be preserved and retrieved).[14] Even if the same script is presented, it would be with modern actors, who were increasingly professional, and it could reasonably be seen as a new production.

The coincidence of these plays with those Aeschylean works singled out in *Frogs* is substantial, and does potentially risk circularity of argument. We have not mentioned *Niobe*, for instance, sitting immobile, though it, too, was clearly known to the *Frogs* audience somehow. This risk is mitigated substantially by *Acharnians* 9–11, with its expectation in 425 of Aeschylean revivals, and the amount of allusion to the *Oresteia* in particular within

Euripides' and Aristophanes' plays prior to *Frogs*. Allusion does not require universal recognition – no reference will be understood by 100 per cent of an audience – but to be persuasive we want some meaningful overlap between the present audience and those who will understand an allusion to a specific earlier passage.

I suggest that when the *Oresteia* was first reperformed in the 420s, it was in competition at the Dionysia, and that it won the prize that year. Whether it was directed by Euphorion or not, we cannot say, but we have no other lead as a potential *didaskalos*. I further want to suggest that Euripides was part of that competition. Euripides lost a contest to a dead Aeschylus. That would understandably be irksome to Euripides, especially if it was the first time that Aeschylus had been reperformed (at least at the major contest). It then becomes possible that part of the explanation behind Euripides' sustained engagement with the *Oresteia* can be traced to this event.

The competitive context of these reperformances has not been sufficiently explored. We only know of *didsakaloi* rivalling one another for a prize at the Lenaia and Dionysia. At rural Dionysia it may be that a deme could mount a single play to celebrate a god without a competitive context. The Suda's claim about Euphorion presumes that he is entering his father's plays in competition, and the use of tetralogy and dilogy in some of the proposed reperformances might suggest that at least some of these were competitive. If Euripides were to lose in a competition to a reperformed Aeschylus, that would provide an additional level of motivation to Aristophanes for choosing the *agōn* participants in *Frogs*.

On one level, the contest in *Frogs* is the contest that never happened: in the traditional biographical accounts, Aeschylus dies in 456, and Euripides begins competing in 455 – two poets whose competitive careers straddle the fifth century but never meet. At the same time, the two have met in competition, in the 420s, and Aeschylus in the underworld had been victorious. Whether subsequent Aeschylean reperformances also were competitive or not, we cannot say, though the passage in *Life* 13, claiming 'not a few' posthumous victories, may be an exaggeration from the event I have proposed.

If this is plausible, we have a motivation both for a principal aspect of Euripides' dramaturgy throughout the last two decades of his working life, and a partial explanation of the genesis of the *agōn* in *Frogs*. Drawing on the scholiast tradition, Biles essentially argues the reverse: 'Philostratus' formulation of the decree, with the Athenians actually summoning the deceased Aeschylus to the Dionysia ... entails the literalization of reperformance as a return from the dead that is central to Aristophanes' plot in *Frogs*.'[15] Though the later biographical tradition could expand fancifully on kernels of truth, that is not happening here. The *Acharnians* passage points to something that the original audience must have understood, and competitive reperformance is, I believe, the most straightforward solution. That same solution also explains the nature of allusion to the *Oresteia* in Euripidean plays beginning in the 420s. Biles can imagine rural reperformances of Aeschylean tragedy and sets his sights against regular reperformance at the City Dionysia. In contrast to this position, if we allow for occasional reperformances at rural Dionysia and the Lenaia (about which Biles is silent), extending it to the City Dionysia as a performance venue, at least once or twice, does fit well with the evidence. If at this event Euripides had been defeated, it is possible to see where Euripides' interest in the *Oresteia* might have generated, as well as Aristophanes' interest in Euripides.

25

Reperformance

In the summer of 405, the Athenian fleet suffered another defeat at Aigospotamoi (Goat River), along the narrow access to the Black Sea of the Hellespont. The Athenian generals did not listen to the unsolicited advice they received from Alcibiades, who was nearby but without any official position at Athens, and they were defeated by the Spartan commander Lysander (Xenophon, *Hellenica* 2.1.25–8; Plutarch, *Alcibiades* 35–6). This signalled the end. Lysander likely executed many of the Athenian captives.[1] The Athenians offered surrender to Sparta, which demanded a dismantling of the democracy, destruction of the protective Long Walls and an imposition in 404 of another group of oligarchs known as the Thirty (or the Thirty Tyrants). Among the Thirty were Critias (whom some believe to be the author of *Pirithous* [**8**]) and Theramenes [**5, 9, 14**]. The violence and cruelty of the Thirty, who were in power for only thirteen months, cannot be underestimated. Perhaps 1,500 (male) citizens were killed, the victims having been targeted specifically for political purposes (Aristotle, *Athenian Constitution* 35.4; Lysias 30.13), with many more driven to exile, with physical assault and confiscated property frequent. The democracy was crushed, and there was blood on the streets, as Spartan-imposed oligarchs ruled.

In the brief window of time between *Frogs* and the Thirty, a proposal was made that *Frogs* be given a repeat performance: 'The play was so amazing, because of its *parabasis*, that it was even remounted [*anedidachthē*], according to Dicaearchus' (*Frogs* hypothesis 1.39–40). Such an encore performance is, so far as we know, a unique honour,[2] and different from the posthumous reproductions accorded to Aeschylus [**23**]. Here there was the possibility of the same actors, same costumes and props, being used, and there is no suggestion that it was anything other than a commendation of the play and its message. It would be an extra performance, outside of the competitive context (or so I believe). Sommerstein has suggested that the occasion for that reperformance was most likely at the Lenaia in 404, a year after the initial production.[3] That would place it after Aigospotamoi, but still before the Thirty. Since the hypothesis (a short plot summary written in the Hellenistic period and attached at the start of a play) identifies the *parabasis* as the impetus, Sommerstein suggests that the reperformance is to be associated with a decree proposed by Patrokleides in the autumn of 405 to restore those citizens disenfranchised after the Four Hundred (Andocides 1.73–80, Xenophon *Hellenica* 2.2.11) – i.e. to follow at least part of the advice of the *Frogs parabasis*. The Lenaia would be the first major festival after that, placing the reperformance after Aigospotamoi, and before the Thirty were installed (an ancient *Life of Aristophanes* additionally says that Aristophanes was awarded a crown of sacred olive because of the text on the disenfranchised).[4]

In the end, only part of Aeschylus' advice at the end of *Frogs* was accepted, and it came too late. The Athenians did not find a place for Alcibiades in their city, and he was killed by Persian soldiers in 404, perhaps at the instigation of Lysander or the Thirty. Similarly, Cleophon **[5, 9, 15]**, still opposing peace even after Aigospotamoi, was condemned to death, and his execution, if it had not yet taken place, was at least expected at the second performance (should the instrument of death he is offered at 1504 be a mortar and pestle for hemlock?).[5] Arnott ties the recall of the disenfranchised oligarchs to establishment of the Thirty, but MacDowell believes this is overstated, noting that neither Critias or Theramenes had been disenfranchised or exiled in 411; nevertheless 'the *parabasis* must have contributed to a current of opinion which led eventually to the establishment of the Thirty'.[6]

Rosen has challenged this, reviving Weil's nineteenth-century proposal that *parabasin* in the hypothesis should be read as *katabasin*:[7] 'The play was so amazing, because of its underworld-descent, that it was even remounted . . .'. If this is right, the reperformance might have occurred as early as the Dionysia of 405 (two months after the original performance), and so still before the loss of the fleet, and the play is being celebrated on aesthetic grounds rather than political ones. This is possible, though I do not think that, even with the earlier performance, aesthetic and political should be separated quite so easily.

That the reperformance occurred should not be doubted, however. The text records indications of performance doublets at 1431 (a or b) and 1442–50 **[22]**. A question then arises as to whether there have been other alterations which are not as easily identified. I suggest that there could be, and in fact there are. One concerns Plouton, whose participation in the *agōn* was limited. Since we believe the text was adapted for reperformance outside of the restrictions of the competition, which include a limited number of actors **[16]**, I think it is reasonable to consider the deletion of nine more lines in the original performance in 405 (1414–17, 1467–8 and 1479–81) in order to keep Plouton a silent figure throughout the *agōn* – if indeed he appears at all. Plouton's other speeches, 1500–14 and 1524–7, could as easily be delivered by Aeacus returning to the stage (played by the Euripides actor), or by Plouton coming onstage only at 1500 (and of course the alterations could have been more extensive than this). Such changes would imply that Aristophanes and Philonides chose to enhance the play in a way that the unique performance circumstances of the encore would allow, by using a fourth actor in a surprise (and fundamentally Aeschylean) way.[8] In that light, the only remaining scene apparently needing four actors is at 549–77 [**14**], where a fourth actor is needed for eight lines or partial lines, as the text currently stands. Given that the text was adapted elsewhere, this is not enough for me to believe that four actors were required in the competitive production of 405. Some minor changes in this short, confused passage, either due to reperformance or in the history of transmission, seem more probable to me than a momentary exception to the limit on three actors.

26

Afterlife

The plays of Old Comedy were not regularly restaged in Athens, and the history of the reception of *Frogs* after 404 in antiquity is sparse: new comedies were written, and the tastes of later centuries did not always favour Athenian political comedy from an earlier age. Nevertheless, a number of touchstones can be identified that demonstrate *Frogs* continued to be known in antiquity. The first piece of evidence is the vase once in Berlin [**6**], which attests to the fact that the play was performed in Apulia, and commemorated in the second quarter of the fourth century, thirty to fifty years after its performance in Athens. It is increasingly recognized that Greek colonies in South Italy regularly remounted Athenian plays, and that associated with this theatre culture was a desire to commemorate them in vase-painting; additionally, many of these vases were found in rural tombs, which suggests the desire to be buried with Greek theatrical scenes was present, especially among non-Greeks.[1]

Literary sources show that the play was known, not just by the elite, throughout the Greek and Roman worlds:

- In the mid third century BCE, the prologue to Callimachus' *Aetia* builds a complex intertextual relationship with *Frogs* based on its presentation of poetic rivalry.[2]
- The contest between Hipponax and Herodas in Herodas' *Mimiamb* 8, judged by Dionysus, is meant to evoke *Frogs*.[3]
- A first-century statue base excavated on the island of Rhodes in 1938 dedicated to Bacchic Dionysus presents an excerpt from the second *parodos*, lines 454–9. This passage, which expects blessings for the initiated if they also lead a good life, is repurposed from comedy in order to celebrate the real Dionysus in worship.[4]
- Horace, *Sermones* 1 (*c.* 35 BCE, esp. 1.4 and 1.5) presumes some familiarity with the play, as Cucchiarelli has shown.[5] Both Horace and Xanthias and Dionysus are on a metaliterary journey, and poetry is deeply entangled in contemporary politics.
- Aeschylus' advice at 1431b–32 is known to Valerius Maximus in the first century CE, who quotes it in Latin [**22**].[6]
- Aulus Gellius, writing in Latin in the second century CE, 'seems certain to have read only *Frogs* in its entirety'.[7]

- Also in the second century, Apuleius appears to show knowledge of *Frogs* 130 in *The Golden Ass* 6.17–19, with the suggestion that Psyche leap from a tall tower.[8]
- And again, in Greek, in Lucian's *Menippus* or *Nekeuomanteia* 1, the satirist Menippus wears a lionskin among other accoutrements of katabatic heroes to protect himself. Given this, it is possible that allusions to *Frogs* are intended in *Kataplous* (*Sailing Down*, or *The Tyrant*).[9]
- Other references from Greek authors in the Roman period include Plutarch (*Alcibiades* 16.3 to lines 1425 and 1432–3, and see Mor. 348D), Aelius Aristides (29.28 to 736, 32.34 to 785, 32.34 to 1515), Maximius of Tyre (25.3 to 92–3). Athenaeus refers to the play at 66B (134), 566E (294) and 636E (1304).[10]

None of these, I should stress, require that the play was known through performance; and many of them might emerge only indirectly or through knowledge of a hypothesis (plot summary). This uncertainty extends back to Athens as well. Though there was a contest for restaged comedies at the City Dionysia from 340/339, we do not know if *Frogs* ever received this distinction. Possibly the regular contest was preceded by occasional performances of remounted comedies. In that case, there would be a reasonable means for the orator Demosthenes' audience to appreciate allusions to *Frogs* in his speech *On the False Embassy* (Demosthenes 19, 343 BCE).[11]

After the second century CE, the works of Aristophanes continued to be read, and *Frogs*, along with *Clouds* and *Wealth*, was prominent in the later education system as a 'Byzantine triad' for Greek comedy. As a result, there are many manuscripts and a rich scholiastic tradition for these plays.[12] Four late papyri survive, from the fourth to the sixth centuries CE.[13]

I suggest that the greatest impact of *Frogs* is not in the scattered references across antiquity, but in the way Aristophanes presented in *Frogs* a view of fifth-century tragedy at a crucial moment, immediately following the deaths of two of its greatest practitioners, Sophocles and Euripides. *Frogs* helped to frame the first century of tragedy's history by canonizing Sophocles, Euripides and Aeschylus, even if Sophocles is left to the side:[14] 'The history of tragedy adumbrated in the *Frogs* was to become the received wisdom about Greek literary history more generally.'[15] When the Dionysia added a new contest in 386, likely a year or two after the death of Aristophanes, for the reperformance of an 'Old Tragedy', this provided an ongoing venue for the reperformance of tragedies in Athens.[16] This ensured a means for the continued life of these plays: in the third quarter of the fourth century, Lycurgus ensured that these three tragedians had statues erected, and that the city had 'official' copies of their tragedies (ps-Plutarch, *Lives of the Ten Orators* 7, 841F). This helped determine the plays that were sent to the Library of Alexandria and which were selected for the educational curriculum and consequently for preservation in the manuscript tradition. *Frogs* did not cause that canonization (that would be too reductive), but it was a factor in the process: five of the seven Aeschylean plays that survive are the plays mentioned by name in *Frogs* [**23**]; of the ten Euripidean plays that were selected for preservation, the three that were in Euripides' Byzantine Triad – *Hecuba*, *Phoenician Women* and *Orestes* – were each tied to the Aeschylean select plays, as was Sophocles' *Electra*. The retrospective understanding of this proto-canon marks the end of an era: as Hanink writes, '*Frogs* marks an early dramatisation of a deep nostalgia for the three great tragedians, but one which continued to regard the deceased poets as at odds and in competition with each other, even within the Underworld.'[17] More than anything else, *Frogs* serves to mark this period, rightly or wrongly, as an end of something significant.

27

Translations

The first printed text of *Frogs* was published in Venice, in 1498, in the Aldine edition of nine Aristophanic plays (*Thesmophoriazusae* and *Lysistrata* were added in Florence in 1516). This edition included a Latin translation, with *Frogs* becoming *Ranae*. In 1524 'the best among Aristophanes' comedies' was published on its own in Basel. Several Latin translations appeared, usually with the Greek text, beginning in 1538 (Venice), and followed by 1561 (Utrecht), 1586 (Frankfurt), 1596 (Leiden), 1607 (Geneva), 1624 (Leiden), 1670 (Amsterdam), 1710 (Amsterdam), 1760 (Leiden). In 1545 the first vernacular translation was published in Italian (in Venice, by Bartolomeo and Pietro Rositini). It was not until 1783 that the first German translation was published (in Basel, by Johann Georg Schlosser), with an English version by Charles Dunster appearing two years later (Oxford, 1785).[1]

By the nineteenth century, *Frogs* had entered the popular imaginary. Mary Shelley describes the origins of Percy Bysshe Shelley's *Swellfoot the Tyrant* (1820), a satirical version of *Oedipus*, in which Percy recited the 'Ode to Liberty' and 'compared it to the "chorus of frogs" in the satiric drama of Aristophanes; and, it being an hour of merriment, and one ludicrous association suggesting another, he imagined a political-satirical drama on the circumstances of the day, to which the pigs would serve as chorus – and "Swellfoot" was begun.'[2] In the play, the goddess Famine presides over a contest between liberty and forms of tyranny.[3] The familiar cry of the frog-swans, *Brekekekex koax koax*, was by now proverbial: it is the voice given to the toad in Hans Christian Anderson's 'Thumbelina' (1835), for example.[4] The 1855 pro-slavery novel *The Forayers* by William Gilmore Simms describes the appeal of a 'frog concert' in which 'The frogs should furnish a running commentary on the follies and vices of society as in Aristophanes, only adapted to our times! ... Of course, the frogs are not less fortunate than their betters.'[5] It is an unexpected intrusion into the story of Captain Porgy, which for its symbolism to be effective requires some familiarity of the reader in the American South with what Aristophanes represents.[6]

More translations appeared in the nineteenth century, as did small editions of the play for use in schools and universities. Of the latter, the 1839 edition by Thomas Mitchell 'became a chief conduit through which Victorian men had access to that play at school and university'.[7] Among translations, by far the most influential was that of John Hookham Frere, finished by 1830, which shared with Mitchell a profound anti-democratic sentiment.[8] The play is presented with extended excurses from the translator throughout the text, interrupting the flow of the drama, but ensuring that the play is interpreted as Frere understood it. For example, in the whipping scene the reader is told,

> It should appear that, in the preceding scenes in the infernal regions, Xanthias is the representative of Alcibiades, and Bacchus [Dionysus] of the Athenian people, and that the changes of character represent the changes in their political relation to each other.[9]

Frere's translation was staged for a short run in a private home theatre production in 1873, directed by Professor of Engineering Charles Fleeming Jenkin in Edinburgh, in which young Robert Louis Stevenson played Aeschylus.[10] When the Oxford University Dramatic Society performed *Frogs* in Greek in 1892, an adapted version of Frere's translation appeared opposite the Greek text in the programme.[11]

Though Frere's translation continued to be in print into the twentieth century, the most influential translation of the play has been that of Gilbert Murray (1902).[12] Murray was Regius Professor of Greek at Oxford University, and his popularizing translations of Greek drama sold remarkably well. He would not return to translating Aristophanes until *Birds* in 1950. The Aristophanic elements of George Bernard Shaw's *Major Barbara* (1905) show the immediate impact of Murray's *Frogs*.[13] When Oxford's Somerville College staged *Frogs* with all women but directed by Murray in 1911, '"numerous topical allusions" were introduced into Murray's translation of *Frogs*: for example, "mention was made of the Registration Fee, which had penetrated to Hades under the guidance of Miss Rogers."'[14] In 1946, *Frogs* was chosen as the first post-war production at Somerville, with Murray again present. It was Murray's translation that was broadcast on BBC radio in 1947, which at the time was associated with the Cambridge Greek Play production directed by J. T. Sheppard, who had also directed *Frogs* in Greek in 1935.[15]

Translating Aristophanes is a challenge, and no translation is entirely satisfactory. It should reflect the Greek clearly and be speakable aloud, and a successful academic translation will often not work on the stage, and vice versa. Translations themselves can have political agendas, as did Douglas Young's 1958 brilliant nationalistic translation into Scots.[16] A particular challenge for translating Aristophanes are references to contemporary Athenians [5]: do you leave them as is, or find a local equivalent? The latter dates immediately, and may not be comprehensible in a different city or country; the former is already dated, even if it is accurate. Substituting generic nouns for specific names means missing a crucial component of Aristophanic humour. Should poetry always be translated into verse? Prose can be clearer, but inevitably loses the inherent musicality. And is it funny? Reading translations of Aristophanes can be dire, and one thing we know about the playwright is that he had a sense of humour.

In what follows I am looking at some of the most popular English translations of the twentieth and twenty-first centuries, but I have been selective and drawn on seven translations, from what might be seen as three generations of translations.[17] Gilbert Murray's 1902 translation was rivalled in the first half of the century only by B. B. Rogers, who published an edition of several plays (*Frogs* 1902, 2nd ed. 1919), and whose translation was included in the Loeb Classical Library in 1924. After the Second World War, as universities increasingly offered literature-in-translation courses and publishers increasingly offered classical texts to a wider readership, a new market emerged. Richmond Lattimore's 1962 translation and David Barrett's 1964 Penguin translation have been widely read and appreciated. More recently, Jeff Henderson has produced a new Loeb (2002), and Paul Roche a complete translation for Signet and the New American Library (2005), and Stephen Halliwell a translation in the Oxford World's Classics (2015), with Barrett's Penguin slightly revised in 2007. The point of this comparison is not a scorecard, and other passages could be chosen as examples. Nevertheless, this might show some of the choices that have been made.

The play's first joke (line 2) is a refusal to tell one of the standards. Dionysus encourages any joke, except . . .

Murray
'I'm overloaded'

Rogers
'I'm getting crushed'

Lattimore
'What a day!'

Barrett
'God, what a heavy load!'

Henderson
'I'm hard pressed.'

Roche
'I'm in a jam.'

Halliwell
'I'm all hard-pressed'

All of these represent the Greek *piezomai*, which can mean 'weighed down' (by the props he carries), 'oppressed' (with a slave's existence) and 'needing to defecate' (or, 'experiencing gastrointestinal distress', a meaning not in the standard lexicon, but present, as seen by the other examples that follow). Arnott leans into the last of these with 'I've sprung a leak',[18] but all of these will only be funny with a footnote or an explanatory gesture from an actor; none is funny on its own.

My next example is the first mention of Cleisthenes, as Dionysus begins his explanation for his get-up (48 *embateuon Kleisthenei*).

Murray
I've been at sea, serving with Cleisthenes.

Rogers
I was serving lately aboard the–Cleisthenes.

Lattimore
Well, I served aboard a kind of
Dreamboat named the Kleisthenes.
(Heracles responds to this with, 'And did you engage?' making the double entendre a bit clearer.)

Barrett
Well, it's like this. I climbed aboard Cleisthenes' vessel. . . .
(Heracles: 'Saw a bit of action, I expect, one way or another.')

Henderson
I was serving topside with Cleisthenes.
(Heracles: 'And did you engage?')

Roche
I've been on board with Cleisthenes.
(Heracles: 'See any action?')

Halliwell
I was sailing on Kleisthenes' boat.

For my tastes, the only one of these that captures the range of meanings is Lattimore, which is the freest with the Greek (poetic, but not worrying about the same line-ends), using 'dreamboat' to capture both the erotic appeal and the naval context, allowing the proper name to stand for both the individual and as a potential ship name. While several translations include a footnote marking Cleisthenes' supposed effeminacy, only Roche's note is explicit that it is a 'euphemism for "I buggered him."'[19] Frere's translation holds up surprisingly well: when asked, 'Have you been abroad?', Dionysus answers,

I've been aboard – in the Fleet – with Cleisthenes.

The substitution of aboard for abroad introduces another kind of humour, and the hurried clarification 'in the Fleet' signals the double meaning. None of these published translations substitutes the name of a contemporary politician in a position of leadership who might secretly or openly be sexually non-normative (as Cleisthenes was perceived in 405), but a modern production could, and perhaps should try to capture the transgressive element of naming *kōmōdoumnoi* [**5**].

A final example comes from Dionysus' sudden introduction of the name Alcibiades at 1422–3:

Murray

Advise me first of Alcibiades,
Whose birth gives travail still to mother Athens.

Rogers

And first of Alcibiades, let each
Say what he thinks; the city travails sore.

Lattimore

Alkibiades is a baby who's giving
our state delivery-pains. What shall we do with him?

Barrett

Here's my first question: what should be done about Alcibiades? The city's in a tricky situation.

Henderson

So for starters, which of you has an opinion about Alcibiades? The city's in travail about him.

Roche

So first things first. Which of you, if either,
Is able to make head or tail of Alcibiades?
The city's in a turmoil. Because of him.

Halliwell

Tell me first the view that each of you holds about
Alkibiades. The city's in pangs over him.

Murray, Lattimore and Halliwell keep the birth imagery present in the Greek verb *dustokei*, the last word of his speech: Murray explicitly makes Athens a mother city; Lattimore provides some context for the treacherous Alcibiades, even if it is only by reductively calling him a baby. Frere also captures the maternal imagery:

First then of Alcibiades, what think ye?
The City is in hard labour with the question.

Every translation keeps Euripides and Aeschylus as the rivals in the *agōn*, but different choices might be made in production. How to present the old generation and the new? A modern production would seem to need to choose between music, playwriting and politics, and choose between presenting jokes more than twenty-four centuries old, mapping contemporary artistic styles onto the names of the Athenian playwrights, or substituting contemporary figures and rewriting the contest completely.[20] Frere, writing in 1839, suggests to any reader with musical ability, 'perhaps his imagination might be more amusingly employed in conceiving a similar scene of contest between the great musical favourites of the last and the present century, between Gluck or Handel, for instance, and Rossini.'[21] Is this the same as comparing the Beatles with the Backstreet Boys, Elvis with Eminem, or Tina Turner with Rhianna? No, of course not, but for different audiences all of these might be meaningful. Playwrights have less cultural clout today, though Shakespeare vs Shaw has been successful [**27**], and Ley describes his university performance with Brecht for Euripides and Artaud for Aeschylus (with a croaking chorus of Ar-Toadians).[22] Dudouyt describes a French adaptation where both dramatists are from an earlier generation:

> in Alain Badiout's rewriting of *Frogs*, *Les Citrouilles* (Pumpkins), staged by Christian Schiaretti in 1996, Aeschylus and Euripides become Brecht and [Paul] Claudel and the protagonist, Achmed, guides the (female) minister of culture, and the spectators, through a literary inferno in which only contact with the great works of the past can save contemporary societies from becoming a cultural 'pumpkin soup'.[23]

A 2019 university production at Winona State University in Minnesota, directed by Jim Williams, staged the contest between two past presidents (Lincoln and Nixon) in order to see whose advice was more relevant today.[24] Productions can also choose to play to generic types, such as upper class vs lower class in a touring production by the London Small Theatre, short and tall clowns in a Cape Town production, and multiple hipster/Bohemian vs tweedy-professor-type imaginings.[25] Every production, and every translation, will have to make choices that are invariably limiting and incomplete. They should at least be funny.

28

Twentieth-Century Frogs

One can point to many productions of *Frogs* in the modern period (since Murray's translation, perhaps), where directorial choices shape the presentation and interpretation of the play. Many of these productions remain under-documented: school productions often represent a tradition of staging classics in an ongoing effort to present the plays as living theatre; university productions draw on dynamic creative energies, often with the freedom and institutional support to risk commercial failure for creative benefits; annual theatre festivals in the Mediterranean present series of plays for tourists, often with overly reverential deference to perceived continuities of practice over time, but with budgets that allow helpful photographic record; experimental theatre can use Greek plays as a foundation for exploring the limits of theatrical practice; rare productions in Ancient Greek present novelties that can nevertheless unite audiences and show that comprehension does not always depend on hearing the script; and, rarely, professional productions by non-specialized companies can bring recognition to a script that is not familiar from the performance repertoire and show that audiences can continue to be affected by ancient plays.

In Greece, for example, *Frogs* was performed at the Epidauros Festival first in 1959 (the Syracuse Festival, which began in 1921, only produced *Frogs* in 1976). Karolos Koun's 1966 production presented a *parabasis* that sided with the political Left, as Koun's politics as director replace those of Aristophanes.[1] A 1977 production, following the 1967–74 military junta and directed by Spyros Euangelatos, favoured the political Right; historical specificity for Aristophanic comedy is both crucial and divisive. A production with shadow puppets by Evgenios Spatharis took place in 1978.[2]

In the following discussion, I have restricted myself to three plays that show the influence of *Frogs*, only one of which is *Frogs* in name, to show ways creative minds have engaged with the play over the past century. As of this writing, video recordings of *Frogs* are few. The 1991–5 production by the London Small Theatre company (tr. Fiona Laird) was made available on VHS. The 2013 Cambridge Greek Play production (in Ancient Greek; dir. Helen Eastman), an image from which appears on the cover of this book, and the 2019 Warwick University production (in English; dir. Kelsi Russell) are available on YouTube.[3]

Shaw

The last play of George Bernard Shaw (1856–1950) is a short (five-page) work entitled *Shakes Versus Shav: A Puppet Play* (1949), first produced by the Lanchester Marionette Theatre in Malvern, England (figure 28.1).[4] Following a preface in which he disposes of the Shakespeare Question with disdainful wit, Shaw presents two playwrights, himself and Shakespeare, in a quick and light-hearted debate for theatrical supremacy. Shakes is unaware of the more recent playwright ('Who art thou | That rearst a forehead almost rivalling mine?'[5]), and when they meet, they box, and Shav ('G.B.S.') is knocked down, as expectations from the British tradition of Punch and Judy puppet shows are transferred to the literary arena. This is arguably the most Aristophanic touch in the short play. After Walter Scott's Rob Roy decapitates Macbeth in a duel ('Whaur's your Wullie Shaxper the noo?'[6]), Macbeth gets up, retrieves his head and returns to Stratford.

As in *Frogs*, the contest has playwrights choosing representative works. Shakes says of his *Macbeth* 'one line of whom | Is worth a thousand of your

Figure 28.1 Promotional postcard for Shakes v Shaw, a ten-minute puppet play by George Bernard Shaw. First produced at the Lyttleton Hall, Malvern, 9 August 1949 and Riverside Theatre, Festival Gardens, 10 June 1951. The play was staged by the Lanchester Marionette Theatre. The voices of the puppets were recorded. © The Michael Diamond Collection / Mary Evans Picture Library.

piffling plays', a challenge Shav accepts.[7] Shakes produces, 'The shardborn beetle with his drowsy hum' (III.ii.43), a ridiculously bathetic line, especially out of context. Shav responds to this by quoting a couplet on beetles by Australian poet Ada Lindsay Gordon, which delights Shakes so much that he immediately learns the couplet by heart. Opening himself to criticism, Shav offers *Heartbreak House* (1919), with the words 'Behold my Lear.' In the end there is no decision: Shav declares a truce ('We are both mortal. For a moment suffer | My glittering light to shine.') and the play ends abruptly.

Aristophanes is nowhere mentioned, but *Frogs* had influenced *Major Barbara* by Shaw [**27**], and the impact continues here. Though Shaw is deferential, using himself as one of the agonizing poets changes the crucial dynamic that Aristophanes had achieved, losing the ostensible impartiality the Greek playwright had maintained. The playwrights do not critique each other's style through emulation, which helped showcase the distinctive lyrics in *Frogs*. The use of puppets is striking, and (for Shaw) is likely mediated through a play from more than two centuries earlier, by Henry Fielding.

In 1730, Henry Fielding (1707–54) first staged *The Author's Farce* in which the hero Luckless strives to mount his play 'The Pleasures of the Town'.[8] It is eventually staged in Act III as a puppet show, and the puppets are played by actors from the first two acts. Fielding satirizes London theatre-going (and his own frustrated efforts, as a coded Luckless) and the degrading tastes in literature. Tragedy and Comedy have given way to other, inferior genres, and puppet roles include Signior Opera, Don Tragedio, Monsieur Pantomime and Sir Farcical Comick, all of whom wish to woo the goddess Nonsense (the pan-European stereotyping of genres is funny in itself). The metatheatrical context is certainly in the spirit of Aristophanes, and Fielding seems to have cultivated this association generally, even if a specific connection to *Frogs* is not usually claimed.[9] 'The Pleasures of the Town', however, is set in the underworld, and Nonsense rules there. The competing genres seeking Nonsense's favour would seem to evoke the *agōn* of *Frogs*, which in turn suggests that Dionysus is to be seen perhaps as a personification of Old Comedy itself (with the gender switch perhaps being evoked in Dionysus' *krōkotos* and *kothornoi* [**6**]). As in *Frogs*, Charon provides access to Nonsense's realm, and his initial appearance is with a poet. *Frogs* also seems to inform an earlier tavern scene where two comedians are criticizing Luckless's script:

Luckless
What faults do you find?
Marplay
Sir, there is nothing in it that pleases me, so I am sure
there is nothing in it that will please the town.

Sparkish
There is nothing in it that will please the town.
Luckless
Methinks you should find some particular fault.
Marplay
Truly, sir, it is so full of faults that the eye of my
judgement is so distracted with the variety of objects,
that it cannot fix on any.
Sparkish
No, no, no. Cannot fix on any.

II.i

Though the details of the supposed faults are not enumerated, and Luckless's play is not an established text familiar to at least some in the audience, the language here recalls Euripides finding 'more than a dozen' faults in the first three lines of Aeschylus' *Libation Bearers* (1120–40 [**19**]).

Drawing the line from Fielding's pseudo-autobiographical puppet show to Shaw's semi-autobiographical puppet show, despite all the differences, is straightforward. *Shakes versus Shav* is not a substantial work, but in its brief ten-minute runtime, it wears its literary pedigree clearly.[10]

Sondheim

For a Yale production in 1974, Burt Shevelove took his 1941 adaptation of *Frogs*, which had been performed in the university's Exhibition Pool with the swim team as the chorus, and remounted it with music composed by Stephen Sondheim. The script is sanitized, losing bawdy and political references, but the (current) swim team and pool were again used.[11] The two playwrights offering advice are Shakespeare and Shaw, an idea that therefore predates the Shaw puppet play (and here it is the younger Shaw who is characterized as fierce, and Shakespeare gentle, reversing the Aristophanic associations).[12] Sondheim's music and lyrics are filled with characteristic wordplay, rhyme and elegant syncopation: 'As a lyricist Sondheim is one of the very few able to equal Aristophanes' linguistic and poetic brilliance.'[13] Though there were challenges with staging *Frogs* in a swimming pool – 'The echo sometimes lasts for days (days, days, days . . .)'[14] – this production represents one of the most important Aristophanic productions of the century.

In one song, 'Parabasis: It's Only a Play', Sondheim ironically stresses the inability of theatre to act politically: 'from the perspective of death, lived reality is evanescent and not worth getting excited about; on the other, passivity and failure to act are deadly.'[15] This is the opposite of the stated intention of an Aristophanic *parabasis*, and yet it represents a mainstream view of the place of art in society that is both provocative and (politically) challenging. Sondheim provides an anti-*parabasis*. The naive opinions ('Things fix themselves') are not a call to inaction. If we, like Dionysus, do not want this to be true, we need to change it.

Shevelove/Sondheim's *Frogs* did receive a commercial production on Broadway in 2004, with new songs and an expanded script by Nathan Lane, who also played Dionysus.[16] Lane added a romantic subplot with Ariadne, and many jokes about theatre culture (and so re-introducing Aristophanes' metatheatre) and politics. While the only *kōmōdoumenos* named is President Bush, the production remains very consciously a post-9/11 work.[17] Though Lane had released a studio album of the 1974 *Frogs* (in October 2001), and his interest in the play predates the attacks, the revisions and added material are shaped by the immediate experience of that period. The need to defend the city in a production in New York, and the failure of modern politicians as America was under threat of further attack, were both real concerns for Lane, even if the venue for this discussion is not typically the American musical.

Stoppard

Tom Stoppard's *The Invention of Love* (1997) is a memory play, as classical scholar and poet A. E. Housman, hovering between life and death at the Evelyn Nursing Home, recalls his youth as a student at Oxford in the 1870s. It is a beautiful, passionate, densely layered work that explores the contradictions in a human life, the intrinsic value of art and the melancholy of contemplating the past. It is also a play greatly indebted to Aristophanes' *Frogs*, perhaps more so than any other work that is not a direct adaptation of Aristophanes. The elder Housman, sitting on the banks of a river, awaits a boatman, who is Charon. In *Frogs*, Charon would only take one passenger, but here he awaits another:

Charon
A poet and a scholar is what I was told.
AEH
I think that must be me.[18]

Housman, Kennedy Professor of Latin at Cambridge University and notoriously acerbic textual critic, was also the author of *A Shropshire Lad*

(1896), among other books of verse. His was a life of contradictions. While talking to Charon, another boat appears, this one with three friends rowing on the Thames at Oxford. One of them is the young Housman, and the heart of the play is a long conversation between AEH and Housman (as Stoppard distinguishes the two), in which they discuss the nature of poetry, of love, and the purpose of reading and emending a Latin text. In an unpublished essay, Moritz frames this scene as a version of the playwrights' *agōn*, with an Aeschylean AEH (suitably-attired-in-leather-boots) and a Euripidean Housman.[19] The men learn from each other, with all the paradoxes that entails.

Stoppard uses the image of a boat on the river to connect the dying AEH to his younger self, but also to introduce allusions to Jerome K. Jerome's *Three Men in a Boat* (1889, with Jerome's characters mapping onto Charon, a scholar, and a poet, to say nothing of Cerberus), and to Oscar Wilde, perhaps stepping into a Venetian gondola.[20] Wilde is a key figure in the play, as an anti-type for Housman. Both studied at Oxford at the same time, but while Wilde embraced a literary persona, Housman preferred the scholarly. Both elements were present in each man, but while Wilde confidently and outrageously presented himself to the world, Housman's confidence and outrage were reserved for other textual critics (Stoppard cites liberally from the historical Housman's scathing prose). Wilde appears at the end of the play as a kind of god-from-the-machine (a feature associated particularly with Euripides).

Though most of the ancient poetry examined is Latin, a handful of Greek works are mentioned explicitly. *Frogs* is one: Charon boasts that he was in a play once ('That needs thinking about,' says AEH drily), and when *Frogs* is named, Housman says, 'You speak the truth. I saw you.'[21] It is not clear which performance Stoppard means, but it is likely that the 1892 production in Greek at Oxford is intended,[22] though there are other possibilities (such as any of several performances of Gilbert Murray's translation [**27**]). Tragedies of both Euripides and Aeschylus are mentioned. For Aeschylus, it is *Myrmidons*, cited explicitly even if Charon is unable to remember anything beyond the two lines that had survived regardless.[23] Our knowledge of the play comes almost exclusively from *Frogs* [**18, 20**], and the play presented a loving relationship between Achilles and Patroclus. For Euripides, it is *Pirithous*, mentioned briefly for the deep friendship between Theseus and Pirithous.[24] *Pirithous* also involves a *katabasis* [**6**], and was itself programmatic for *Frogs*; Stoppard has Housman extol the heroes' mutual love to his friend and flatmate, Moses Jackson, who was never his lover, as their lives in the end sadly separate.[25] More directly relevant, however, their friendship is isolated in the final two lines of Horace, *Odes* 4.7, *diffugere nives* ('The snows have fled . . .'), meditating on the transience of all things, but especially human life.

As Housman says, 'I think it's the most beautiful poem in Latin or Greek there ever was.'[26]

Both *Myrmidons* and *Pirithous* are about male love, and both are resonant with *Frogs*. Housman's friendship with Jackson never achieves this degree of singular elevation, and consequently it also lacked the extreme, notorious conclusion that was seen with Wilde and Lord Alfred Douglas. In a way, suggests Stoppard, that is Housman's tragedy, that he was repressed in an age when the understanding of love was changing.

There is an urgency to *The Invention of Love*: that poetry and its study is, in itself, a significant activity. This, too, is a truth from *Frogs*. No earlier work of Greek literature was so intent on displaying the author's deep understanding from spending time with poetry and theatre. For both Aristophanes and Stoppard, this appreciation of the beauty of words is framed in a political context. Inevitably, that cheapens it, sullying it with the narrow views of others.[27] This is what poetry does, collapsing the gulf of time between the poet and the listener, as we marvel at the mystery that 'We catch our breath at the same place where the breath was always caught.'[28] This, precisely, is what Dionysus feels when he is reading *Andromeda*.

29

Seriously

What is the purpose of poetry? Amid the buffoonery, the slapstick, the wordplay, the music, the caricature and the fun, *Frogs* presents a serious engagement with this question. Do we genuinely believe that art can change the world? That it can save us? We might say it, or want to believe, but very few would accept that it can or does in any substantial way without any qualification. Aristophanes, if we look at the body of his work, seems to believe that influence was possible, and wrote his plays continually aspiring to effect some sort of political change, whether he believed such change was possible or not.

Theatre was publicly performed poetry for the *polis*, and it spoke to all levels of society. We tend to discount comedy as a venue for serious thought, and in some ways the deference of *Frogs* to tragedy might be part of the reason why. As Silk discusses, the tendency to see these genres as opposites generates false assumptions, that comedy is secondary and derivative, or that only tragedy is serious while comedy seeks to amuse.[1] As this book has tried to demonstrate, just because *Frogs* is funny (and it is) does not mean it is unimportant.

That importance exists in part because of the play's historical situation. Though contests for comedy continue, the nature of comedy seems to change after *Frogs*, drifting from the direct political comedy that the radical democracy of Athens espoused. *Frogs* helped establish the canon of tragedians that would survive beyond antiquity, and that was only possible with the death of Sophocles and Euripides, who had dominated the performance scene for decades. Aristophanes understood Euripides, and I believe wanted to dramatize a crucial moment in the tragedian's theatrical career. But there is more. Though it is often presented in terms of its representation and mediation of tragedy, the structure and content of *Frogs* have been deeply shaped by the history of earlier comedy:[2]

- Cratinus' *Dionysalexandros* (437 or 431–430) had presented Dionysus as a judge [**1**].
- Eupolis' *Taxiarchs* (428 [415?]) had presented Dionysus learning to row (as perhaps did Aristophanes' *Babylonians* (426) [**1, 9**].
- Eupolis' *Demes* (417 [412?]) had political heroes from the past returned from the underworld to help Athens [**8**].

- Aristophanes' *Gerytades* (*c.* 407) sent a delegation, of 'slight' poets, to the underworld [**8**].
- Pherecrates' *Shiners* (pre-405) had a journey to the underworld to meet Aeschylus, who claims to have established tragic poetry as a *technē* (craft) [**8**].
- Finally, both Callias and Magnes had used frog choruses [**10**].

Immediate contemporaries are also illuminating: Platon competed at the Lenaia in 405 with a political comedy called *Cleophon* [**5, 9, 15**]; Phrynichus, who had also written a comedy called *Initiates* and who had Dionysus as a character in his *Kronos*, competed at the Lenaia in 405 with *Muses*, which had a character, perhaps Euripides, on trial [**5**]. This does not make Aristophanes derivative: *Frogs* braids the threads of previous comedy, and his creativity draws these ideas together in a critical attempt to influence his fellow citizens.

Tastes, of course, change. Edward Gibbon, author of *The Decline and Fall of the Roman Empire*, once wrote, 'The gross language of a boatman, and the ribaldry of two buffoons, surely belong only to the lowest species of comedy.'[3] Surprisingly, he is not speaking of *Frogs* here, but of Horace, *Sermones* 1.5. One wonders how for Gibbon any comedy could be anything other than the lowest species. While different manifestations of comedy over the years exhibit a wide range of qualities, there remain elements that can allow us to perceive a family resemblance.[4] Comedy focuses on the material, not the metaphysical: from gross bodies, to oversize props, to individuals sitting in the audience right now. Comedy is amusing: finding distance in despair and engaging the intellect in ways that lead spectators to laugh and nod in identification. Comedy ends on survival: it is inherently hopeful, imagining a future where the world goes on, and happily-ever-after is possible.

By imagining a future for Athens in which it is saved, even if through the unrealizable rescue of a dead poet, Aristophanes and Philonides and their creative team, working together, achieved a unique honour. The reperformance of *Frogs* marks its significance, and it shows the willingness of some individuals in Athens (admittedly, perhaps the wrong individuals) to listen and act (admittedly, perhaps too late) on what Aristophanes' characters suggest. To make this happen, *Frogs* distorted the expected narrative structure of Old Comedy. Aristophanes' earlier extant dramas began with an *agōn* evaluating the merits of the Great Idea [**5**] between the *parodos* and *parabasis*, and following the *parabasis* presented a series of short scenes revealing the comic implications of the Great Idea's enactment. *Frogs* reverses this, placing the short comic scenes before the *parabasis*, and the *agōn* after it.[5] As a result, the audience does not see the Great Idea falter as it is put into practice.

Aristophanes closes his play looking upwards to the light of an Athens he wants to survive.

Why then should we read or stage *Frogs* today? *Frogs* is a comedy that speaks to Athens directly, months before its final defeat and surrender to Sparta after a protracted and costly war, before the bloody oligarchic junta of the Thirty. Its playful irreverence demonstrates that civic religion, and even mystery cults, are insufficient, as an all-too-human Dionysus, a broken, flawed, cowardly, selfish individual, decides to try to fix things. The play's existence and reception have shaped a key period in Athenian literary history, and helped establish what classical literature is. *Frogs* preserves the value of the old-fashioned alongside the new and learns from previous generations. It wants literature to challenge and influence its audiences, and accepts that literary and artistic agendas can change over time. *Frogs* genuinely believes that a shared knowledge of the past and of poetry can improve the present. Do you?

Readings

Three recent and reliable scholarly translations of Aristophanes's plays are available in English:

- Sommerstein, Alan. 1980–2002. *The Comedies of Aristophanes*, 12 volumes. Warminster. [Text, translation and commentary; now reissued. *Frogs* is in Sommerstein 1996a.]
- Henderson, Jeffrey. 1998–2007. *Aristophanes*, 5 volumes. Cambridge MA. [Text and translation. *Frogs* is in Henderson 2002. Volume 5 contains *testimonia* for the life of Aristophanes and fragments.]
- Halliwell, Stephen. 1997–. *Aristophanes*, 3 volumes. Oxford. [Translation with introduction and notes. *Frogs* is in Halliwell 2015.]

All have line numbers indicated, which is crucial for any serious study of an ancient play. Henderson and Sommerstein have published other versions of their translations with selected presses. Storey 2011a, b, c provides texts and translations of other surviving Old Comedy. Dover 1993a is the most substantial commentary on *Frogs*, though there remains much of value in Stanford 1963. MacDowell 1995 is the best introduction to Aristophanes, though see also Russo 1994 and Lowe 2007: 21–62. Wilson 2007 provides the most recent Greek text.

Griffith 2013 offers an introduction to the play on a scale comparable to this volume. His is a great book, but the emphases and the conclusions are different from mine. Littlefield 1968 stands as a monument collecting some of the best scholarship of the time, but its chief virtue now is to show how new analytical techniques have helped transform the study of comedy over the past fifty years. Some favourite articles or chapters that have challenged me or taught me about *Frogs* include Borthwick 1994, Dobrov 2001: 133–61, Edmonds 2003, Hooker 1960, Moorton 1987, Segal 1961, Silk 2000: 42–97, Slater 2002: 181–206, Torrance 2013: 14–61 (expanded from 2011) and Wrigley 2007. Goad 2018 provides an excellent and wide-ranging discussion of the reception of the play in the 20th century that came to my attention only after this book was written.

Notes

1 Dionysus

1 Henrichs 1984 traces the development of Dionysus in modern (mis-) understanding, from 1872 (Nietszche's *The Birth of Tragedy*) to 1972 (René Girard's *Violence and the Sacred* and Walter Burkert's *Homo Necans*); see also Henrichs 1993.
2 Henrichs 1984: 240.
3 Csapo and Wilson 2020: 2–274, with a summary on 7–8; see also Pickard-Cambridge 1968: 42–56 and Csapo and Slater 1995: 124–32. It seems the timing of Rural Dionysia was staggered to allow theatre fans to travel around (Plato, *Republic* 475d). Ikarion is now the best understood of these festivals, thanks to an analysis of an inscription dating *c.* 440 BCE (Wilson 2015).
4 Habash 1996: 560–7, and see Henrichs 1990: 269–70. Herodotus 2.48–9 describes how phallic processions were begun by the mythical Melampous.
5 Csapo 2012: 28–9.
6 Parker 2005: 316 (italics in original), and, on dramatic festivals, 316–26; another Dionysiac festival, the Oschophoria, occurred sometime in the autumn (211–17). Henrichs 1990: 260–4 traces Dionysus in deme worship.
7 Parker 2005: 313, and see 290–316, Pickard-Cambridge 1968: 1–25, Burkert 1985: 237–42, Hamilton 1992. Parker 2005: 306–12 describes the so-called Lenaia vases, which depicted a mask of (bearded) Dionysus lifted on a pole, which Parker connects to the Anthesteria (and see Pickard-Cambridge 1968: 30–4).
8 Carpenter 1997: 107.
9 Parker 2005: 326: 'The god himself is unimaginable without his followers but does not resemble them. He is seldom drunk, seldom mad, never sexually aroused.' Nevertheless, at *Frogs* 740 **[16]**, Xanthias does claim that all his master knows is how to drink and fuck [*pinein kai binein*].
10 Carpenter 1993, esp. 204–6. For *Edonians*, see Sommerstein 2008: 60–7.
11 Carpenter 1997: 85–103.
12 *Bacchae* 53–4, 240–1, 453–9; and see Carpenter 1997: 104–18. The identification of Dionysus has been questioned (see Traficante 2007: 77–89) but seems very probable (Isler-Kerényi 2015: 166–77).
13 Storey 2011a: 284–95, and see Storey 2006 (and 113–16 on an early date) and Bakola 2005, 2010: 81–102, 181–208, 253–72, 285–94, 299–304, and Farioli 1994 for its influence.
14 Translations in this paragraph are from Storey 2011a. For the chorus as satyrs, see Storey 2006: 119–22. If Dionysus had appeared in the prologue with Hermes, the audience would see both before and after the transformation.

15 Revermann 1997 suggests a portrait mask of sorts was used.
16 Among other titles by Cratinus, *Dionysuses* and *Men* [*Satyrs*?] *of Ida* may be alternative titles for *Dionysalexandros* (Storey 2011a: 294–5, 312–13, and see Luppe 1966: 184–92 and Bakola 2010: 84–6). *Men of Ida* fr. 90 seems to imply an onstage shaving scene, possibly of Dionysus disguising himself (cf. fr. 48).
17 Storey 2006: 122–3, Csapo 2016: 135–6.
18 Henderson 2007: 141–61, and Starkey 2013 for Dionysus as a rower.
19 *Taxiarchs* fr. 268.51–5; Hermippus' *Soldiers* (or *She-Soldiers*) fr. 54; Cratinus fr. 332.

2 Lenaia

1 See Pickard-Cambridge 1968: 57–101, Connor 1989 and Easterling 1997, and, for the origins of Athenian comedy, Csapo 2015.
2 Goldhill 1987: 59–64 describes these ceremonies, which could include the display of tribute from the allies, processions of orphans of the military dead, recognition of civic honours and freed slaves, etc. (and Pickard-Cambridge 1968: 58–9, Wilson and Hartwig 2009). While not all necessarily were presented every year, the function of civic integration and celebration was profound.
3 Pickard-Cambridge 1968: 59–70, esp. 63–7. Tragedies had been part of the City Dionysia since the last decade of the sixth century (Millis and Olson 2012: 141), with comic competition introduced in 487/486 (Millis and Olson 2012: 156–7). Hartwig 2010 and 2012: 195–7 argues against a reduction in the number of comedies produced during the Peloponnesian War to three.
4 Marshall and van Willigenburg 2004 describes how only some of the votes cast are reckoned. For any given result, nothing can be inferred about a given play's quality or the response it met. A play might win with as few as three votes, and lose with as many as seven, and four votes would be enough to secure a victory about half of the time.
5 Wilson 2000 and Makres 2014.
6 Pickard-Cambridge 1968: 25–42.
7 Millis and Olson 2012: 178.
8 This date has been challenged by Millis and Olson (2012: 204); this date is the beginning of competitions for both tragic and comic actors (2012: 193, 208). The evidence for dilogies rests on the entry for the year 419/418 on *IG* II^2 2319 (Pickard-Cambridge 1968: 41).
9 Millis and Olson 2012: 150.
10 Makres 2014: 76, Csapo 2016: 123.
11 Russo 1994: 3.
12 Slater 1986, and see Russo 1994: 1–5.
13 Wycherley 1960; Slater 1986: 258; Slater 1986: 259–60. An inscription (*IG* I^3 84, dating to 418/417) shows a place called the Dionysion in use, and this continued at least until the 340s; Slater 1986: 262–3).

14 Bowie 1993: 26–7, 35–9 and Habash 1995.
15 Csapo 2012.
16 For tragedians at the Lenaia, see Pickard-Cambridge 1968: 51 and Russo 1994: 186–91. Aelian, *True History* 2.13 describes how Socrates would walk to the Piraeus whenever Euripides was competing at the (Rural) festival there.
17 Wiles is persuasive on this understanding of scene-painting (*skēnographia*): 'the purpose of scene-painting was to create out of transient materials the illusion of a stone monument, in accordance with Dionysos' nature as god of illusion and transformation' (1997: 161); 'Detailed verbal descriptions . . . are not surrogate stage directions to the scenographer' (162).
18 On the number of doors, see the concise summary of Lowe 2006: 49 n. 3.
19 Dearden 1976: 13–18, Marshall 2016: 197–200, and see Dearden 1970: 19–20.
20 The image is a screen grab from a YouTube video, 'Assassin's Creed Odyssey: A Tour of Athens' (posted by IGN) https://www.youtube.com/watch?v=-a8cWF-29lI. Thanks to Tim Shea.

3 Aristophanes

1 In spite of his protests of youth early in his career, it is just possible that Aristophanes was born before Pericles' citizenship law of 451/450 came into effect. Testimony exists that his mother's name was Zenodora (Henderson 2007: 16–17), which is not an Athenian name. If true, Aristophanes might have had a non-citizen mother, a detail which could later be used to impugn his own citizenship.
2 *IG* II^2 2325C is a fragment of a monument carved in the 280s, once in the sanctuary of Dionysus Eleutherios, which recorded victors at the Dionysia and Lenaia in tragedy and comedy (for the monument on which the victors lists was displayed, see Millis and Olson 2012: 137–40). This fragment lists comic poets victorious at the City Dionysia and lists Pherecrates, known to have first been victorious in 435 or earlier, immediately before Aristophanes in 426 (lines 23–4; see Biles 2001, Millis and Olson 2012: 158 and Olson 2017: 59–61).
3 Storey 2011a: 6–37.
4 This is not a complete list, but only the plays mentioned in this book. As with *Clouds* (for which the distinction between *Clouds I* and *II* is modern convenience), earlier versions of *Thesmophoriazusae* (date unknown) and *Wealth* (from 408) existed; Storey 2019: 151–3 argues against the possibility of a second *Peace*.
5 Evidence for Aristophanes' life is gathered at Henderson 2007: 2–109 and see Lowe 2007: 32–6.
6 *IG* II^2 1740.21–4.
7 Arnott 2010: 287–9.

8 Halliwell 1980. Ancient production notices use the verb *edidaxe* followed by *dia* and the name of the *didaskalos*. We can translate this, 'He [the poet] mounted [the production] through the *didaskalos*'; but the verb can equally be used (without *dia*) to mean 'He [the *didaskalos*] directed [the production].'
9 MacDowell 1982, who notes that the term *poiētēs* in 425 is just coming into use, and may not yet mean 'author' but the 'maker' (24; cf. the Scots word *makar*). 'Poet' is used in Plato and Aristophanes, and at Herodotus 4.53.2 of those bards preceding Homer and Hesiod.
10 Storey 2011c: 4–17. One source also suggests that he directed *Clouds* (423-D), but this is not generally accepted (*Prol. De Com.* III; see Storey 2011a: 20–1).
11 For example, Eupolis' *Autolykos* in 420 was directed by Demostratus, and Platon the comic poet had this relationship with Cantharus (Hartwig 2010); see also Hunter 1983: 13.
12 Slater 1989.
13 *IG* II^2 2343. See Welsh 1983 and Lind 1985.
14 See Millis 2015: 229–36, describing three monuments which he takes to refer to victories at Rural Dionysia.
15 Storey 2003.
16 Hartwig 2012 argues that Lykis and Amepsias were also Lenaia competitors in this contest.

4 Hero

1 Russo 1994: 215.
2 Whitman 1964: 52, with 228–58 on *Frogs*, and see Rosen 2014: 222–31.
3 Sommerstein 1980: 11, and see 11–13; 'it may well be that this was Aristophanes' own distinctive contribution to the history of Athenian comedy' (13).
4 Kloss 2001: 240–61 demonstrates how the initial plan is often unsuccessful, but then it shifts to a more radical or extreme version, which is fulfilled.
5 Rosen 2014: 231.
6 Padilla 1992: 379.
7 Rosen 2014: 231.
8 If Xanthias were present throughout *Frogs*, one might consider him as a potential comic hero, anticipating the slave Carion in *Wealth* **[16]**; but the Idea in *Frogs* belongs to Dionysus.

5 Names

1 Sommerstein 1996b.
2 Wright 2016: 18–19, 23–5.

3 See also Chantry 2001.
4 Demand 1970 argues that the chorus are meant to be associated with the name Phrynichus, as an allusion to all three individuals. I believe the association can be made without it becoming programmatic for the play as Demand suggests.
5 Franklin 2017.
6 Baldwin 1974.
7 Allan 2012.

6 Costumes (*Frogs* 1–51)

1 See Foley 2000, with some conclusions challenged by Stehle 2002: 372–6; see also Compton-Engle 2015: 16–58. Revermann 2006: 145–59 discusses comic ugliness.
2 Green 2006.
3 *Kothornoi*, 'a term which was used to refer to soft boots which were loose enough to be pulled onto either foot and were associated with women, they are not the same as the platform-heeled tragic boots ([Latin] *cothurni*) which were iconic in the later [Roman] period. In the fifth century it seems to have been the role being played, i.e. female maenads, rather than the type of drama, which dictated the inclusion of these boots in the costume' (Wyles 2011: 13–14).
4 These accounts are preserved in second-century CE Roman sources (Pausanias 2.31.2, 2.37.6, ps. Apollodorus *Library* 3.38, Diodorus Siculus 4.25.4, Hyginus *Fabulae* 251, *Astronomica* 2.5) but may predate *Frogs* (though see Pindar, *Olympian* 2.26).
5 On the baggage, see Compton-Engle 2015: 105–6. I once suggested that the donkey was in fact a costume donkey body-and-head, worn over the shoulders (an idea originally by Jeff Massey; Marshall 1999b: 146). Jokes about Xanthias carrying *skeuē* become more pointed, and Heracles' comment that the door-knocking was 'centaur-like' (38–9) becomes much funnier (though this would require 37, after the caesura, to be assigned to Xanthias). This is still appealing, and it is definitely how I would stage the scene today.
6 Berlin F3046 = *PhV*[2] 22. See Taplin 1993: 45–7, pl. 13 no. 7, Csapo 2010: 58–61, Sells 2018: 60–2 and Csapo and Wilson 2020: 416–18; also Handley 2000: 158 n. 3.
7 Csapo 2010: 58–9 notes that the vase may have been 'touched up' by restorers in the nineteenth century, and that a line drawing which survives contains inaccuracies that can be discounted.
8 South Italian comic vases regularly depict characters as naked, much more than would be expected from the surviving plays of Aristophanes. This appears to be an artistic choice, making the *sōmation* an indicator of theatrical genre.

9 Handley 2000: 157–8. For the Return of Hephaestus and its associations with satyrs, phallic poles and a ship-cart, see Carpenter 1986: 13–29, Hedreen 2004 and Csapo 2012. The 1936 Cambridge Greek Play, directed by J. T. Sheppard, used a pantomime donkey, acted by two undergraduates. Contemporary reviews reveal some of the physical comedy that they were able to generate (Marshall 2015: 191–2).
10 For masks, see Marshall 1999a. There is no indication of a beardless Dionysus in *Frogs* (Dover 1993a: 40).
11 For metatheatre in *Frogs*, see Slater 2002: 181–206 and Rengel 2017.
12 On Phrynichus' *Muses* (405), see Harvey 2000: 100–8.
13 See Carpenter 1986: 98–123 and Lada-Richards 1999: 17–44 on similarities between Dionysus and Heracles. 'Aristophanes portrays a Dionysus who ineptly possesses Heracles' heroic and comic drives' (Padilla 1992: 363).
14 Edmonds 2004: 122.
15 Slater 2002: 184–5.

7 Yearning (*Frogs* 52–107)

1 Collard and Cropp 2008a: 124–55; and see Moorton 1987, Gibert 1999-2000, 2004, and Marshall 2016: 140–87.
2 Seager 1981: 249–50.
3 Dover 1993a: 14.
4 For the so-called minor tragedians whose work survives only in fragments, see Wright 2016: 92–4 and 221 (Iophon, Sophocles' son), 59–90 and 222–5 (Agathon, also a character in *Thesmophoriazusae*), 106–7 and 222 (Xenocles), and 186–7 (Pythangelus).
5 Sommerstein 2012: 115–16, building on Russo 1994: 198–200.
6 Edmonds 2004: 122, and Higgins 1977: 61–2. Sommerstein 1996a: 45 has 'potent'.
7 The first is found in the lost *Alexandros* fr. 42 (415 BCE) and *Bacchae* 889 (also 405 BCE, and so perhaps not known to Aristophanes); the latter is a comic corruption of *Wise Melanippe* fr. 487 (before 411 BCE). Shakespeare's Time has feet in *As You Like It* 3.2 and Sonnet 65, and Sommerstein 2012: 117–18 also remarks that in Greek 'foot' (*pous*) can mean 'penis' (a misunderstanding found at Euripides, *Medea* 679). Since one's bedroom is often a convenient place for sex, both phrases may contain sexual innuendo.
8 Major 2013: 177.
9 Collard and Cropp 2008b: 629–57 (who consider the possibility it is a satyr play), and see Dobrov 2001: 133–57. Though *Pirithous* has been attributed to the oligarch Critias, if the argument here is accepted, that would favour Euripidean authorship (and see Collard and Cropp 2008b: 639). Sfyroeras 2008 argues that the *Andromeda* reference implies Euripides as the Perseus-figure rescuing Dionysus-Andromeda, but I remain unconvinced.

10 Dobrov 2001: 152–4. Euripides is explicitly 'criminal' (*panourgos*) at 80, 1520, and see 781, 1015. The scholion to *Frogs* 142a calls Pirithous a 'thief' (*harpax*; and Dobrov 2001: 136).
11 Dobrov 2001: 147.
12 Dobrov 2001: 145.
13 Collard and Cropp 2008b: 641 n. 1.
14 Hanink 2014: 181–3, Farmer 2017: 44–5.

8 Underworlds (*Frogs* 108–66)

1 Edmonds 2004: 112, and see Santamaría Álvarez 2015: 119–26.
2 For admission, see Aristophanes fr. 575 (*Phoenician Women*), and Pickard-Cambridge 1968: 265–8. The amount had also been introduced as a dole for the unemployed in 410 by Cleophon (*Ath Pol.* 28.3 [**5, 15**]). Roselli 2009 argues that there was no permanent Theoric Fund in 405, but ad hoc dispensations to subsidize theatre admissions were possible, and are attested from 410 to 406 (*IG* I[3] 375).
3 Stanford 1963: 90.
4 Sommerstein 1996a: 169.
5 *Suppliants* 701–9, *Eumenides* 269–72, 538–48 (Sommerstein 1996a: 169).
6 Ceccarelli 2004. Even if the *pyrrhichē* was not held every year, it certainly would have been held at the most recent Panathenaea in 406, which was a larger 'penteteric' celebration, held every four years (Shear 2001: 337 and see 551–2, 810–12).
7 Storey 2011b: 94–129, with an argument for the date (against the more usual 412) at 97 and 2000: 173–5; see also Major 2013: 118–23.
8 Storey 2000: 175–7 and Torello 2008: 41–7.
9 Storey 2011a: 386–93.
10 Storey 2011c: 396–7, 403.
11 Storey 2011c: 120–5. The alternate titles are unexplained.
12 Storey 2011c: 459–67, and see Hanink and Uhlig 2017: 52–3. Jokes on the debased currency in Athens are found at 718–37, and this could suggest a late date for Pherecrates' play.
13 Henderson 2007: 184–99 and Farmer 2017: 195–212. Franklin 2017: 205 n. 180 suggests the play postdates *Frogs*.
14 Fr. 156 is likely the beginning of the play, since it begins with a parody of Euripides' *Hecuba* 1. Farmer 2017: 199 suggests this is a dialogue between *Gerytades* escorting the slight poets to the diarrhoea river and a gatekeeper such as Aeacus.
15 O'Sullivan 1992 suggests that *Frogs* was crucial in the development of the technical vocabulary for ancient literary criticism in the fourth century, and that the contrast between 'grand' and 'thin' styles is already evident in the treatment of tragedians in *Frogs*.

16 Storey 2011c: 220–1 (*Laughter*), and also Aristophanes fr. 117 (*Farmers*; Henderson 2007: 168–9).
17 Storey 2011c: 238–43, and see Steinhart 2007 Kidd 2014: 87–117, esp. 89–93, and Franklin 2017.
18 Franklin 2017: 189–98.
19 Following the play, in the early fourth century, Cinesias was awarded a victory monument in Athens (*IG* II^2 3028).
20 Hooker 1960, and see Slater 2002: 186.

9 Warships (*Frogs* 167–208)

1 Major 2013: 146–62 summarizes this period with a focus on the evidence from tragedy and the courtroom (Lysias 25).
2 Wiles 2011: 33–5, and see Worthington 1989 and Allan 2012: 104–9.
3 They 'became Plataeans' (693–4), referring to another group, enfranchised in the 420s. Though the citizens of Plataea who took citizenship (not all did) were excluded from being archon or priest (Demosthenes 59.104–6; Canevaro 2010 shows this is not straightforward), their children were not. Hunt 2001: 368–9 suggests a number in the thousands, drawing in part from the slaves who worked in the silver mines at Laurion; he also answers the arguments of Worthington 1989 that the evidence is not especially strong (2001: 360–6).
4 While eye injuries can be remarkably painful (and could be used to excuse military service; Herodotus 7.229–31), it is likely that this is an excuse, as if he has avoided military service for conjunctivitis (pink-eye), or bone spurs on the feet.
5 Allan 2012: 103.
6 Between 42 and 159, and so for most of the exchange with Heracles, Xanthias has been relegated to the side of the action. His only lines 51b, 87b–88, 107b, 115b become a refrain on his being ignored; each speech begins mid-line, as Xanthias interrupts whoever is speaking.
7 Taplin 1977: 138.
8 Stanford 1963: 87.
9 Stanford 1963: 88–9 (suggesting 'Charon was rather deaf, being an old man'); Dover 1993a: 214; Sommerstein 1996a: 173.
10 Marshall 1996: 257–9, and see Dearden 1976: 67–9.
11 Tr. Storey 2011b: 215, who dates the play to 415, in immediate response to the Sicilian expedition; the traditionally accepted date is 428. See also Wilson 1974, 1976, and Olson 2015: 209–10, who denies both that a rowing scene is presented and that the play influenced *Frogs*.
12 Tr. Sommerstein 1996a: 55, rendering the three-word poetic line (of three, four, then five syllables), in which each word begins with a negating *a*- (alpha privative). The third word may evoke traditional Salaminian expertise at

rowing (1996: 175, citing *Lysistrata* 59–60 and *Ecclesiazusae* 37–9), but it additionally hearkens back to the loss of warships in Sicily in 413.

10 Croaking (*Frogs* 209–68)

1 You have just memorized 0.7 per cent of the play's lines. Aren't you proud?
2 Both *brekekekex koax koax* and *ō op parabalou* (180 'Heave-ho! Draw up alongside'; naval terminology, again reminding spectators of who is absent among them) were incorporated into the Yale College 'Long Cheer' (as it was called), chanted at football games between its introduction in 1884 and the mid-1960s (Schiff 1998) [**28**].
3 Dover 1993a: 219 and 222.
4 Wilson 1999.
5 In *Birds*, the *aulētēs* is incorporated naturalistically as the Nightingale when music begins (at line 215), the wife of the comic (paratragic) character Tereus.
6 Lowe 2006: 59: 'the spatial logic remains surprisingly clear-cut and focused throughout.'
7 Marshall 1996: 262–3. Truth be told, the live animal is not needed at any point after line 32, and if it could be taken off conveniently before then, that would be more straightforward. Dover 1972: 180 assumes it would be natural for an unmentioned servant to take the donkey in at 44. Dearden 1970 has it remain onstage until Xanthias departs.
8 Wills 1969: 306–8, 310–11 (the reasons given against violence are nevertheless mistaken, I believe).
9 Wills 1969: 308–10.
10 Wills 1969: 313–16. Exactly what Wills suggests is modestly and unhelpfully hidden behind the Latin *crepidus ventri* (fart, literally 'butt-croak') and the Greek *pordē* (fart). How such a sound was made in the theatre is a separate question, but a drum, the actor's voice or (if there was one; see Donelan 2018) the *bronteion* (thunder-machine) are all possibilities.
11 *Phaedo* 109b gives the image of human settlement in the Mediterranean as resembling 'frogs living around a pond' (*batrachous peri tēn thalattan oikountas*).
12 Campbell 1984: 165. Frogs do not have lips (Deb 2011).
13 Edmonds 2004: 132–3.
14 Outside of the city walls, this may not even have been a safe area in 405 (Wiles 2011: 36).
15 MacDowell 1995: 281.
16 This same contrast is established in 'Plato's Stepchildren,' an episode of *Star Trek* (season 3, episode 10; 22 November 1968), in which an alien culture with telekinesis lives in a version of Plato's Republic. One citizen, the dwarf Alexander, lacks superhuman abilities, and is heard quoting the frog chorus (brekekekex) at the end of a song he sings. The episode is discussed by Kovacs 2015: 210–12.

17 *Knights* 523 refers to a chorus of Magnes dyed frog-green for example. Dover 1993a: 56 n. 2, Marshall 1996: 253 n. 8.
18 Ian Storey (personal communication) writes, 'A production of *Frogs* that I saw at Oriel College Oxford in 1972 had the frogs (not 24, however) wear diving gear with flipper and bulging face-masks. The lead frog was in fact the Chaplain of Oriel College. [APGRD 4971] In 1981 I saw a production of *Frogs* at Worcester College where they used the lake for the rowing scene. I can't remember if the frogs were visible – we were seated on bleachers and I THINK that the frog voices came from behind us. Plouton was played by my cousin David Winnington-Ingram. [APGRD 4940].' (APGRD = Archive of Performances of Greek and Roman Drama reference number.)
19 Vickers 2011.
20 Wansbrough 1993. Aristophanes has no obligation to represent frogs with biological precision (though see Dover 1993a: 219 and 222, connecting the species *rana ridibunda*).
21 Allison 1983, answered by Marshall 1996, and see Barbera 1981.
22 MacDowell 1972 raises the question of audibility and articulation of a chorus singing from backstage.
23 Marshall 1996: 262–4.

11 Monsters (*Frogs* 269–322)

1 Padilla 1992: 369–70, 372, and see Santamaría Álvarez 2015: 118–19.
2 *Frogs* 293–4, and see *Ecclesiazusae* 1056–7 'where an ugly and heavily rouged old woman is mistaken for her' (Sommerstein 1996a: 180). Aristophanes fr. 515 (from *Tagenestai* [*Men with Frying-Pans*]) identifies her with Hecate.
3 Borthwick 1993: 35.
4 The name Empousa may derive from her as an obstacle, 'in the way' (*empodos*), but sources suggest that she 'moves on a single leg' (*heni podizein* is the phrase in the Suda, a tenth-century Byzantine encyclopedia; see https://www.cs.uky.edu/~raphael/sol/sol-entries/epsilon/1049). Though not a true etymology, the single leg of bronze (294) appears traditional and perhaps links her to the Erinyes (Furies). The leg of dung here is a joke, replacing a donkey leg; the Suda nevertheless insists that *bolitinon* is the proper word for donkey-dung. Aristophanes' first forms for the creature, a cow and ass, anticipate this confusion; see Bremmer 2011: 13–14.
5 Daitz 1983. Slater 2002: 187 adopts a pun proposed by W. W. Merry in his 1884 commentary: 'After the storm, how weasily we sail!'
6 Borthwick 1968: 200–4.
7 Borthwick 1968: 204–5.
8 Colour words are always a problem in Greek. Possibly the *purros*-stem here means 'brown'. *Purros* is the colour of cows and lions (golden brown? tawny?)

but also yellow-red; in the Hippocratic *Epidemics* 6.1.10 it is the colour of sediment in urine (which might be yellow, or red, or brown). Because he wears a *krōkotos* ([**6**], which is a saffron reddish-brown), the audience will not have visual confirmation of Xanthias' claim. See Franklin 2017: 199–205. Things will get worse for Dionysus's clothing later [**13**].

9 Line assignment here is uncertain, and it might be Xanthias; see Sommerstein 1996a: 182.

10 Brown 1993, and see Lada-Richards 1999: 71 and 90–4 and Santamaría Álvarez 2015: 128–9.

12 Mysteries (*Frogs* 323–459)

1 This is the approach of Bruit Zaidman and Schmitt Pantel 1992.

2 Parker 2005: 327–68, and see Burkert 1985: 285–90.

3 Parker 2005: 344–6. Anthesterion 20 is roughly in early March.

4 Plato, *Gorgias* 497c with scholia. Agrai is the setting of Plato's *Phaedrus* (229c), and possibly near the lost sanctuary of Dionysus in the Marshes (the oldest sanctuary of Dionysus in Athens), tied to the Lenaia (Wycherley 1965: 74 discusses the confusion between Lenaion and Limnaion); and see Simms 2002/3. Tucker 1906: xxviii–xxxiv argued that the Lesser Mysteries were the primary ritual being evoked in *Frogs*, and while they are relevant, the religious landscape of the play is much more heterogeneous than this.

5 See also Stanford 1963: 86.

6 Graf 1974: 48–58, Ford 2011: 345–8, but see Segal 1961: 219 and Burkert 1985: 287–8. This procession occurred on 19 or 20 Boedromion in the Athenian calendar (Parker 2005: 348) – roughly, in early October.

7 Bremmer 2011: 2–11.

8 These were the same individuals as had performed the frog-chorus ([**10**]; even if one wants to argue that the frogs did not appear). The scholia are confused on this point, and unhelpfully use the word *parachorēgēma*, which typically refers to an extra expense (Barbera 1981: 119–21).

9 Graf 1974: 40–51, and see Sommerstein 1996a: 184.

10 Dover 1993b: 187–90 challenges this, and thinks the Mystai are all male.

11 Seager 1981: 250. MacDowell 1995: 283 n. 18 denies the joke.

12 Sommerstein 1996a: 183. Dover 1993b: 173 prefers 'are enjoying themselves' (and see 173–8).

13 See Dover 1993a: 57–69.

14 Bowie 1993: 231.

15 Ford 2011: 352.

16 Sommerstein 1996a: 70–1.

17 Millis 2015: 230.

18 Dover 1993b: 180 n. 6.

19 Dover 1993b: 179–80.

20 We do not know where in the performance area they have been hiding: perhaps partly along an *eisodos*, or at the downstage edge of the perimeter of the *orchēstra*.
21 Edmonds 2004: 138–43.
22 Graf 1974: 45–6 and see Bowie 1993: 239–40. Reference is to a point on the route, where a bridge crosses the river Cephisus.
23 Andocides 1.124–7, and Dover 1993a: 249, 256–7.
24 Dover 1993b: 183–4.
25 Segal 1961: 208.
26 Segal 1961: 217.
27 Bowie 1993: 228–53, Lada-Richards 1999, and see Parker 2005: 349–50.
28 Edmonds 2003, esp. 186 and 188, and 2004: 117–21.
29 Edmonds 2003: 184. Heiden 1991: 97–9 argues he is actively opposed to comedy, but does not recognize that this position is itself comedic, allowing for the generation of humour.
30 Edmonds 2003: 187–8, and see Dover 1993b: 182–3 and MacDowell 1995: 282 n. 16.
31 Dover 1993b: 199, quoted in a discussion that follows Dover's chapter.
32 Hooker 1980: 174–5. For the Eleusinian importance of torches, see Parker 2005: 350.
33 Dover 1993b: 185–7.
34 Bowie 1993: 238–9.

13 Disguise (*Frogs* 460–533)

1 Sommerstein 1996a: 198–9, and see Dover 1993a: 50–5 and Edmonds 2004: 147–9.
2 Thiercy 1986: 363.
3 Rau 1967: 115–18 demonstrates that it is not evocative of any single specific tragic scene, but evokes tragedy more generally.
4 van Der Valk 1980: 75–6.
5 This is a feature of Aristophanes' underworld generally (Santamaría Álvarez 2015).
6 When asked in an interview who his Dream Lover would be, the novelist Douglas Adams replied, 'The Dagenham Girl Pipers. With all due respect and love to my dear wife, there are some things that, however loving or tender your wife may be, only a large pipe band can give you' (Adams 2003: 37).
7 Johnstone 1981: 33–74 and Marshall 1993.

14 Torture (*Frogs* 534–673)

1 Hooker 1980: 174.

2 While Old Comedy demonstrates a greater flexibility of spatial representation, it is not anarchic, and typically becomes fixed after the appearance of the chorus (Thiercy 2000, Lowe 2006).
3 See Sommerstein 2000 for an overview of the 'demagogue comedy', of which one was Platon's *Cleophon*, also produced at the Lenaia of 405.
4 Dover 1993a: 267.
5 For the torture of slave witnesses (*basanos*), see Thür 1977, Gagarin 1996, Mirhady 2007 (with a summary of the debate at 267–8) and Adamidis 2018.
6 Marshall 1993: 59–60.
7 Sommerstein 1996a: 211. See also Edmonds 2004: 153–4.
8 The manuscripts at this point show that copying errors can be funny, too. Readings differ between *iattatai*, *attatai*, *tattatai*, with Aeacus questioning 'What is this *iattatai*?' Some manuscripts extend the shout with extra syllables (without Aeacus' question). There is an entry in the tenth-century encyclopedia Suda for the word *iattatattatattatattatattai*; see https://www.cs.uky.edu/~raphael/sol/sol-entries/iota/56. This does not scan, and is more than the moment requires (the cries are escalating), but shows some copyist's comedic sensibilities clearly.
9 Elderkin 1936: 70 draws a historical connection between Melite (501) and Diomeia, speculating that the worship may have involved flagellation.
10 Elderkin 1936: 69 proposes the thorn is in his back, and neither possibility makes sense if Heracles is not supposed to feel any pain. Context, however, expects the line to be a deflection from the real feeling, and so a displacement from the back to the foot is reasonable, even if the story of Androcles and the Lion, which seems to offer some parallel for the situation, has not yet been written (it is first attested in Aulus Gellius 5.14, where it is given a Roman setting).
11 Konstan 1995: 61–74, esp. 67, where van Gennep's understanding of ritual transition is invoked.
12 Lada-Richards 1999: 315–19 suggests that this scene evokes tragic examples in which Dionysus is mistreated.

15 Parabasis (*Frogs* 674–737)

1 See Storey 2006: 112, with reference to the hypothesis at *POxy* 663, lines 7–9. The same blurring may occur at Cratinus fr. 171 (*Wealth Gods* [*Ploutoi*]).
2 Lowe 2007: 27–9.
3 Hubbard 1991: 199–219, and see Higgins 1977: 65–7, Goldhill 1991: 201–5.
4 Baldwin 1974, esp. 37–9, Major 2013: 164–9.
5 Moorton 1988: 352–3.
6 Storey 2011c: 115.
7 The interpretation that this refers to equal votes is from the scholiast.

8 Moorton 1988: 349–59, and see Arnott 1991.
9 See MacDowell 1995: 284–8. Edmonds 2004: 155–6 stresses the concern is not for universal enfranchisement, but for who gets to be called citizen, and the answer includes some slaves. It is a question of worthiness (cf. Bowie 1993: 243). Sidwell 2009: 283–97 believes the suggestion for re-enfranchisement is being ridiculed because of the way it is presented (see esp. 285), and that Dionysus is characterized as the rival (and now deceased) poet Eupolis.
10 No references; I want this not to be true.

16 Xanthias (*Frogs* 738–829)

1 Lowe 2007: 48, and see McLeish 1980: 140–3.
2 Heiden 1994: 11–12. We do not know that Aristophanes acted in his plays, but the use of other *didaskaloi* might be thought to make it more possible.
3 Marshall 1997, 2013; MacDowell 1994.
4 Pickard-Cambridge 1968: 152–3, Russo 1993: 215–16 (who stresses how equally roles are divided between three performers), Dover 1993a: 104–6. McLeish 1980: 151–2 prefers doubling Euripides and Xanthias.
5 Dover 1993a: 50–5, Sommerstein 1996a: 221.
6 Only barbarians wore trousers, but the idiom is right.
7 For this and the political terminology in the second half of *Frogs*, see Major 2013: 170–8.
8 Rosen 2006: 34–6.
9 Handley 2000: 151–4.
10 Scharffenberger 2007: 236–9.
11 Dover 1993a: 43–50.
12 MacDowell 1995: 278.
13 Dover 1993a: 49–50.

17 Contest (*Frogs* 830–94)

1 The specifically tragic associations are brought out by using it to present the entries of Euripides in *Acharnians* and Agathon in *Thesmophoriazusae*.
2 Parker 2005: 336–7.
3 Sommerstein 1996a: 830, preferring an *ekkyklēma* against Dover 1993a: 295–6; and see Dearden 1976: 69–70.
4 Amendola 2015.
5 Roselli 2005: 19–23. Sidwell 2009: 285 ties this emphasis to the chorus' ragged costumes, described at 404–5.
6 Heath 1987, and see Cropp and Collard 2008b: 185–223.

7 Phaedra had appeared in Euripides' *Hippolytus*; Aerope in *Cretan Women* (*Krēssai*) from 438 BCE, cf. Collard and Cropp 2008a: 516–27; Pasiphae in *Cretan Men* (*Krētes*), cf. Collard and Cropp 2008a: 529–55.
8 This insult is found at *Acharnians* 457, 478, *Knights* 19, *Thesmophoriazusae* 387, 456, and *Frogs* 840, though the bareness of the references in *Acharnians* suggests the joke predates 425. Borthwick 1994: 37–41 plausibly explains it as an unfounded accusation of marketplace prostitution, where one might say she sells her melons. Roselli 2005: 7–19, 22–3 ties the joke to Athenian citizenship laws and the demagogue comedies (cf. Sommerstein 2000), as a form of class criticism from Aristophanes.
9 Tr. Henderson 2002: 139, adapted.
10 Rosen 2006: 45–7.
11 A similar effect is accomplished in Euripides' *Helen* 865 (Marshall 2014: 215–17); the smell of torches was noticed by Dionysus at 314.
12 The scholia on Aristotle list five plays in which it happened (*Iphigenia*, *Oedipus*, *Female Archers* [*Toxotides*], *Priestesses*, and the satyr play *Sisyphus the Rock Roller* [*Petrocylistes*]). Aelian says the Athenians wanted to stone him for the offence (*True History* 5.19); curiously, this is the punishment Xanthias thought was appropriate for Euripides on claiming Aeschylus' Chair at 778.
13 Sutton 1983. Clement of Alexandria, *Stromata* 2, suggests he was absolved because he demonstrated that he was not an initiate. Biographical fictions become more elaborate as time progresses.
14 Note also the simplicity of the sets, and the simple boxes on which the balance woman stands; though the sign behind her reads 'Road to Hades' the detail is completely extraneous to understanding the nature of the dramatic setting.

18 Teachers (*Frogs* 895–1098)

1 Lines 901–4 use what first-year Greek students learn as a *men* . . . *de* construction ('on the one hand . . . on the other hand'), as a means of indicating this balance.
2 But not Jerry Lee Lewis's 'Breathless' (1958).
3 Lada-Richards 1999: 242, cf. 289–92.
4 MacDowell 1995: 289–90.
5 Taplin 1972.
6 The final word on Theramenes, that instead of a Chian, he is a Cean (Keian, which some manuscripts instead give as Kōian, i.e. from Cos) is a complex joke about dice and islands. The one on a die was called 'Chian' and the six was 'Coan'. However, instead of saying something like 'he's not a zero, he's a ten' (or 'he's not a deuce, he's an ace', but with dice as the referent), Aristophanes substitutes Ceos for Cos, the island from which Theramenes'

teacher Prodicus came, and an island where the inhabitants had a reputation for honesty (Dover 1993a: 314, Sommerstein 1996a: 243, and see van der Valk 1980: 71–3, who additionally casts aspersions on Theramenes' birth). 'He's not a zero, he's a ten-tive.

7 Heiden 1991: 101–3.

8 Scharffenberger 2007: 239–40.

9 For problems with the *Persians* reference, see Broggiato 2014. Sidwell 2009: 295–6 observes that these are the only two plays explicitly parodied in the fragments of Eupolis (fr. 231, 207).

10 Sommerstein 1996a: 246, and see Stanford 1963: 162 and Dover 1993a: 320.

11 For the scholia on 1028–9, see Broggiato 2014.

19 Prologues (*Frogs* 1099–1247)

1 MacDowell 1995: 289.

2 Allison 1978 revives van Leeuven's suggestion of reading *tin'* for *ton* in 1124: '. . . something from the *Oresteia*'.

3 Marshall 2017: 27–8, 51.

4 One distinctive feature of this play is, apparently, that Oedipus was blinded when he killed Laius (fr. 541; Collard and Cropp 2008b: 15, and see 9–27). He would never have seen that his new wife was old enough to be his mother.

5 Goldhill 1991: 216.

6 See *Meleager*, fr. 215 and 216, Collard and Cropp 2008a: 618–21 and see 613–31.

7 Dover 1993a: 338.

8 Sansone 2016, with references to previous discussions.

9 Whitman 1969, Borthwick 1993 (35 compares the name 'Sex Pistols' for a punk band), and see Dover 1993a: 338. See also *Thesmophoriazusae* 139–40.

10 This is the opposite of the view that *lēkuthion* suggests an elevated turgid style, which Sommerstein (1996: 264) rightly eliminates (and see Sansone 2016: 321).

11 Henderson 1972 and Bain 1985.

20 Songs (*Frogs* 1248–1364)

1 Dover 1993a: 343–4, Sommerstein 1996a: 134, 268–9.

2 Csapo and Wilson 2009.

3 Wilson 1999.

4 *Frogs* 1269–70 (Aeschylus fr. 238) is from either *Iphigenia* or *Telephus*; 1273–4 (Aeschylus fr. 87) is from *Priestesses*; 1276 is from Aeschylus'

Agamemnon 104. See Rau 1967: 125–6 for the nature of the paratragedy in this and the next song.

5 Steinhart 2007 draws the connection of this phrase with Strattis' fragmentary comedy *Cinesias*, but not *Frogs*.

6 See Moritz 1979 and Scharffenberger 2007: 241–4 on how the Aeschylean songs contribute to the sound-portrait of the playwright.

7 That's five more lines you've just memorized, which with *brekekekex koax koax* makes over 1 per cent of the play. The manuscripts all read *tophlattothrat tophlattothrat*, but editors feel the initial *to*- was added on analogy with 1296, where *to* is the definite article. In imitating a strum across strings, the *phlat*- and *thrat*- syllables are the downbeats, and the *to*- are the upbeats. We would be comfortable with an initial upbeat ('and-a-one . . .'), and I am not sure the removal of the syllable is needed.

8 Borthwick 1994: 23–6 argues that 'rope-winders' refers to a carnival-bet, 'fast and loose'; Sommerstein 1996a: 272 suggests work songs.

9 An emendation by Tyrell changes *kalou* to *kalō*, 'for the good, from the ropes' (O'Sullivan 2000), which resonates with 'rope winders' in the previous line.

10 Sommerstein 1996a: 139.

11 Dover 1993a: 351.

12 *Acharnians* 1198–end, *Knights* 1389–end, *Wasps* 1326–86, *Peace* 517–728, 819–908, 1329–end, *Birds* 1720–end, *Lysistrata* 1114–88, *Thesmophoriazusae* 1172–201, and *Ecclesiazusae* 1128–end; and see Zweig 1992 and Marshall 2000. This is the only possible context in which women (always non-citizens, always unspeaking) might be allowed onstage.

13 Borthwick 1994: 26–7 accepts the attractiveness of the Muse, and the best explanation for an ugly Muse is provided by De Simone 2008: 482.

14 Henderson 1991: 183–4, and see Borthwick 1994: 28. The modern sexual associations with the island of Lesbos are not found in antiquity (and see De Simone 2008: 483).

15 De Simone 2008: 487–8.

16 Danielewicz 1990: 135–7.

17 Heiden 1994: 8–11 connects Aeschylus with the Spartan poet/singer Tyrtaeus. While this is overstated, the connection with Dorian poetry is present.

18 *Frogs* 1317–18 are taken from *Electra* 435–7. See Borthwick 1994: 29–33, and Rau 1967: 127–36 for the nature of the paratragedy in this and the next song. The scholia claim the beginning draws on *Iphigenia in Aulis* (which had not been performed by the time of the Lenaia in 405), but there are no similarities in the surviving text (Hooker 1980: 179–80).

19 Borthwick 1994: 33.

20 Sommerstein 1996a: 139 and 276.

21 Borthwick 1994: 34–6.

22 Storey 2011b: 494–505, and see De Simone 2008: 480–8.

23 Borthwick 1994: 36–7, Slater 2002: 200.

24 Sells 2019: 173–5.

25 Stanford 1963: 185.

21 Scales (*Frogs* 1365–1410)

1 Sommerstein 1996a: 101 assumes the balance is brought on during the song at 814–30, but this telegraphs the final stage of the *agōn*, and draws focus for the second half of the play; it is better if the scales appear after Aeschylus has introduced the idea, during the song at 1370–7.
2 Stanford 1963: 190.
3 See https://www.metmuseum.org/toah/works-of-art/47.11.5/.
4 In Homer, *Iliad* 8.68–74, Zeus places the fates of the Greeks and Trojans in the balance, and the sinking of the balance indicates their doom, as the fate of the Trojans is lifted up. *Frogs* operates with the opposite connotation (see Slater 2002: 201–2).
5 Sommerstein 2008: 274–5, and see Farioli 2004 and Slater 2002: 201–2. West 2000 suggests the play was written by Euphorion, Aeschylus' son, but its presence here argues against that.
6 Dover 1993a: 367: Aeschylus' scale 'must be weighted, but the fact must be concealed from the audience'.
7 Mauromoustakos 2008: 296–301.
8 Kovacs 1990.
9 Stanford 1963: 192, Dover 1993a: 19, Sommerstein 1996a: 283.

22 Alcibiades (*Frogs* 1414–66)

1 Plato, *Symposium* 219e–221b (Socrates saves Alcibiades' life) and 220d–221c.
2 It was the owner of the horses who was accorded the victory, not the charioteer.
3 MacDowell 1995: 293–7.
4 Moorton 1988: 350.
5 Moorton 1988: 352.
6 Moorton 1988: 353–5.
7 See Vickers 2019: 4–6.
8 Lada-Richards 1999: 216–30 traces this theme.
9 Sommerstein 1993, 1996a: 148–51, 286–92, 2001: 317–18, Henderson 2002: 220–7, Wilson 2007a: 200–1. This solution is largely anticipated by Tucker 1906: 77–9, 255–8.
10 Dover 1993a: 373–6.
11 Previous discussions do not accept both transposition of lines and performance doublets, and resort to assuming lacunae, gaps where passages have dropped from the text.
12 MacDowell 1995: 296, and see 293–7.
13 Moorton 1988: 358.
14 Vickers 2001: 188–90 draws several connections.
15 Shackleton-Bailey 2000: 118–21.

16 Vickers 2000 extends this analysis broadly, so that Euripides and Dionysus are to be understood as Alcibiades, which leads him to ask, 'Why should an Alcibiadean Dionysus reject an Alcibiadean Euripides in favour of a Periclean Aeschylus?' (200). In the end **[23]**, Dionysus' decision is based on neither poetry nor politics.

23 Aeschylus (*Frogs* 1467–1533)

1 Whitman 1964: 256. Heiden suggests that Aristophanes' solution is 'doubly impossible' (1991: 105) because even if Aeschylus could be resurrected, he would not provide the necessary advice. I am not convinced this layer of irony is operating.
2 More charitable estimations of the development of Dionysus' character can be found at Higgins 1977 (see 62–5 on his confidence, 67 on his easy grace, 76 a hearty rogue) and Habash 2002.
3 Tarkow 1982: 11.
4 Avery 1968: 20–5. Another source suggests the demagogue Cleon prosecuted Euripides for impiety (Satyrus, Life of Euripides, *POxy.* 9.1176, col. x, lines 15–22).
5 See Goldhill 1991: 217–20. Rosen 2004 draws a parallel with another fictional literary contest from antiquity, the *Certamen* or *Contest of Homer and Hesiod.*
6 Lada-Richards 1999: 154–5 (on hospitality) and 327 (on Plouton treating them as equals).
7 Dover 1993a: 379. Sommerstein 1996a: 153 and 203 suggests a more grandiose paratragic scenario with Euripides dying or collapsing on the *ekkyklēma*, and being drawn inside at 1478, similar to *Knights* 1248–52 and *Wasps* 750–7. This requires Plouton to have stood and dismounted the *ekkyklēma* before this. If the *ekkyklēma* is not withdrawn with Euripides, it is retracted at 1481 as Aeschylus and Dionysus follow.
8 Sommerstein 1996a: 153.
9 Moorton 1988: 352–53, and see Baldwin 1974.
10 Suter 1977: 6.
11 Sommerstein 1996a: 295.

24 Euripides: A Heresy

1 Dobrov 2001: 145.
2 Lefkowitz 2012: 70–7.
3 Since Euphorion won against Euripides' *Medea* and its tetralogy in 431, West 1990: 67–72 has suggested that this victory was due to him competing with his father's *Prometheus Bound* (and *Prometheus Unbound*). Prometheus seems to be familiar to the audience of Cratinus' *Wealth-gods* (429), which

fits this scenario, and that of *Birds* (414), but these allusions do not bear on the authorship question.

4 A good starting point on Euripides' relationship with the *Oresteia* is Torrance 2013: 14–61.

5 Marshall 2014: 79–95.

6 Zuckerberg 2018.

7 Torrance 2007: 112–17, and see Scharffenberger 1995, Hanink and Uhlig 2017: 68–9. See also Lech 2008, for a reperformance between *Lysistrata* and *Frogs*.

8 West 2000: 340–7.

9 West 2000: 343 n. 26.

10 Biles 2006–7: 226–7; also recitation of tragic passages at symposia (229–30).

11 Biles 2006–7: 230, 232.

12 For this list, see also Marshall *forthcoming*.

13 Biles 2006–7: 234–7, but see Hanink and Uhlig 2017: 54–9.

14 Marshall 2001 argues that the prop with which Clytemnestra is said to have killed Agamemnon when the *Oresteia* was reperformed was an axe, but that this need not reflect the choice made in 458.

15 Biles 2006–7: 240. I attach no weight to Biles's argument that the scholia (which emerge in Hellenistic Alexandria, where the plays were not known to be performed) are silent on reperformance (237: 'Whereas for modern scholars such allusions amount to reliable and abundant confirmation of the decree, ancient commentators never once go further on these occasions than to identify the Aeschylean play in question').

25 Reperformance

1 Kapellos 2013.

2 A Roman inscription appears to preserve mention of a reperformed *Sterroi* (*Stiffies*) by Teleclides (Storey 2011c: 288–9, and see 300–3), a comic poet from the 430s and 420s.

3 Sommerstein 1993, Dover 1993a: 73–6, MacDowell 1995: 297–300, Hanink 2014: 50–1, and see Dover 1972: 180–3.

4 Henderson 2007: 6–7.

5 Sommerstein 1996a: 21–3.

6 MacDowell 1995: 299, and see Sommerstein 1993: 466–9.

7 Rosen 2015.

8 This is a variation of an idea suggested at Marshall 1996: 149–50.

26 Afterlife

1 Taplin 1993, Carpenter 2009: 32–4.

2 Nelson 2018: 245–51.

3 Zanker 2009: 235.
4 Pugliesi Carratella 1940, Robert and Robert 1946: 335–6.
5 Cucchiarelli 2001: 25–31, 41–3, 48–51.
6 Vickers 2019: 7 n. 16.
7 Slater 2016:14, and see Holford-Strevans 2004, esp. 236.
8 May 2006: 198–201.
9 Bowie 2007: 37–8 and Slater 2016: 16–17. In Lucian's *Charon*, there is a reverse *katabasis*, as the underworld figure comes to the surface.
10 Bowie 2007: 34 and 46–7.
11 Pontani 2009: 410–14, and see Hanink 2014: 143–51.
12 For a (not particularly easy-going) history of the manuscripts, see Dover 1993a: 76–104. The scholia are collected (untranslated) in Koster 1962.
13 Wilson 2007: 126.
14 'A tragic canon of Aeschylus, Sophocles and Euripides had already begun to show signs of emergence in 405 BC, at the premiere of Aristophanes' *Frogs*' (Hanink 2014: 82, and see 3–4, 8–9, 64–5).
15 Hunter 2009: 36 (and 10–52 trace how *Frogs* offers a retrospective understanding that helps later authors formulate their critical perspectives); and see Rosen 2006.
16 Hanink 2015.
17 Hanink 2014: 3.

27 Translations

1 See Giannopoulou 2007; however, 'Pierre Brumoy's *Dissertation on Ancient Comedy* had been translated into English by 1759 and contained a version of *Frogs*' (Griffith 2013: 235).
2 Shelley 1905. Erkelenz 1996: 500 suggests the 'Ode to Naples' is meant.
3 Erkelenz 1996: 507.
4 Hall 2007a: 29 n. 71.
5 See Heatherington 1966: 197–201; quotations are from 197 and 198. Thanks to Graham Butler for this reference.
6 The parody proposed ('On your knees, O, Not a sneeze, O . . .' [198], 'Such a moaning, such intoning, So much groaning, honing, droning, Calling, falling, bawling, drawling . . .' [199]; etc.) evokes Edgar Allen Poe at his most cloying, and is perhaps meant as a homage, since Poe had praised Simms's novels.
7 Hall 2007b: 76 (and see 76–7).
8 Hall 2007b: 77–9, 85.
9 Frere 1872: 256.
10 Masson 1922: 116–18, 140 and 143 (where William A. Herdman writes, 'I recall the air of pride and conscious superiority with which he declaimed his verses, pouring forth line after line with increasing triumph as the scale descended in his favour').

11 Wrigley 2007.
12 Lippman 2016: 287–8, Wrigley 2011: 91–2. *Frogs* was initially published with Euripides' *Hippolytus* and *Bacchae*; and then by itself in 1908.
13 Macintosh 1998, esp. 82–4, and Hall 2007b: 86.
14 Adams 1996: 118. Annie Rogers (1856–1937) was an educator who had the offer of a place as a student at Oxford withdrawn when it was discovered she was female. Topical allusions were encouraged by Murray, who is said to have 'allowed himself to be smuggled secretly into [Somerville] college to direct and stage-manage the second-year play . . . which had, traditionally, to be kept as a surprise for the rest of the college; as an official guest on the night of the | actual performance, he rose from his seat beside the Principal to express his thanks with the words "it was so good that we all felt we really *were* in Hell"' (118–19).
15 Radio: Morris: 2007: 303–4, Wrigley 2014: 853–7. Sheppard: Marshall 2015.
16 Marshall 2010–11, Baker 2016: 321–8.
17 See Murray 1902, Rogers 1924, Lattimore 1962, Barrett 2007, Henderson 2002, Roche 2005, Halliwell 2015.
18 Arnott 1961: 133.
19 Roche 2005: 542.
20 See Eissen and Gondicas 2014 on troubles translating the *agōn*. Van Steen 2014 describes a Greek production in the 1880s where the *agōn* was simply cut.
21 Frere 1872: 284.
22 Ley 2014: 882–5.
23 Dudouyt 2016: 253.
24 Nelson 2019.
25 For the first two, see Keen 1996 (reviewing a Belfast performance; see also Griffith 2013: 251 and 257) and Mezzabotta 1994; for the last see, e.g., Hoffer 2004 (with thanks to Joy A. R. Elliot and Al Duncan).

28 Twentieth-Century Frogs

1 Van Steen 2000: 178–80, Varakis 2007: 186–8 (on masks), Mauromoustakos 2008: 296–301.
2 Kannelakis 2018.
3 Cambridge 2013: https://www.youtube.com/watch?v=yYYQIn_sC-4. Warwick 2019: https://www.youtube.com/watch?v=DM7JfS4Q_ww.
4 Laurence 1974: 467–77.
5 Laurence 1974: 473.
6 Laurence 1974: 474.
7 Laurence 1974: 475.
8 Lockwood 2002: 185–338 (including both the 1730 text and the revised 1734 text), and see Hall 2007: 72–4, who notes the presence of new musical features like melismas in the songs, and a castanet dancer [**20**].

9 Knight 1981 and Kinservik 2016. In 1742, Fielding and William Young published a prose translation of *Plutus*.
10 Peter Arnott's 1961 translation of *Frogs* also was first performed by him with marionettes.
11 Gamel 2007: 212. See also Goad 2018: 279–300.
12 Gamel 2007: 213–14.
13 Gamel 2007: 218, and see 214–19.
14 Gamel 2007: 229 n. 47.
15 Gamel 2007: 218.
16 See English 2005, Weimer 2009, Beta 2014: 831–3, Ley 2014: 873–81; Goad 2018: 301–13.
17 Gamel 2007: 220–3; at 224–5, she criticizes some of director Susan Stroman's choices as not challenging audience perceptions sufficiently.
18 Stoppard 1997: 2, and see Reckford 2001: 110–18.
19 Stoppard 1997: 30–45, and see 97–9; Moritz (n.d.).
20 The Boatman who appears for Wilde (Stoppard 1997: 97) is not explicitly Charon, though no separate actor is found in the cast lists of the UK, US and Canadian premieres. Reckford 2001: 131–6 frames the AEH–Wilde encounter as an *agōn*.
21 Stoppard 1997: 27.
22 See Wrigley 2007 and 2011: 60–80.
23 Stoppard 1997: 27–8, a lovely scene where Housman is desperate to recover a further single line to the play, but Charon (and Stoppard) are unable to provide.
24 Stoppard 1997: 42.
25 Stoppard 1997: 76.
26 Stoppard 1997: 71, and see 39–41 and Reckford 2001: 125–31. Housman's translation of the poem appeared in the posthumous collection, *More Poems* (1936).
27 Stoppard's earlier plays can also be tied to Aristophanes: see Reckford 1987, esp. 143–61, and Scharffenberger 1997 on *Clouds* and *Jumpers*.
28 Stoppard 1997: 36.

29 Seriously

1 Silk 2000: 59–60, 77–84.
2 Young 1933 recognized this pattern and suggested a subgenre.
3 Gibbon 1837: 567 and see Cucchiarelli 2001: 15.
4 Silk 2000: 93.
5 Fraenkel 1962: 163–88 (and see Hooker 1980: 169–73, 178–82). To solve the apparent disunity, scholars have rested on Segal 1961 and Lada-Richards 1999, which Edmonds 2003 and 2004: 113–17 says is insufficient.

Bibliography

Adamidis, V. 2018. 'The Theory and Practice of Torture in Ancient Athenian Courts', *Schole* 12.2: 6–18.

Adams, Douglas. 2003. *The Salmon of Doubt: Hitchhiking the Galaxy One Last Time*. London.

Adams, Pauline. 1996. *Somerville for Women: An Oxford College, 1879–1993*. Oxford.

Allan, Arlene. 2012. 'Turning Remorse to Good Effect? Arginusae, Theramenes and Aristophanes' *Frogs*', in Marshall and Kovacs 2012: 101–14.

Allison Richard H. 1978. 'Aristophanes, *Frogs* 1124', *LCM* 3: 75.

Allison Richard H. 1983. 'Amphibian Ambiguities: Aristophanes and his Frogs', *G&R* 30: 8–20.

Amendola, Stefano. 2015. 'Aeschylus, Euripides and the Conquest of a Re[g]al Throne: Reflections on the Staging of Aristophanes' *Frogs*', *Logeion* 5: 183–96.

Arnott, Peter D. 1961. *Three Greek Plays for the Theatre*. Bloomington, IN. [119–220 = *Frogs*]

Arnott, W.G. 2010. 'Middle Comedy', in Gregory W. Dobrov (ed.), *Brill's Companion to the Study of Comedy* (Leiden/Boston): 279–331.

Avery, Harry C. 1968. '"My Tongue Swore, but my Mind is Unsworn"', *TAPA* 99: 19–35.

Bain, David. 1985. 'Ληκύθιον ἀπώλεσεν: Some Reservations', *CQ* 35: 31–7.

Baker, Gregory. 2016. '"Attic Salt into an Undiluted Scots": Aristophanes and the Modernism of Douglas Young', in Walsh (ed.) 2016: 307–30.

Bakola, Emmanuela. 2005. 'Old Comedy Disguised as Satyr-Play: A New Reading of Cratinus' *Dionysalexandros (*P.Oxy. 663)', *ZPE* 154: 46–58.

Bakola, Emmanuela. 2010. *Cratinus and the Art of Comedy*. Oxford.

Baldwin, Barry. 1974. 'Notes on Cleophon', *Acta Classica* 17: 35–47.

Barbera, P. 1981. 'Le rane invisibili', *Pan* 7: 119–33.

Barrett, David. 2007 [orig. 1964]. *Aristophanes: Frogs and Other Plays*, revised by Shomit Dutta. London.

Beta, Simone, '"Attend, O Muse, Our Holy Dances and Come to Rejoice in Our Songs": The Reception of Aristophanes in the Modern Musical Theatre', in Olson (ed.) 2014: 824–48.

Biles, Zachary P. 2001. 'Aristophanes' Victory Dance: Old Poets in the Parabasis of *Knights*', *ZPE* 136: 195–200.

Biles, Zachary P. 2006–7. 'Aeschylus' Afterlife Reperformance by Decree in 5th C. Athens?' *ICS* 31/32: 206–42.

Borthwick, E. K. 1968. 'Seeing Weasels: The Superstitious Background of the Empusa Scene in the *Frogs*', *CQ* 18: 200–6.

Borthwick, E. K. 1993. 'Autolekythos and Lekythion in Demosthenes and Aristophanes', *LCM* 18.3: 34–7.

Borthwick, E. K. 1994. 'New Interpretations of Aristophanes *Frogs* 1249-1328', *Phoenix* 48: 21–41.

Bowie, A. M. 1993. *Aristophanes: Myth, Ritual and Comedy*. Cambridge.

Bowie, Ewen. 2007. 'The Ups and Downs of Aristophanic Travel', in Hall and Wrigley 2007: 32–51.

Bremmer, Jan N. 2011. 'Initiation into the Eleusinian Mysteries: A "Thin" Description', in Bull, Lied, and Turner 2011: 375–97.

Broggiato, Maria. 2014. 'Aristophanes and Aeschylus' *Persians*: Hellenistic Discussions on Ar. Ran. 1028f', *RhM* 157: 1–15.

Brown, Christopher G. 1991. 'Empousa, Dionysus and the Mysteries: Aristophanes, *Frogs* 285ff', *CQ* 41: 41–50.

Bruit Zaidman, Louise, and Pauline Schmitt Pantel. 1992. *Religion in the Ancient Greek City*. Cambridge.

Budelmann, Felix, ed. 2009. *The Cambridge Companion to Greek Lyric*. Cambridge.

Bull, Christian H., Liv Lied and John D. Turner. 2011. *Mystery and Secrecy in the Nag Hammadi Collection and Other Ancient Literature: Ideas and Practices*. Leiden.

Burkert, Walter. 1985. *Greek Religion: Archaic and Classical*. London.

Campbell, David A. 1984. 'The Frogs in the *Frogs*', *JHS* 104: 163–5.

Canevaro, Mirko. 2010. 'The Decree Awarding Citizenship to the Plataeans ([Dem.] 59.104)', *GRBS* 50: 337–69.

Carpenter, Thomas H. 1986. *Dionysian Imagery in Ancient Greek Art*. Oxford.

Carpenter, Thomas H. 1993. 'On the Beardless Dionysus', in Carpenter and Faraone 1993: 185–206.

Carpenter, Thomas H. 1997. *Dionysian Imagery in Fifth-Century Athens*. Oxford.

Carpenter, Thomas H. 2009. 'Prolegomenon to the Study of Apulian Red-Figure Pottery', *AJA* 113: 27–38.

Carpenter, Thomas H and Christopher A. Faraone (eds.). 1993. *Masks of Dionysus*. Ithaca, NY and London.

Ceccarelli, Paola. 2004. 'Dancing the *Pyrrhichē* in Athens', in Murray and Wilson 2004: 91–117.

Chantry, Marcel. 2001. 'Phrynichos dans les Scholies d'Aristophane', *Revue de philologie* 75: 239–47.

Chronopoulos, S. and C. Orth (eds.). 2015. *Fragmente einer Geschichte der griechischen Komödie/Fragmentary History of Greek Comedy*. Heidelberg.

Collard, Christopher and Martin Cropp. 2008a. *Euripides Fragments: Aegeus-Meleager*. Cambridge, MA.

Collard, Christopher and Martin Cropp. 2008b. *Euripides Fragments: Oedipus-Chrysippus, Other Fragments*. Cambridge, MA.

Compton-Engle, Gwendolyn. 2015. *Costume in the Comedies of Aristophanes*. Cambridge.

Connor, W. R. 1989. 'City Dionysia and Athenian Democracy', *Classica and Mediaevalia* 40: 7–32.

Constantinidis, Stratos E., ed. 2017. *The Reception of Aeschylus' Plays through Shifting Models and Frontiers*. Leiden.

Csapo, Eric. 2010. *Actors and Icons of the Ancient Theater*. Chichester.

Csapo, Eric. 2012. '"Parade Abuse", "From the Wagons"', in Marshall and Kovacs, 2012: 19–33.

Csapo, Eric. 2015. 'The Earliest Phase of "Comic" Choral Entertainments in Athens: The Dionysian Pompe and the "Birth" of Comedy', in Chronopoulos and Orth 2015: 66–108.

Csapo, Eric. 2016. 'The "Theology" of the Dionysia and Old Comedy', in Esther Eidinow, Julia Kindt and Robin Osborne (eds.), *Theologies of Ancient Greek Religion* (Cambridge) 117–52.

Csapo, Eric and William J. Slater. 1995. *The Context of Ancient Drama*. Ann Arbor, MI.

Csapo, Eric and Peter Wilson. 2009. 'Timotheus the New Musician', in Budelmann (ed.) 2009: 277–93.

Cucchiarelli, Andrea. 2001. *La satira e il poeta: Orazio tra Epodi e Sermones*. Pisa.

Cucchiarelli, Andrea. 2020. *A Social and Economic History of the Theatre to 300 BC. Vol. II. Theatre beyond Athens: Documents with Translation and Commentary*. Cambridge.

Daitz, Stephen G. 1983. 'Euripides, *Orestes* 279 γαλήν' γαλῆν, Or How A Blue Sky Turned into A Pussycat', *CQ* 33: 294–5.

Danielewicz, J. 1990. 'Il *nomos* nella parodia di Aristofane (*Ran*. 1264 sgg)', *AION* 12: 131–42.

Dearden, C. W. 1970. 'What Happened to the Donkey? Aristophanes' *Frogs* 172f.', *Mnemosyne* 23: 17–21.

Dearden, C. W. 1976. *The Stage of Aristophanes*. London.

Deb. 2011. 'Kid Questions: Do Frogs Have Lips?' *Science@Home*, 7 December 2011. Online: http://science-at-home.org/kid-questions-do-frogs-have-lips/ (accessed 19 July 2019).

Demand, Nancy. 1970. 'The Identity of the Frogs', *CP* 65: 83–7.

Dobrov, Gregory W. 2001. *Figures of Play: Greek Drama and Metafictional Poetics*. Oxford.

Donelan, Jasper F. 2018. 'Did the classical theatre have a thunder machine?' *Hermes* 146: 110–15.

Dover, Kenneth J. 1972. *Aristophanic Comedy*. Berkeley, CA.

Dover, Kenneth J. 1993a. *Aristophanes: Frogs*. Oxford.

Dover, Kenneth J. 1993b. 'The Chorus of Initiates in Aristophanes' *Frogs*', in J. M. Bremer and E. W. Handley (eds.), *Aristophane* (*Fondation Hardt Entretiens 38*; Geneva) 173–201.

Dudouyt, Cécile. 2016. 'The Reception of Greek Theatre in France since 1700', in van Zyl Smit (ed.) 2016: 238–56.

Easterling, P. E. 1997. 'A Show for Dionysus,' in P. E. Easterling (ed.) *The Cambridge Companion to Greek Tragedy* (Cambridge) 36–53.

Eastman, Helen. 2015 (recorded 2013). *Aristophanes' Frogs (Cambridge Greek Play 2013)*. Cambridge (online at https://www.youtube.com/watch?time_continue=2796&v=yYYQIn_sC-4, retrieved 19 August 2019).

Edmonds, Radcliffe. 2003. 'Who in Hell is Heracles? Dionysus' Disastrous Disguise in Aristophanes' *Frogs*', in D. B. Dodd and C. A. Faraone (eds.), *Initiation in Ancient Greek Rituals and Narratives: New Critical Perspectives* (London) 181–200.

Edmonds, Radcliffe. 2004. *Myths of the Underworld Journey: Plato, Aristophanes, and the 'Orphic' Gold Tablets*. Cambridge.

Eissen, Ariane and Myrto Gondicas. 2014. 'Eschyle et Euripide entre tragédie et comédie: polyphonie et interpretation dans quelques traductions récentes des *Grenouilles* d'Aristophane', in Olson (ed.) 2014: 1022–39.

Elderkin, G. W. 1936. 'Xanthias and Herakles', *CP* 31: 69–70.

English, Mary. 2005. 'Aristophanes' *Frogs*: Brek-kek-kek-kak! On Broadway', *AJP* 126: 127–33.

Erkelenz, Michael. 1996. 'The Genre and Politics of Shelley's Swellfoot the Tyrant', *Review of English Studies* 47: 500–20.

Farioli, M. 1994. 'Cratino "Modello" di Aristofane: Il Caso del *Dionysalessandro* e della *Rane*', *Aevum Antiquum* 7: 119–36.

Farioli, M. 2004. 'Due parodie comiche della "psychostasia": Ar. *Ran*. 1364–1413 e fr. 504 K.-A.', *Lexis* 22: 251–67.

Farmer, Matthew C. 2017. *Tragedy on the Comic Stage*. Oxford.

Foley, Helene P. 2000. 'The Comic Body in Greek Art and Drama', in Beth Cohen (ed.) *Not the Classical Ideal: Athens and the Construction of the Other in Greek Art* (Leiden) 275–311.

Ford, Andrew L. 2011. 'Dionysus' Many Names in Aristophanes' *Frogs*', in Renate Schlesier (ed.) *A Different God? Dionysos and Ancient Polytheism* (Berlin/Boston) 343–55.

Fraenkel, Eduard. 1962. *Beobachtungen zu Aristophanes*. Rome.

Franklin, John C. 2017. '"Skatabasis": The Rise and Fall of Kinesias', in Gostoli 2017: 163–221.

Frere, John Hookham. 1872. *The Works of John Hookham Frere*, vol. 2. London.

Gagarin, Michael. 1996. 'The Torture of Slaves in Athenian Law', *CP* 91: 1–18.

Gamel, Mary-Kay. 2007. 'Sondheim Floats *Frogs*', in Hall and Wrigley (eds.) 2007: 209–30.

Giannopoulou, Vasiliki. 2007. 'Aristophanes in Translation before 1920', in Hall and Wrigley (eds.) 2007: 309–42.

Gibbon, Edward. 1837. *The Miscellaneous Works*. London.

Gibert, John. 1999–2000. 'Falling in Love with Euripides (*Andromeda*)', *ICS* 24–5: 75–91.

Gibert, John. 2004. 'Andromeda', in Collard et al. (eds.), *Euripides: Selected Fragmentary Plays vol. 2* (Warminster), 133–68.

Goad, Daniel. 2018. *The Performance Reception of Frogs in the English Language, Past and Potential*. London (Ph.D. dissertation, Royal Holloway, University of London).

Goldhill, Simon. 1987. 'The Great Dionysia and Civic Ideology', *JHS* 107: 58–76.

Goldhill, Simon. 1991. *The Poet's Voice: Essays on Poetics and Greek Literature*. Cambridge.

Graf, Friz. 1974. *Eleusis und die orphische Dichtung Athens in vorhellenistischer Zeit*. Berlin/New York.

Green, J. Richard. 2006. 'The Persistent Phallus: Regional Variability in the Performance Style of Comedy', in John Davidson, Frances Muecke and Peter J. Wilson (eds.) *Greek Drama III: Essays in Honour of Kevin Lee* (London) 141–62.

Griffith, Mark. 2013. *Aristophanes'* Frogs. Oxford.

Habash, Martha. 1995. 'Two Complementary Festivals in Aristophanes' *Acharnians*', *AJP* 116: 559–77.

Habash, Martha. 2002. 'Dionysos' Roles in Aristophanes' *Frogs*', *Mnemosyne* 55: 1–17.

Hall, Edith. 2007a. 'Introduction. Aristophanic Laughter across the Centuries', in Hall and Wrigley 2007: 1–29.

Hall, Edith. 2007b. 'The English-Speaking Aristophanes, 1650–1914', in Hall and Wrigley 2007: 66–92.

Hall, Edith and Amanda Wrigley, eds. 2007. *Aristophanes in Performance 421 BC–AD 2007:* Peace, Birds, *and* Frogs. Oxford.

Halliwell, S. 1980. 'Aristophanes' Apprenticeship', *CQ* 30: 33–45.

Halliwell, S. 2015. *Aristophanes: Frogs and Other Plays*. Oxford.

Hamilton, Richard. 1992. *Anthesteria and Choes: Athenian Iconography and Ritual*. Ann Arbor, MI.

Handley, Eric W. 2000. 'Going to Hades: Two Passages in Aristophanes, *Frogs* (786–94, 1–37)', *Act. Ant. Hung.* 40: 151–60.

Hanink, Johanna. 2014. *Lycurgan Athens and the Making of Classical Tragedy*. Cambridge.

Hanink, Johanna. 2015. '"Why 386 BC?" Lost Empire, Old Tragedy, and Reperformance in the Era of the Corinthian War', *Trends in Classics* 7: 277–96.

Hanink, Johanna and Anna Uhlig. 2017. 'Aeschylus and His Afterlife in the Classical Period: "My Poetry Did Not Die with Me"', in Constantinidis (ed.) 2017: 51–79.

Harder, M. A., R. F. Regtuit and G. C. Wakker 2018. *Drama and Performance in Hellenistic Poetry*. Amsterdam.

Hartwig, Andrew. 2010. 'The date of the *Rhabdouchoi* and the early career of Plato Comicus', *ZPE* 174: 19–31.

Hartwig, Andrew. 2012. 'Comic Rivalry and the Number of Comic Poets at the Lenaia of 405 B.C.', *Philologus* 156: 195–206.

Harvey, David. 2000. 'Phrynichos and his Muses', in Harvey and Wilkins (eds.) 2000: 91–134.

Harvey, David and John Wilkins, eds. 2000. *The Rivals of Aristophanes: Studies in Athenian Old Comedy*. Swansea.

Heath, Malcolm. 1987. 'Euripides' *Telephus*', *CQ* 37: 272–80.

Hetherington, Hugh W. 1966. *Cavalier of Old South Carolina: William Gilmore Simms's Captain Porgy*. Chapel Hill.

Hedreen, Guy. 2004. 'The return of Hephaistos: Dionysiac processional ritual and the creation of a visual narrative', *JHS* 124: 38–64.

Heiden, Bruce. 1991. 'Tragedy and Comedy in the Frogs of Aristophanes', *Ramus* 20: 95–111.

Heiden, Bruce. 1994. 'Two Notes on the *Frogs*', *LCM* 19.1: 8–12.

Henderson, Jeffrey. 1972. 'The *lekythos* and *Frogs* 1200–48', *HSCP* 76: 133–43.

Henderson, Jeffrey. 1991. *The Maculate Muse: Obscene Language in Attic Comedy*, 2nd ed. Oxford.

Henderson, Jeffrey. 2002. *Aristophanes: Frogs, Assemblywomen, Wealth*. Cambridge, MA.

Henderson, Jeffrey. 2007. *Aristophanes: Fragments*. Cambridge, MA.

Henrichs, Albert. 1984. 'Loss of Self, Suffering, Violence: The Modern View of Dionysus from Nitzsche to Girard', *HSCP* 88: 205–40.

Henrichs, Albert. 1990. 'Between City and Country: Cultic Dimensions of Dionysus in Athens and Attica', in M. Griffith and D. J. Mastronarde (eds.), *Cabinet of the Muses* (Atlanta) 257–77.

Henrichs, Albert. 1993. '"He Has a God in Him": Human and Divine in the Modern Perception of Dionysus', in Carpenter and Faraone 1993: 13–43.

Higgins, W. E. 1977. 'A Passage to Hades: The Frogs of Aristophanes', *Ramus* 6: 160–81.

Hoffer, Alexandra D. 2004. '"Frogs" Breaks from Classical Tradition', *The Harvard Crimson*, 22 March 2004. Online https://www.thecrimson.com/article/2004/3/22/review-frogs-breaks-from-classical-tradition/ (accessed 19 August 2019).

Holford-Strevans, Leofranc. 2004. *Aulus Gellius: An Antonine Scholar and his Achievement*, rev. ed. Oxford.

Hooker, G. T. W. 1960. 'The Topography of the *Frogs*', *JHS* 80: 112–17.

Hooker, G. T. W. 1980. 'The Composition of the *Frogs*', *Hermes* 108: 169–82.

Hubbard, Thomas K. 1991. *The Masks of Comedy: Aristophanes and the Intertextual Parabasis*. Ithaca, NY.

Hunt, Peter. 2001. 'The Slaves and the Generals of Arginusae', *AJP* 122: 359–80.

Hunter, R. L. 1983. *Eubulus: The Fragments*. Cambridge.

Hunter, R. L. 2009. *Critical Moments in Classical Literature*. Cambridge.

Isler-Kerényi, Cornelia. 2015. *Dionysus in Classical Athens: An Understanding through Images*, tr. Anna Beerens. Leiden.

Johnstone, Keith. 1981. *Impro: Improvisation and the Theatre*. London.

Kanellakis, Dimitrios. 2018. 'Aristophanes in Greek shadow theatre: codification and adaptation of Peace and Frogs performed by Evgenios Spatharis', *Byzantine and Modern Greek Studies* 42: 151–71.

Kapellos, Aggelos. 2013. 'Xenophon and the Execution of the Athenian Captives after Aegospotami', *Mnem*. 66 464–72.

Keen, Antony. 1996. 'Laird's *Frogs*', *Didaskalia* 3.1. Online: https://www.didaskalia.net/issues/vol3no1/keen.html (accessed 19 August 2019).

Kidd, Stephen E. 2014. *Nonsense and Meaning in Ancient Greek Comedy.* Cambridge.

Kinservk, Matthew J. 2016. 'The "English Aristophanes": Fielding, Foote, and Debates over Literary Satire,' in Walsh (ed.) 2016: 109–28.

Kloss, G. 2001. *Ercheinungsformen komischen Sprechens bei Aristophanes.* Berlin.

Knight, Charles A. 1981. 'Fielding and Aristophanes', *SEL* 21: 481–98.

Konstan, David. 1995. *Greek Comedy and Ideology.* Oxford.

Koster, W. J. W. 1962. *Scholia in Aristophanem. Pars IV.3. Io. Tzetzae, Commentarium in Ranas et in Aves, Argumentum Equitum.* Groningen.

Kovacs, David. 1990. '*De Cephisophonte Verna, Ut Perhibent*', *ZPE* 84: 15–18.

Kovacs, George. 2015. 'Moral and Mortal in *Star Trek: The Original Series*', in Brett M. Rogers and Benjamin Eldon Stevens (eds.), *Classical Traditions in Science Fiction* (Oxford) 199–216.

Kozak, L. and John Rich, eds. 2007. *Playing around Aristophanes.* Oxford.

Kyriakou, Poulheria and Antonios Rengakos, eds. 2016. *Wisdom and Folly in Euripides.* Berlin.

Lada-Richards, Ismene. 1999. *Initiating Dionysus: Ritual and Theatre in Aristophanes' Frogs.* Oxford.

Lattimore, Richmond. 1962. *The Frogs by Aristophanes.* New York.

Laurence, Dan H. 1974. *The Bodley Head Bernard Shaw: Collected Plays with their Prefaces*, vol. VII. London.

Lech, Marcel L. 2008. 'A Possible Date of the Revival of Aeschylus' *The Seven Against Thebes*', *CQ* 58: 661–4.

Lefkowitz, Mary R. 2012. *The Lives of the Greek Poets*, 2nd ed. London.

Ley, Graham. 2014. 'Cultural Politics and Aesthetic Debate in Two Modern Versions of Aristophanes' *Frogs*', in Olson (ed.) 2014: 871–86.

Lippmann, Mike. 2016. 'Murray's Aristophanes', in Walsh (ed.) 2016: 284–306.

Lind, Hermann. 1985. 'Neues aus Kydathen: Beobachtungen zum Hintergrund der "Daitales" und der "Ritter" des Aristophanes', *MH* 42: 249–61.

Littlefield, David J., ed. 1968. *Twentieth Century Interpretations of The Frogs.* Englewood Cliffs, NJ.

Lowe, N. J. 2006. 'Aristophanic Spacecraft,' in Kozak and Rich 2006: 48–64.

Lowe, N. J. 2007. *Comedy.* Cambridge (Greece and Rome New Surveys in the Classics 37).

Luppe, W. 1966. 'Die Hypothesis zu Kratinos' *Dionysalexandros*', *Philologus* 110: 169–93.

MacDowell, Douglas M. 1972. 'The Frogs' Chorus', *CR* 22: 3–5.

MacDowell, Douglas M. 1982. 'Aristophanes and Kallistratos', *CQ* 32: 21–6.

MacDowell, Douglas M. 1994. 'The Number of Speaking Actors in Old Comedy', *CQ* 44: 325–35.

MacDowell, Douglas M. 1995. *Aristophanes and Athens.* Oxford.

Macintosh, Fiona. 1998. 'The Shavian Murray and the Euripidean Shaw: *Major Barbara* and the *Bacchae*', *Classics Ireland* 5: 64–84.

Major, Wilfred E. 2013. *The Court of Comedy: Aristophanes, Rhetoric, and Democrracy in Fifth-Century Athens.* Columbus, OH.

Makres, Andronike. 2014. 'Dionysiac Festivals in Athens and the Financing of Comic Performances', in M. Fontaine and A. C. Scafuro (eds.), *The Oxford Handbook to Greek and Roman Comedy* (Oxford) 70–92.
Marshall, C. W. 1993. 'Status Transactions in Aristophanes' *Frogs*', *Text & Presentation* 14: 57–61.
Marshall, C. W. 1996. 'Amphibian Ambiguities Answered', *Echos du Monde Classique/Classical Views* 15: 251–65.
Marshall, C. W. 1997. 'Comic Technique and the Fourth Actor', *CQ* 47: 77–84.
Marshall, C. W. 1999a. 'Some Fifth-Century Masking Conventions', *G&R* 46: 188–202.
Marshall, C. W. 1999b. Review of Sommerstein 1996a, *EMC* 18: 145–50
Marshall, C. W. 2000. 'Female Performers on Stage? (*PhV* 96 [*RVP* 2/33])', *Text & Presentation* 21: 13–25.
Marshall, C. W. 2001. 'The Next Time Agamemnon Died', *Classical World* 95 (2001) 59–63.
Marshall, C. W. 2010–11. 'Aristophanes and Douglas Young', *Comparative Drama* 44.4–45.1: 539–44.
Marshall, C. W. 2013. 'Three Actors in Old Comedy, Again', in G. W. M. Harrison and V. Liapis (eds.), *Performance in Greek and Roman Theatre* (Leiden) 257–78.
Marshall, C. W. 2015. 'Performance Reception and the Cambridge Greek Play: Aristophanes' *Frogs* in 1936 and 1947', *Classical Receptions Journal* 7: 177–201.
Marshall, C. W. 2016. *The Structure and Performance of Euripides'* Helen. Cambridge.
Marshall, C. W. 2017. *Aeschylus: Libation Bearers*. London.
Marshall, C. W. *forthcoming*. 'The Reception of Aeschylus in the Fifth and Fourth Centuries,' in J. Bromberg and P. Burian (eds.), *A Companion to Aeschylus*. Blackwell.
Marshall, C. W and George Kovacs, eds. 2012. *No Laughing Matter: Studies in Athenian Comedy*. London.
Marshall, C. W and S. van Willigenberg. 2004. 'Judging Athenian Dramatic Competitions', *JHS* 124: 90–107.
Masson, Rosaline, ed. 1922. *I Can Remember Robert Louis Stevenson*. Edinburgh.
Mauromoustakos, Platon. 2008. Κάρολος Κουν· Οι Παραστάσεις. Athens.
May, Regine. 2006. *Apuleius and Drama: The Ass on Stage*. Oxford.
McLeish, Kenneth. 1980. *The Theatre of Aristophanes*. New York.
Mezzabotta, Margaret. 1994. 'Frolicking Frogs Rap in Cape Town', *Didaskalia* 1.3. Online: https://www.didaskalia.net/issues/vol1no3/mezzabotta.html (accessed 19 August 2019).
Millis, Benjamin W. 2015. 'Out of Athens: Greek Comedy at the Rural Dionysia and Elsewhere', in Chronopoulos and Orth (eds.) 2015: 228–49.
Millis, Benjamin W and S. Douglas Olson. 2012. *Inscriptional Records for the Dramatic Festivals in Athens:* IG *II*^{2} *2318-25 and Related Texts*. Leiden/Boston.
Mirhady, David C. 2007. 'Torture and Rhetoric in Athens', in Edward Carawan (ed.), *Oxford Readings in the Attic Orators* (Oxford) 247–68.

Moorton, Richard F. 1987. 'Euripides' *Andromeda* in Aristophanes' *Frogs*', *AJP* 108: 434–6.

Moorton, Richard F. 1988. 'Aristophanes on Alcibiades', *GRBS* 29: 345–59.

Moritz, Helen E. 1979. 'Refrain in Aeschylus: Literary Adaptation of Traditional Form', *CP* 74: 187–213.

Moritz, Helen E. n.d. 'Aristophanes' *Frogs* in Tom Stoppard's *The Invention of Love*.' Unpublished essay.

Morris, Mick. 2007. '"That Living Voice": Gilbert Murray at the BBC', in Stray (ed.) 2007: 293–317.

Murray, Gilbert. 1908. *The Frogs of Aristophanes*. London.

Murray, Penelope, and Peter Wilson, eds. 2004. *Music and the Muses: The Culture of* Mousikē *in the Classical Athenian City*. Oxford.

Nelson, Nathaniel. 2019. '"The Frogs" Lampoon U.S. Politics', *Winona Post*, 10 April 2019. Online: http://www.winonapost.com/Article/ArticleID/63725/The-Frogs-lampoons-US-politics (accessed 19 August 2019).

Nelson, Thomas J. 2018. 'The Shadow of Aristophanes: Hellenistic Poetry's Reception of Comic Poetics', in Harder, Regtuit and Wakker (eds.) 2018: 225–71.

O'Sullivan, Neil. 1992. *Alcidamas, Aristophanes, and the Beginnings of Greek Stylistic Theory*. Stuttgart.

O'Sullivan, Neil. 2000. 'Poetry from Old Rope: A Neglected Emendation in Aristophanes, *Frogs* 1298', *CQ* 50: 297–8.

Olson, S. Douglas, ed. 2014. *Ancient Comedy and Reception: Essays in Honor of Jeffrey Henderson*. Berlin.

Olson, S. Douglas. 2015. 'On the Fragments of Eupolis' *Taxiarchoi*', in M. Taufer (ed.), *Studi sulla commedia attica* (Freiburg) 201–13.

Padilla, Mark. 1992. 'The Heraclean Dionysus: Theatrical and Social Renewal in Aristophanes' *Frogs*', *Arethusa* 25: 359–84.

Parker, Robert. 2005. *Polytheism and Society at Athens*. Oxford.

Pickard-Cambridge, Arthur. 1968 (additions in 1988). *The Dramatic Festivals of Athens*, second ed. rev. by John Gould and D. M. Lewis. Oxford.

Pontani, Filippomaria. 2009. 'Demosthenes, Parody and the *Frogs*', *Mnem.* 62: 401–16.

Pugliesi Carratelli, Giovanni. 1940. 'Versi di un coro delle «Rane» in un'epigrafe rodia', *Dioniso* 8: 119–23.

Rau, Peter. 1967. *Paratragodia: Untersuchun einer komischen Form des Aristophanes*. Munich.

Reckford, Kenneth J. 1987. *Aristophanes' Old-and-New Comedy, Volume 1: Six Essays in Perspective*. Chapel Hill, NC.

Reckford, Kenneth J. 2001. 'Stoppard's Housman', *Arion* 9.2: 108–49.

Rengel, Milo. 2017. 'Metatheatre in Aristophanes' *Frogs*: Dionysos, Immortality, and the *agon* as a Play-within-a-Play', *Logeion* 7: 145–69.

Revermann, M. 1997. 'Cratinus' Διονυσαλέξανδρος and the Head of Pericles', *JHS* 117: 197–200.

Richlin, Amy, ed. 1992. *Pornography and Representation in Greece and Rome*. Oxford.

Robert, Jeanne and Louis Robert. 1946. 'Bulletin épigraphique', *REG* 59–60: 298–372.

Roche, Paul. 2005. *Aristophanes: The Complete Plays*. New York.

Rogers, Benjamin Bickley. 1924. *Aristophanes III*. Cambridge, MA.

Roselli, D. K. 2005. 'Vegetable-Hawking Mom and Fortunate Son: Euripides, Tragic Style, and Reception', *Phoenix* 59: 1–49.

Roselli, D. K. 2009. '*Theorika* in Fifth-Century Athens', *GRBS* 49: 5–30.

Rosen, Ralph M. 2004. 'Aristophanes' *Frogs* and the *Contest of Homer and Hesiod*', *TAPA* 134: 295–322.

Rosen, Ralph M. 2006. 'Aristophanes, fandom, and the classicizing of Greek Tragedy', in Kozak and Rich 2006: 27–47.

Rosen, Ralph M. 2014. 'The Greek "comic hero"', in Martin Revermann (ed.), *The Cambridge Companion to Greek Comedy* (Cambridge) 222–40.

Rosen, Ralph M. 2015. 'Reconsidering the Reperformance of Aristophanes' *Frogs*', *Trends in Classics* 7.2: 237–56.

Russo, C. F. 1994. *Aristophanes: An Author for the Stage*. London.

Santamaría Álvarez, Marco Antonio. 2015. 'The Parody of the *Katábasis*-Motif in Aristophanes' *Frogs*', *Les Études classiques* 83: 117–36.

Sansone, David. 2016. 'Whatever Happened to Euripides' *Lekythion* (*Frogs* 1198-1247)?' in Kyriakou and Rengakos 2016: 319–34.

Scharffenberger, E. W. 1995. 'A Tragic Lysistrata? Jocasta in the "Reconciliation Scene" of the *Phoenician Women*', *RhM* 138: 312–36.

Scharffenberger, E. W. 1997. 'Jumping into the Clouds: Morality and Intellectual Radicalism in Aristophanes and Tom Stoppard', *Text and Presentation* 18: 119–30.

Scharffenberger, E. W. 2007. '*Deinon eribremetas*: The Sound and Sense of Aeschylus in Aristophanes' *Frogs*', *CW* 100: 229–49.

Schiff, Judith Anne. 1998. 'The Greatest College Cheer', *Yale Alumni Magazine*, May 1998; online at http://archives.yalealumnimagazine.com/issues/98_05/old_yale.html; see also (unsigned) 'Readers Remember the Long Cheer', July/August 2008; online at http://archive.yalealumnimagazine.com/issues/2008_07/notebook_comments.html (both accessed 19 July 2019).

Seager, Robin. 1981. 'Notes on Aristophanes', *CQ* 31: 244–51.

Segal, C. P. 1961. 'The Character and Cults of Dionysus and the Unity of the *Frogs*', *HSCP* 65: 207–42.

Sells, D. 2018. *Parody, Politics and the Populace in Greek Old Comedy*. Bloomsbury.

Sfyroeras, Pavlos. 2008. 'Πόθος Εὐριπίδου: Reading *Andromeda* in Aristophanes' *Frogs*', *AJP* 129: 299–317.

Shackleton Bailey, D. R. 2000. *Valerius Maximus. Memorable Doings and Sayings, Volume II: Books 6–9*. Cambridge, MA.

Shear, Julia Louise. 2001. *Polis and Panathenaia: The History and Development of Athena's Festival*. Philadelphia (PhD dissertation, University of Pennsylvania).

Shelley, Mary. 1905. 'Note on *Oedipus Tyrannus*', in *Shelley: Poetical Works*, ed. T. Hutchinson (Oxford) 410.

Sidwell, Keith. 2009. *Aristophanes the Democrat: The Politics of Satirical Comedy during the Peloponnesian War*. Cambridge.
Silk, M. S. 2000. *Aristophanes and the Definition of Comedy*. Oxford.
Simms, Robert. 2002/3. 'Argra and Agrai', *GRBS* 43: 219–29.
Slater, N. W. 1986. 'The Lenaian Theatre', *ZPE* 66: 255–64.
Slater, N. W. 1989. 'Aristophanes' Apprenticeship Again', *GRBS* 30: 67–82.
Slater, N. W. 2002. *Spectator Politics: Metatheatre and Performance in Aristophanes*. Philadelphia.
Slater, N. W. 2016. 'Aristophanes in Antiquity: Reputation and Reception', in Walsh (ed.) 2016: 3–21.
Sommerstein, Alan H. 1980. *The Comedies of Aristophanes, vol. 1: Acharnians*. Warminster.
Sommerstein, Alan H. 1993. 'Kleophon and the Restaging of *Frogs*', in Sommerstein et. al. (eds.) 1993: 461–76.
Sommerstein, Alan H. 1996a. *The Comedies of Aristophanes, vol. 9: Frogs*. Warminster.
Sommerstein, Alan H. 1996b. 'How to Avoid Being a *Komodoumenos*', *CQ* 46: 327–56.
Sommerstein, Alan H. 2000. 'Platon, Eupolis and the "demagogue-comedy"', in Harvey and Wilkins (eds.), 2000: 437–51.
Sommerstein, Alan H. 2001. *The Comedies of Aristophanes, vol. 11: Wealth*. Warminster [311–18 = 'Addenda: Frogs']
Sommerstein, Alan H. 2008. *Aeschylus: Fragments*. Cambridge, MA.
Sommerstein, Alan H. 2012. 'Notes on Aristophanes' *Frogs*', in Marshall and Kovacs (eds.) 2000: 115–25.
Sommerstein, Alan H, Stephen Halliwell, Jeffrey Henderson and Bernhard Zimmermann (eds.) 1993. *Tragedy, Comedy, and the Polis*. Bari.
Stanford, W. B. 1963 [with alterations, 1971]. *Aristophanes, The Frogs*, 2nd ed. London.
Starkey, Jennifer S. 2013. 'Soldiers and Sailors in Aristophanes' *Babylonians*', *CQ* 63: 501–10.
Stehle, Eva. 2002. 'The Male Body in Aristophanes' *Thesmophoriazusae*: Where Does Costume End?', *AJP* 123: 369–406.
Steinhart, Matthias. 2007. 'Phthian Achilles', *CQ* 51: 283–4.
Stoppard, Tom. 1997. *The Invention of Love*. London.
Storey, Ian C. 2000. 'Some problems in Eupolis' *Demoi*', in D. Harvey and J. Wilkins (eds.), *The Rivals of Aristophanes: Studies in Athenian Old Comedy* (Swansea) 173–90.
Storey, Ian C. 2003. 'The curious matter of the Lenaia festival of 422 BC', in D. J. Phillips and D. M. Pritchard (eds.), *Sport and festival in the ancient Greek world* (Swansea), 281–92.
Storey, Ian C. 2006. 'On First Looking into Kratinos' *Dionysalexandros*', in L. Kozak and J. Rich (eds.), *Playing around Aristophanes* (Oxford) 105–25.
Storey, Ian C. 2011a. *Fragments of Old Comedy, vol. 1. Alcaeus to Diocles*. Cambridge, MA.

Storey, Ian C. 2011b. *Fragments of Old Comedy, vol. 11. Diopeithes to Pherecrates*. Cambridge, MA.
Storey, Ian C. 2011c. *Fragments of Old Comedy, vol. 111. Philonicus to Xenophon, Adespota*. Cambridge, MA.
Storey, Ian C. 2019. *Aristophanes: Peace*. London.
Stray, Christopher, ed. 2007. *Gilbert Murray Reassessed: Hellenism, Theatre, and International Politics*. Oxford.
Suter, Anne. 1977. 'Back from the Dead: Euripides' *Orestes* and Aristophanes' *Frogs*', *NECJ* 25.1: 3–7.
Sutton, D. F. 1983. 'Aeschylus and the Mysteries: A Suggestion', *Hermes* 111: 249–51.
Taplin, Oliver. 1972. 'Aeschylean Silences and Silences in Aeschylus', *HSCP* 76: 57–97.
Taplin, Oliver. 1993. *Comic Angels and Other Approaches to Greek Drama through Vase-Paintings*. Oxford.
Tarkow, Theodore A. 1982. 'Achilles and the Ghost of Aeschyles [sic] in Aristophanes' *Frogs*', *Traditio* 38: 1–16.
Thiercy, P. 1986. *Aristophane. Fiction et dramaturgie*. Paris.
Thiercy, P. 2000. 'L'unité de lieu chez Aristophane', *Pallas* 54: 15–24.
Thür, G. 1977. *Beweisfürung vor den Schwurgerischtshöfen Athens: Die Proklesis zue Basanos*. Vienna.
Torrance, Isabelle. 2007. *Aeschylus: Seven Against Thebes*. London.
Torrance, Isabelle. 2011. 'In the Footprints of Aeschylus: Recognition, Allusion, and Metapoetics in Euripides', *AJP* 132: 177–204.
Torrance, Isabelle. 2013. *Metapoetry in Euripides*. Oxford.
Torello, Giulia. 2008. 'The resurrection of Aristeides, Miltiades, Solon and Perikles in Eupolis' *Demes*', *Antichthon* 42: 40–55.
Traficante, V. 2007. 'Quale Dioniso nelle Baccanti di Euripide? Nota iconografica sull'evoluzione dell'immagine di Dioniso nel V sec. a. C.', in A. Beltrametti (ed.) *Studi e materiali per le Baccanti di Euripide. Storia Memorie Spettacoli* (Como/Pavia) 65–93.
Tucker, T. G. 1906. *The Frogs of Aristopanes*. London.
van der Valk, M. 1980. 'On a Few Passages of Aristophanes' *Ranae*', *WJA* 6a: 71–6.
Van Steen, Gonda A. H. 2000. *Venom in Verse: Aristophanes in Modern Greece*. Princeton.
Van Steen, Gonda A. H. 2014. 'Close Encounters of the Comic Kind: Aristophanes' *Frogs* and *Lysistrata* in Athenian Mythological Burlesque of the 1880s', in Olson (ed.) 2014: 747–61.
Van Zyl Smit, Betine, ed. 2016. *A Handbook to the Reception of Greek Drama*. Chichester.
Varakis, Angeliki. 2007. 'The Use of Masks in Koun's Stage Interpretations of *Birds*, *Frogs*, and *Peace*', in Hall and Wrigley 2007: 179–93.
Vickers, J. 2011. *Tumbling in Choral Dance: Aristophanes' Frogs*. London, ON (MA thesis, University of Western Ontario).
Vickers, J. 2019. 'The Lion Cub Ainos, Suppositious Children, and *Thesmophoriazusae*', *RhM* 162: 1–34.

Vickers, M. 2001. 'Aristophanes' *Frogs*: Nothing to do with Literature', *Athenaeum* 89: 187–201.
Walsh, Philip, ed. 2016. *Brill's Companion to the Reception of Aristophanes*. Leiden.
Wansbrough, Henry. 1993. 'Two Choruses of Frogs?' *JHS* 113: 162.
Weimer, Christopher. 2009. 'A Classic Journey', *Sondheim Review* 16.2: 25–6.
Welsh, D. 1983. '*IG* ii^2 2343: Philonides and Aristophanes' *Banqueters*', *CQ* 33: 51–5.
West, M.L 2000. '*Iliad* and *Aithiopis* on Stage: Aeschylus and Son', *CQ* 50: 338–52.
Whitman, Cedric H. 1964. *Aristophanes and the Comic Hero*. Cambridge, MA.
Whitman, Cedric H. 1969. 'Ληκύθιον ἀπώλεσεν', *HSCP* 73: 109–12.
Wiles, David. 2011. *Theatre and Citizenship: The History of a Practice*. Cambridge.
Wills, Garry. 1969. 'Why are the Frogs in *The Frogs*?' *Hermes* 97: 306–17.
Wilson, A. M. 1974. 'A Eupolidean Precedent for the Rowing Scene in Aristophanes' *Frogs*?' *CQ* 24: 250–2.
Wilson, A. M. 1976. 'Addendum to "A Eupolidean Precedent for the Rowing Scene in Aristophanes' *Frogs*?"', *CQ* 26: 318.
Wilson, N. G. 2007a. *Aristophanis Fabulae*, vol. 2. Oxford
Wilson, N. G. 2007b. *Aristophanea: Studies on the Text of Aristophanes*. Oxford.
Wilson, Peter. 1999. 'The *aulos* in Athens', in S. Goldhill and R. Osborne (eds.), *Performance Culture and Athenian Democracy* (Cambridge) 58–95.
Wilson, Peter. 2000. *The Athenian Institution of the Khoregia: The Chorus, the City, and the Stage*. Cambridge.
Wilson, Peter. 2015. 'The Festival of Dionysus in Ikarion: A New Study of *IG* I^3 254', *Hesperia* 84: 97–147.
Wilson, Peter and Andrew Hartwig. 2009. '*IG* I^3 102 and the Tradition of Proclaiming Honours at the Tragic Agon of the Athenian City Dionysia', *ZPE* 169: 17–27.
Worthington, I. 1989. 'Aristophanes' *Frogs* and Arginusae', *Hermes* 117: 359–63.
Wright, Matthew. 2016. *The Lost Plays of Greek Tragedy, Volume 1: Neglected Authors*. London.
Wrigley, Amanda. 2007. 'Aristophanes Revitalized! Music and Spectacle on the Academic Stage', in Hall and Wrigley (eds.) 2007: 136–54.
Wrigley, Amanda. 2011. *Performing Greek Drama in Oxford and on tour with the Balliol Players*. Exeter.
Wrigley, Amanda. 2014. 'Aristophanes at the BBC, 1940s–1960s', in Olson (ed.) 2014: 849–70.
Wycherley, R. E. 1965. 'Lenaion', *Hesperia* 34: 72–76.
Wyles, Rosie. 2011. *Costume in Greek Tragedy*. London.
Young, Arthur M. 1933. 'The *Frogs* of Aristophanes as a Type of Play', *CJ* 29: 23–32.
Zanker, Graham. 2009. *Herodas: Mimiambs*. Oxford.
Zuckerberg, Donna. 2018. 'The Curious Incident of the Intertextual Debt in the *Frogs*', *Didaskalia* 14.02: 2–9.
Zweig, Bella. 1992. 'The Mute Nude Female Characters in Aristophanes' Plays', in Richlin (ed.) 1992: 73–89.

Index